Who's Running America?

Who's Running America?
The Clinton Years

SIXTH EDITION

Thomas R. Dye
Florida State University

 PRENTICE HALL, Englewood Cliffs, New Jersey 07632

Library of Congress Cataloging-in-Publication Data

Dye, Thomas R.
    Who's running America? : The Clinton years / Thomas R. Dye — 6th ed.
      p.   cm.
    Includes index.
    ISBN 0-13-123241-X
      1. Elite (Social sciences)—United States.   2. United States—Politics and government—1993-
3. Power (Social sciences)   4. Leadership.   I. Title
HN90.E4D93   1995   94-9675
305.5'2'0973—dc20   CIP

Project Manager and
   interior design: Serena Hoffman
Cover design: Laurel Marx
Production Coordinator: Mary Ann Gloriande
Copy Editor: Nancy Marcello

Printed in the United States of America
10 9 8 7 6 5 4 3 2 1

ISBN 0-13-123241-X

Prentice-Hall International (UK) Limited, *London*
Prentice-Hall of Australia Pty. Limited, *Sydney*
Prentice-Hall Canada Inc., *Toronto*
Prentice-Hall Hispanoamericana, S.A., *Mexico*
Prentice-Hall of India Private Limited, *New Delhi*
Prentice-Hall of Japan, Inc., *Tokyo*
Simon & Schuster Asia Pte. Ltd., *Singapore*
Editora Prentice-Hall do Brasil, Ltda., *Rio de Janeiro*

Contents

PART III
THE STRUCTURE OF INSTITUTIONAL ELITES

6 Interlocking and Specialization at the Top 150

7 Elite Recruitment: Getting to the Top 168

8 Conflict and Consensus among Institutional Leaders 195

9   How Institutional Leaders Make Public Policy

10   Institutional Elites in America

Index

Preface

Who's Running America? has *not* been supported by any grant or contract from any institution, public or private. It grew out of a graduate seminar "Research on Power and Elites" at Florida State University. Initially, biographical data for over 5,000 members of various institutional elites were collected and coded by students. These computerized biographies constituted the original data base for the continuing project *Who's Running America?* The data base has been revised periodically, and data on over 7,000 institutional elites have been collected and coded.

Two articles based on this data from the early 1970s were published in social science journals:

Thomas R. Dye, Eugene R. DeClercq, and John W. Pickering, "Concentration, Specialization, and Interlocking among Institutional Elites," *Social Science Quarterly* (June 1973), pp. 8–28.

Thomas R. Dye and John W. Pickering, "Governmental and Corporate Elites: Convergence and Specialization," *Journal of Politics* (November 1974), pp. 900–25.

We are indebted to a number of commentators who wrote to us before and after publication of these articles, including scholars G. William Domhoff, Suzanne Keller, John Walton, Robert Lineberry, Harmon Zeigler, and Charles Bonjean.

The First Edition of this book was published in 1976 and described national leadership in the Nixon-Ford years. The First Edition was subtitled *Institutional Leadership in the United States.*

The Second Edition of this volume, *The Carter Years,* reflected changes in national leadership which occurred with the election of Jimmy Carter to the presidency and the advent of a new Democratic administration.

The Third Edition of this book, *The Reagan Years,* involved the collection of an entire new data base for national leaders in 1980–81. Special topics were addressed in several articles in professional journals, including:

Thomas R. Dye, "Obligarchic Tendencies in National Policy-Making: The Role of the Private Policy-Planning Organization," *Journal of Politics,* 40 (May 1978), 309–31.

Thomas R. Dye and Julie Strickland, "Women at the Top," *Social Science Quarterly*, 63 (March 1982).

The Fourth Edition, *The Conservative Years*, discussed changes in national leadership during the 1980s. Additional research on corporate ownership was examined in professional journals:

Thomas R. Dye, "Who Owns America?" *Social Science Quarterly*, 64 (December 1983), 862–70.

Thomas R. Dye, "Strategic Ownership Positions in U.S. Industry and Banking," *American Journal of Economics and Sociology*, 44 (January 1985), 9–22.

The Fifth Edition, *The Bush Era*, updated both corporate and governmental leadership to 1990. Additional detailed analysis of institutional power was published in:

Thomas R. Dye, "Organizing Power for Policy Planning," in *Power Elites and Organizations*, eds. G. William Domhoff and Thomas R. Dye (Beverly Hills: Sage, 1987).

The Sixth Edition, *The Clinton Years*, not only chronicles changes in leadership in Washington accompanying the arrival of the first Democratic administration in twelve years but also assesses important recent developments in corporate governance in America. In Washington, we observe that the "Friends of Bill and Hillary" differ from previous administrations in their lack of experience outside of government. Almost all top Clinton officials are lawyers, lobbyists, politicians, and bureaucrats; very few have any background in business, banking, the media, or the military. In corporate boardrooms, we observe a new willingness by outside directors and large stockholders to confront poorly performing managers. Decades of management control of corporate America are currently being challenged by both aggressive directors and corporate raiders. New sections, "Inside the Boardroom," take a close look at the people who run IBM, Du Pont, Chase Manhattan, and the *Washington Post*. The Sixth Edition also records the continuing struggles of the great entrepreneurial families, notably the Rockfellers and the Fords, to retain their power over generations; and it also describes how changes in technology, especially in the mass media, have inspired challenges to established elites. An article developed in conjunction with the Sixth Edition appeared as:

Thomas R. Dye, "The Friends of Bill and Hillary," *P.S. Political Science and Politics*, 26 (December, 1993), 693–695.

This volume is divided into three parts. Part I, Power in American Society, sets forth our questions for research, defines terms and concepts, and explains our method of identifying the nation's institutional elite. Part II,

Institutional Leadership in America, describes the concentration of power in industry, banking, insurance, utilities, government, the news media, the law, investment finance, foundations, civic and cultural organizations, and universities. It also describes the type of persons who occupy top institutional leadership positions in these various sectors of society; it "names names," and in so doing, makes use of brief biographical sketches. These sketches are designed to give a general introduction to the characteristics of elites: the schools they attend, their early careers, their records of achievement, and the multiple positions of leadership they occupy. These sketches are updated with each new edition of the book. These sketches are derived from a wide variety of sources: *Who's Who in America, Current Biography, Forbes, Fortune, Congressional Quarterly,* and individual articles and books.[1] The sketches in Part II are designed to pave the way for more systematic analysis of biographical data, which follows in Part III.

Part III, The Structure of Institutional Elites, is a systematic investigation of interlocking and specialization among elites, overlapping elite membership, recruitment paths, socioeconomic backgrounds, previous experience, racial and gender bias, club memberships and life styles, attitudes and opinions, competition and consensus, factionalism, and patterns of interaction in policy-making. Part III relies on computerized biographical files which we compiled at Florida State University on thousands of top institutional elites in 1970–71 and in 1980–81.

The decision to "name names" was carefully considered. We know that occupants of top institutional positions change over time, and that some of our information will be out of date by the time of publication. And with thousands of names, some mistakes are inevitable. However, the biographical sketches provide "flesh and bones" to the statistical analysis; they "personalize" the numbers and percentages in our research. The people who run America *are* real people, and we know of no better way to impress this fact upon our readers.

Thomas R. Dye

---

[1] *Who's Who in America,* published biannually by Marquis Who's Who, Inc., Chicago; *Current Biography,* published monthly and annually by H. L. Wilson Co., New York; *Forbes,* published biweekly by Malcom S. Forbes, New York; *Fortune,* published monthly by Time-Life, Inc., New York; *Congressional Quarterly Weekly Report,* published weekly by Congressional Quarterly, Inc., Washington, D.C.

1 Elitism in a Democracy

Great power in America is concentrated in a handful of people. A few thousand individuals out of 250 million Americans decide about war and peace, wages and prices, consumption and investment, employment and production, law and justice, taxes and benefits, education and learning, health and welfare, advertising and communication, life and leisure. In all societies—primitive and advanced, totalitarian and democratic, capitalist and socialist—only a few people exercise great power. This is true whether or not such power is exercised in the name of "the people."

Who's Running America? is about those at the top of the institutional structure in America—who they are, how much power they wield, how they came to power, and what they do with it. In a modern, complex industrial society, power is concentrated in large institutions: corporations, banks, utilities, insurance companies, broadcasting networks, the White House, Congress and the Washington bureaucracy, the military establishment, the prestigious law firms, the large investment houses, the foundations, the universities, and the private policy-planning organizations. The people at the top of these institutions—the presidents and principal officers and directors, the senior partners, the governing trustees, the congressional committee chairpersons, the Cabinet and senior presidential advisers, the Supreme Court Justices, the four-star generals and admirals—are the objects of our study in this book.

We want to ask: Who occupies the top positions of authority in America? How concentrated or dispersed is power in this nation? How do these institutional leaders attain their positions? What are their backgrounds, attitudes, and goals? What relationships exist among these people of power? How much cohesion or competition characterizes their relationships? Do they agree or disagree on crucial issues confronting the nation? How do they go about making important decisions or undertaking new programs or policies?

We also want to ask about stability and change: Is America's leadership changing over time? Is there a true "changing of the guard" occurring at the top of the nation's institutional structure, or do top leaders today resemble those of a decade or more ago in terms of social origins, education, attitudes, and experiences? Is power gradually dispersing over time to larger and more diverse leadership groups, or do we find even greater concentrations of power today than years ago? Are women and blacks making significant inroads into top positions in America, or are "the higher circles" still nearly all male and all white?

THE INEVITABILITY OF ELITES

The *elite* are the few who have power in society; the *masses* are the many who do not. We shall call our national leaders "elites" because they possess formal authority over large institutions that shape the lives of all Americans.

America is by no means unique in its concentration of great power in the hands of a few. The universality of elites has been a prominent theme in the works of scholars throughout the ages. The Italian sociologist Vilfredo Pareto put it succinctly: "Every people is governed by an elite, by a chosen element of the population."[1]

Traditional social theorizing about elites views them as essential, functional components of social organization. The necessity of elites derives from the general need for *order* in society. Whenever human beings find themselves living together, they establish a set of ordered relationships so that they can know how others around them will behave. Without ordered behavior, the concept of society itself would be impossible. Among these ordered relationships is the expectation that a few people will make decisions on behalf of the group. Even in primitive societies someone has to decide when the hunt will begin, how it will proceed, and what will be done with the catch.

Nearly two centuries ago Alexander Hamilton defended the existence of the elite by writing:

> All communities divide themselves into the few and the many. The first are the rich and well-born, the other the masses of people. The voice of the people has been said to be the voice of God; and however generally this maxim has been quoted and believed, it is not true in fact. The people are turbulent and changing, they seldom judge or determine right.[2]

The Italian political scientist Gaetano Mosca agreed:

> In all societies—from societies that are very underdeveloped and have largely attained the dawnings of civilization, down to the most advanced and powerful societies—two classes of people appear—a class that rules and a class that is ruled. The first class, always the less numerous, performs all of the political functions, monopolizes power, and enjoys the advantages that power brings, whereas the second, the more numerous class, is directed and controlled by the first, in a manner that is now more or less legal, now more or less arbitrary and violent.[3]

[1] Vilfredo Pareto, *Mind and Society* (New York: Harcourt Brace Jovanovich, 1935), p. 246.

[2] Alexander Hamilton, *Records of the Federal Convention* of 1787.

[3] Gaetano Mosca, *The Ruling Class* (New York: McGraw-Hill, 1939), p. 50.

Contemporary social scientists have echoed the same theme. Sociologist Robert Lynd writes:

> It is the necessity in each society—if it is to be a society, not a rabble—to order the relations of men and their institutional ways of achieving needed ends. . . . Organized power exists—always and everywhere, in societies large or small, primitive or modern—because it performs the necessary function of establishing and maintaining the version of order by which a given society in a given time and place lives.[4]

Political scientists Harold Lasswell and Daniel Lerner are even more explicit: "The discovery that in all large-scale societies the decisions at any given time are typically in the hands of a small number of people confirms a basic fact: Government is always government by the few, whether in the name of the few, the one, or the many."[5]

Elitism is *not* a result of inadequate education of the masses or of poverty or of a "military-industrial complex" or of capitalist control of the mass media or of any special problem in society. The necessity for leadership in social organizations applies universally. Robert Michels, who as a student was active in socialist politics in Europe in the early 1900s, concluded reluctantly that elitism was *not* a product of capitalism. *All* large organizations—political parties, labor unions, governments—are oligarchies, even radical *socialist* parties. In Michels's words, "He who says organization says oligarchy." Michels explains his famous "iron law of oligarchy" as a characteristic of *any* social system.[6]

Thus, the elitist character of American society is not a product of political conspiracy, capitalist exploitation, or any specific malfunction of democracy. *All* societies are elitist. There cannot be large institutions without great power being concentrated within the hands of the few at the top of these institutions.

THE INSTITUTIONAL BASIS OF POWER

Power is not an attribute of individuals, but of social organizations. Power is the potential for control in society that accompanies certain roles in the social system. This notion reflects Max Weber's classic formulation of the definition of power:

[4] Robert Lynd, "Power in American Society," in *Problems of Power in American Society*, ed. Arthur Kornhauser (Detroit: Wayne State University Press, 1957), pp. 3–4.

[5] Harold Lasswell and Daniel Lerner, *The Comparative Study of Elites* (Stanford, Calif.: Stanford University Press, 1952), p. 7.

[6] Robert Michels, *Political Parties: A Sociological Study of the Oligarchical Tendencies of Modern Democracy* (1915) (New York: Free Press, 1962), p. 70.

> In general, we understand by "power" the *chance* of a number of men to realize their own will in a communal act even against the resistance of others who are participating in the action.[7]

"Chance" in this context means the opportunity or capacity for effecting one's will. Viewed in this fashion, power is not so much the *act* of control as the *potential to act*—the social *expectation* that such control is possible and legitimate—that defines power.

Power is simply the capacity or potential of persons in certain roles to make decisions that affect the conduct of others in the social system. Sociologist Robert O. Schultze puts it in these words:

> . . . a few have emphasized that *act as such* rather than the *potential to act* is the crucial aspect of power. It seems far more sociologically sound to accept a Weberian definition which stresses the potential to act. Power may thus be conceived as an inherently group-linked property, an attribute of social statuses rather than of individual persons. . . . Accordingly, power will denote the *capacity* or *potential* of persons *in certain statuses* to set conditions, make decisions, and/or take actions which are determinative for the existence of others within a given social system.[8]

Thus, elites are people who occupy power roles in society. In a modern, complex society, these roles are institutionalized; the elite are the individuals who occupy positions of authority in large institutions. Authority is the expected and legitimate capacity to direct, manage, and guide programs, policies, and activities of the major institutions of society.

It is true, of course, that not all power is institutionalized. Power can be exercised in transitory and informal groups and in interpersonal interactions. Power is exercised, for example, when a mugger stops a pedestrian on the street and forces him to give up his wallet, or when a political assassin murders a President. But great power is found only in institutional roles. C. Wright Mills, a socialist critic of the structure of power in American society, observed:

> No one . . . can be truly powerful unless he has access to the command of major institutions, for it is over these institutional means of power that the truly powerful are, in the first instance, powerful.[9]

Adolf A. Berle, who spent a lifetime studying private property and the American corporation, was equally impressed with the institutional basis of power:

> Power is invariably organized and transmitted through institutions. Top power

---

[7] Hans Gerth and C. Wright Mill, eds., *From Max Weber* (New York: Oxford University Press, 1946), p. 180.

[8] Robert O. Schultze, "The Bifurcation of Power in a Satellite City," in *Community Political Systems*, ed. Morris Janowitz (Glencoe: Free Press, 1961), p. 20.

[9] C. Wright Mills, *The Power Elite* (New York: Oxford University Press, 1956), p. 9.

holders must work through existing institutions, perhaps extending or modifying them, or must at once create new institutions. There is no other way of exercising power—unless it is limited to the range of the power holder's fist or his gun.[10]

Individuals do not become powerful simply because they have particular qualities, valuable skills, burning ambitions, or sparkling personalities. These assets may be helpful in gaining positions of power, but it is the position itself that gives an individual control over the activities of other individuals. This relationship between power and institutional authority in modern society is described by Mills:

> If we took the one hundred most powerful men in America, the one hundred wealthiest, and the one hundred most celebrated away from the institutional positions they now occupy, away from their resources of men and women and money, away from the media of mass communication . . . then they would be powerless and poor and uncelebrated. For power is not of a man. Wealth does not center in the person of the wealthy. Celebrity is not inherent in any personality. To be celebrated, to be wealthy, to have power, requires access to major institutions, for the institutional positions men occupy determine in large part their chances to have and to hold these valued experiences.[11]

Power, then, is an attribute of *roles* in a social system, not an attribute of individuals. People are powerful when they occupy positions of authority and control in social organizations. Once they occupy these positions, their power is felt as a result not only in their actions but in their failures to act as well. Both have great impact on the behaviors of others. Elites "are in positions to make decisions having major consequences. Whether they do or do not make such decisions is less important than the fact that they do occupy such pivotal positions: Their failure to act, their failure to make a decision, is itself an act that is often of greater consequence than the decisions they do make."[12]

People in top institutional positions exercise power whether they act overtly to influence particular decisions or not.[13] When the social, economic, and political values of elite groups, or, more importantly, the structures of the institutions themselves, limit the scope of decision-making to only those issues which do not threaten top elites, then power is being exercised. Political scientists Peter Bachrach and Morton S. Baratz refer to this phenomenon as "*non*–decision-making." A has power over B when he or she succeeds in suppressing issues that might in their resolution be detrimental to A's preferences. In short, the institutional structure of our society, and the people at the top of that structure, encourage the development of some kinds of public

---

[10] Adolph A. Berle, *Power* (New York: Harcourt Brace Jovanovich, 1967), p. 92.

[11] Mills, *The Power Elite*, p. 9.

[12] Ibid., p. 4.

[13] Peter Bachrach and Morton S. Baratz, "Decisions and Non-Decisions," *American Political Science Review*, 57 (September 1963), 632–42.

issues but prevent other kinds of issues from ever being considered by the American public. Such "non–decision-making" provides still another reason for studying institutional leadership.

POWER AS DECISION-MAKING: AN ALTERNATIVE VIEW

It is our contention, then, that great power is institutionalized—that it derives from roles in social organizations and that individuals who occupy top institutional positions possess power whether they act directly to influence particular decisions or not. But these views—often labeled as "elitist"—are not universally shared among social scientists. We are aware that our institutional approach to power conflicts with the approach of many scholars who believe that power can be viewed only in a decision-making context.

This alternative approach to power—often labeled as "pluralist"— defines power as *active participation in decision-making*. Persons are said to have power *only* when they participate directly in particular decisions. Pluralist scholars would object to our presumption that people who occupy institutional positions and who have formal authority over economic, governmental, or social affairs necessarily have power. Pluralists differentiate between the "potential" for power (which is generally associated with top institutional positions) and "actual" power (which assumes active participation in decision-making). Political scientist Robert A. Dahl writes:

> Suppose a set of individuals in a political system has the following property: there is a high probability that if they agree on a key political alternative, and if they all act in some specified way, then that alternative will be chosen. We may say of such a group that it has a high *potential* for control. . . . But a *potential* for control is not, except in a peculiarly Hobbesian world, equivalent to *actual* control.[14]

Pluralists contend that the potential for power is not power itself. Power occurs in individual interactions: "A has power over B to the extent that he can get B to do something that B would not otherwise do."[15] We should not simply assume that power attaches to high office. Top institutional officeholders may or may not exercise power—their "power" depends upon their active participation in particular decisions. They may choose not to participate in certain decisions; their influence may be limited to specific kinds of decisions; they may be constrained by formal and informal checks on their discretion; they may be forced to respond to the demands of individuals or groups within or outside the institutions they lead; they may have little real discretion in their choice among alternative courses of action.

Pluralists would argue that research into institutional leadership can

---

[14] Robert A. Dahl, "Critique of the Ruling Elite Model," *American Political Science Review*, 52 (June 1958), 66 {italics mine}.

[15] Robert A. Dahl, "The Concept of Power," *Behavioral Science*, 2 (1957), 202.

describe at best only the *potential* for control that exists within American society. They would insist that research on national leadership should proceed by careful examination of a series of important national decisions—that the individuals who took an active part in these decisions be identified and a full account of their decision-making behavior be obtained. Political scientist Nelson Polsby, a former student of Robert A. Dahl at Yale, reflects the interests of pluralists in observing specific decisions:

> How can one tell, after all, whether or not an actor is powerful unless some sequence of events, competently observed, attests to his power? If these events take place, then the power of the actor is not "potential" but actual. If these events do not occur, then what grounds have we to suppose that the actor is powerful?[16]

And, indeed, much of the best research and writing in political science has proceeded by studying specific cases in the uses of power.

Pluralism, of course, is more than a definition of power and a method of study—it is an integrated body of theory that seeks to reaffirm the fundamental democratic character of American society. Pluralism arose in response to criticisms of the American political system to the effect that individual participation in a large, complex, bureaucratic society was increasingly difficult. Traditional notions of democracy had stressed individual participation of all citizens in the decisions that shape their own lives. But it was clear to scholars of all persuasions that relatively few individuals in America have any *direct* impact on national decision-making.

Pluralism developed as an ideology designed to reconcile the *ideals* of democracy with the *realities* of a large-scale, industrial, technocratic society. Jack L. Walker writes that the "principal aim" of the pluralists "has been to make the theory of democracy more realistic, to bring it into closer correspondence with empirical reality. They are convinced that the classical theory does not account for 'much of the real machinery' by which the system operates."[17]

Pluralists recognize that an elite few, rather than the masses, rule America and that "it is difficult—nay impossible—to see how it could be otherwise in large political systems."[18] However, they reassert the essentially democratic character of America by arguing that competition between leadership groups protects the individual—that is, countervailing centers of power check each other and guard against abuse of power. Leadership groups are not closed; new groups can be formed and gain access to the political system. The existence of multiple leadership groups in society gives

[16] Nelson Polsby, *Community Power and Political Theory* (New Haven: Yale University Press, 1963), p. 60.

[17] Jack L. Walker, "A Critique of the Elitist Theory of Democracy," *American Political Science Review*, 60 (June 1966), 286.

[18] Robert A. Dahl, "Power, Pluralism and Democracy," paper delivered at the Annual Meeting of the American Political Science Association, 1966, p. 3.

rise to a "polyarchy"—leaders who exercise power over some kinds of decisions do not necessarily exercise power over other kinds of decisions. Finally, pluralists acknowledge that public policy may not be majority preference, but they claim it is the rough equilibrium of group influence and, therefore, a reasonable approximation of society's preferences.

IDENTIFYING POSITIONS OF POWER

We are committed in this volume to the study of institutional power. It is *not* our purpose to assert the superiority of our approach to power in America over the approaches recommended by others. We do *not* intend to debate the merits of pluralism or elitism as political philosophies. Abstract arguments over conceptualizations, definitions, and method of study already abound in the literature on power. Rather, working within an *institutional* paradigm, we intend to present systematic evidence about the concentration of resources in the nation's largest institutions, to find out who occupies top positions in these institutions, to explore interlocking and convergence among these top position-holders, to learn how they rose to their positions, to investigate the extent of their consensus or disagreement over the major issues confronting the nation, to explore the extent of competition and factionalism among various segments of the nation's institutional leadership, and to learn how institutional leadership interacts in national policy-making.

We hope to avoid elaborate theorizing about power, pluralism, and elitism. We propose to present what we believe to be interesting data on national institutional elites and to permit our readers to relate it to their own theories of power.

A great deal has been said about "the power elite," "the ruling class," "the liberal establishment," "the military-industrial complex," "the powers that be," and so on. But even though many of these notions are interesting and insightful, we never really encounter a systematic definition of precisely *who* these people are, how we can identify them, how they came to power, and what they do with their power.

We know that power is elusive and that elites are not easy to identify. Scholars have encountered great difficulty in finding a specific working definition of a national elite—a definition that can be used to actually identify powerful people. However, this is the necessary starting place for any serious inquiry into power in America.

Our first task, therefore, is to develop an operational *definition* of a national elite. We must formulate a definition that is consistent with our theoretical notions about the institutional basis of power and that will enable us to identify, by name and position, those individuals who possess great power in America.

Our institutional elites will be individuals who occupy *the top positions in the institutional structure of American society.* These are the individuals who possess the formal authority to formulate, direct, and manage programs, policies, and activities of the major corporate, governmental, legal, educational, civic, and cultural institutions in the nation. Our definition of a national elite, then, is consistent with the notion that great power in America resides in large institutions.

For purposes of analysis, we have divided American society into twelve sectors: (1) industrial corporations, (2) utilities and communications, (3) banking, (4) insurance, (5) investments, (6) mass media, (7) law, (8) education, (9) foundations, (10) civic and cultural organizations, (11) government, and (12) the military.

In the corporate sectors, our operational definition of the elite is *those individuals who occupy formal positions of authority in institutions which control more than half of the nation's total corporate assets.* Our procedure in identifying the largest institutions was to rank corporations by the size of their assets, and to cumulate these assets, moving from the top of the rankings down, until at least 50 percent of the nation's total assets in each sector are included (see Tables 2–1, 2–2, 2–3, and 2–4). We also identified the nation's fifteen largest Wall Street investment firms (see Table 2–5). Then we identified by name the presidents, officer-directors, and directors of these corporations.

We also included in our definition of the elite *those individuals who occupy formal positions of authority in the mass media, the large prestigious New York and Washington law firms, the well-endowed private universities, the major philanthropic foundations, and the most influential civic and cultural organizations.* The identification of these institutions involved some subjective judgments. These judgments can be defended, but we recognize that other judgments could be made. In the *mass media,* we include three television networks (CBS, ABC, and NBC); the *New York Times*; Time, Inc.; *Washington Post–Newsweek*; and fifteen newspaper empires which account for over one half of the nation's daily newspaper circulation. Because of the great influence of the news media in America's elite structure, we have devoted a special chapter to "The Newsmakers."

Leadership in a variety of sectors is considered under the general heading of "The Civic Establishment." In *education,* we identify the twenty-five colleges and universities with the largest private endowment funds; we exclude public universities. Our twenty-five universities control two thirds of all private endowment funds in higher education, and they are consistently ranked among the nation's most "prestigious" private colleges and universities. Our leadership group includes their presidents and trustees. Our selection of foundations is based on *The Foundation Directory*'s data on the nation's fifty largest foundations. These foundations, and their trustees/directors, control over 40 percent of all foundation assets. Identifying top positions in the *law* was an even more subjective task. Our definition of positions of authority in the law includes the senior partners of twenty-five large and influential New York and Washington law firms. Top positions in *civic and cultural affairs* were identified by qualitative evaluations of the prestige and influence of various well-known organizations. The civic organizations are the Council on Foreign Relations, the Business Round-table, and the Brookings Institution. The cultural organizations are the Metropolitan Museum of Art, the Museum of Modern Art, the Smithsonian Institution, the Lincoln Center for the Performing Arts, and the John F. Kennedy Center for the Performing Arts. The members of the governing boards of trustees or directors were included in our definition of institutional leadership.

In the governmental sectors, the operational definition of the elite is *those individuals who occupy formal positions of authority in the major institutions of the national government.* Positions of authority in government were defined as the President and Vice-President; secretaries, undersecretaries, and assistant secretaries of all executive departments; senior White House presidential advisers and ambassadors-at-large; congressional committee chairpersons and ranking minority committee members in the House and Senate; House and Senate majority and minority party leaders and whips; Supreme Court Justices; and members of the Federal Reserve Board and the Council of Economic Advisers. Positions of authority in *the military* include both civilian offices and top military commands: secretaries, undersecretaries, and assis-tant secretaries of the Departments of the Army, Navy, and Air Force; all four-star generals and admirals in the Army, Navy, Air Force, and Marine Corps, including the chairman of the Joint Chiefs of Staff; and the Chiefs of Staff and vice-chiefs of staff of the Army and Air Force, the chief and vice-chief of Naval Operations, and the commanding officers of the major mili-tary commands.

Any effort to operationalize a concept as broad as a national institu-tional elite is bound to generate discussion over the inclusion or exclusion of specific sectors, institutions, or positions. (Why law, but not medicine? Why not law firms in Chicago, Houston, or Atlanta? Why not religious institutions or labor unions? Why not governors or mayors of big cities?) There are no explicit guidelines to *systematic* research on national elites. Our choices involve many subjective judgments. Let us see, however, what we can learn about concentration, specialization, and interlocking using the definitions above; perhaps other researchers can improve upon our attempt to opera-tionalize this elusive notion of a national institutional elite. In the analysis to follow, we will present findings for our aggregate elites, and for specific sec-tors of these elites. Clearly, findings for specific sectors will be free of what-ever bias might exist in the aggregate elite as a result of our inclusion or exclusion of specific sectors.

DIMENSIONS OF AMERICA'S ELITE

Our definition of a national institutional elite resulted in the identification of 7,314 elite positions:

Corporate Sectors	Number of Leadership Positions
1. Industrial corporations (100)	1,475
2. Utilities, communications, transportation (50)	668
3. Banks (50)	1,092
4. Insurance (50)	611
5. Investments (15)	479
Total	4,325
Public Interest Sectors	
6. Mass media (18)	220
7. Law (25)	758
8. Education (25)	892
9. Foundations (50)	402
10. Civic and cultural organizations (12)	433
Total	2,705
Governmental Sectors	
11. Legislative, executive, judicial	236
12. Military	48
Total	284
Total	**7,314**

These top positions, taken collectively, control almost three quarters of the nation's industrial assets; one half of all assets in communication and utilities; over one half of all U.S. banking assets; over three quarters of all insurance assets; and they direct Wall Street's largest investment firms. They control the television networks, the influential news agencies, and the major newspaper chains. They control nearly 40 percent of all the assets of private foundations and two thirds of all private university endowments. They direct the nation's largest and best-known New York and Washington law firms as well as the nation's major civic and cultural organizations. They occupy key federal governmental positions in the executive, legislative, and judicial branches. And they occupy all the top command positions in the Army, Navy, Air Force, and Marines.

These aggregate figures—roughly 7,300 positions—are themselves important indicators of the concentration of authority and control in American society. Of course, these figures are the direct product of our specific definition of top institutional positions.[19] Yet these aggregate statistics provide us with an explicit definition and quantitative estimate of the size of the national elite in America.

[19] In earlier editions of this volume, using data from 1970–71, we included only 5,416 positions. In recent editions, using data from 1980–81, we added the investment firms and expanded the number of utilities, insurance companies, universities, and foundations. This produced 7,314 positions. Thus, even minor changes in the definition of an elite can produce substantial differences in the overall size of the elite.

SOME QUESTIONS FOR RESEARCH

Our definition of America's institutional elite provides a starting place for exploring some of the central questions confronting students of power. How concentrated are institutional resources in America? How much concentration exists in industry and finance, in government, in the mass media, in education, in the law, in the foundations, and in civic and cultural affairs? Who are the people at the top of the nation's institutional structure? How did they get there? Did they inherit their positions or work their way up through the ranks of the institutional hierarchy? What are their general attitudes, beliefs, and goals? Do elites in America generally agree about major national goals and the general directions of foreign and domestic policy, and limit their disagreements to the *means* of achieving their goals and the details of policy implementation? Or do leaders disagree over fundamental *ends* and values and the future character of American society?

Are institutional elites in America "interlocked" or "specialized"? That is, is there convergence at the "top" of the institutional structure in America, with the same group of people dominating decision-making in industry, finance, education, government, the mass media, foundations, law, investments, and civic and cultural affairs? Or is there a separate elite in each sector of society with little or no overlap in authority? Are there opportunities to rise to the top of the leadership structure for individuals from both sexes, all classes, races, religions, and ethnic groups, through multiple career paths in different sectors of society? Or are opportunities to acquire key leadership roles generally limited to white, Anglo-Saxon, Protestant, upper-class and upper-middle-class males whose careers are based primarily in industry and finance? Is the nation's institutional leadership recruited primarily from private "name" prep schools and "Ivy League" universities? Do leaders join the same clubs, intermarry, and enjoy the same life styles? Or is there diversity in educational backgrounds, social ties, club memberships, and life styles among the elite?

How much competition and conflict take place among America's institutional elite? Are there clear-cut factions within the nation's leadership struggling for preeminence and power, and if so, what are the underlying sources of this factionalism? Do different segments of the nation's institutional elite accommodate each other in a system of bargaining, negotiation, and compromising based on a widely shared consensus of values?

How do institutional elites make national policy? Are there established institutions and procedures for elite interaction, communication, and consensus-building on national policy questions? Or are such questions decided in a relatively unstructured process of competition, bargaining, and compromise among a large number of diverse individuals and interest groups? Do the "proximate policy-makers"—the President, Congress, the courts—respond to mass opinions, or do they respond primarily to initiatives originating from the elite policy-planning organizations?

Is America's leadership changing over time, and if so, how? Is power becoming more or less concentrated or dispersed over time? Is there more or less "interlocking" today than a decade ago? Do the same types of people occupy top leadership positions today as compared to a decade ago? Have blacks and women gained significant representation among top positions over the last ten years? These are the questions that we will tackle in the pages to follow.

2 The Corporate Directors

Control of economic resources provides a continuous and important base of power in any society. A great deal of power is organized into large economic institutions—industrial corporations, banks, utilities, insurance companies, and investment firms. These economic organizations decide what will be produced, how much it will cost, how many people will be employed, and what their wages will be. They determine how goods and services will be distributed, what technology will be developed, what profits will be made and how they will be distributed, how much money will be available for capital investment, what interest rates will be charged, and many similarly important questions.

ECONOMIC POWER IN AMERICA

Decisions made in corporate boardrooms affect our lives as much as, or perhaps even more than, those typically made by governments. Traditionally, pluralism portrayed business as just another interest group, competing with all the other interest groups to influence public policy. Corporate power, according to the pluralists, depended on the political skills and resources of particular individuals, groups, and industries within the corporate world, the performance of the economy, the climate of public opinion, and the relative strength of competing groups.

In contrast, we view economic elites as distinctively powerful, not only in shaping government policy, but also more importantly in making decisions themselves which directly influence the lives of all of us. Even some of the leading pluralist scholars have revised their views about corporate power in America. Robert A. Dahl and Charles E. Lindblom have publicly confessed their "error":

> . . . in our discussion of pluralism we made another error—and it is a continuing error in social science—in regarding business and business groups as playing the same interest-group role as other groups in polyarchal systems, though more powerful. Businessmen play a distinctive role in polyarchal politics that is

qualitatively different from that of any interest group. It is also much more powerful than an interest-group role.[1]

Today these scholars lament that the private corporation is "hierarchical" and not governed democratically by its employees. Of course, this is true. But what these pluralists still do not understand is that *all organizations are hierarchical.* Corporate governance is not unique. "Virtually all nongovernment institutions can be described in similar terms. Universities, foundations, labor unions, many professional and trade associations, religious institutions and organizations, charitable organizations—even public-interest groups—all exercise political power, and yet none is governed according to democratic principles or precepts. In its internal system of authority, the corporation is actually quite typical of the social structures that characterize democratic societies."[2]

Since business and financial leaders make decisions about "who gets what when and how,"[3] studies of power in society must include economic power.

THE CONCENTRATION OF ECONOMIC POWER

Economic power in America is highly concentrated. Indeed, only about 4,300 individuals—two one-thousandths of 1 percent of the population—exercise formal authority over more than one half of the nation's industrial assets, two thirds of all banking assets, one half of all assets in communications and utilities, and more than two thirds of all insurance assets. These individuals are the presidents, officer-directors, and directors of the largest corporations in these fields. The reason for this concentration of power in the hands of so few people is found in the concentration of industrial and financial assets in a small number of giant corporations. The following statistics can only suggest the scale and concentration of modern corporate enterprise in America.

There are about 200,000 *industrial corporations* in the United States with total assets in 1990 of about $2.6 trillion. The 100 corporations listed in Table 2–1 control 74.6 percent ($1.2 trillion) of all industrial assets. The five largest industrial corporations—General Electric, General Motors, Ford Motors, IBM, and Exxon—control 28 percent of all industrial assets.

The concentration of resources among a relatively few industrial corporations is slowly increasing over time. In a 42-year period, the proportion of all industrial assets controlled by the top 100 corporations grew as follows:

1950	1960	1970	1980	1983	1986	1992
39.8%	46.4%	52.3%	55.0%	58.2%	61.1%	74.6%

[1] Robert A. Dahl and Charles E. Lindblom, *Politics Economics and Welfare*, 2nd ed. (New York: Harper, 1976), preface.

[2] David Vogel, "The New Political Science of Corporate Power," *The Public Interest*, 87 (Spring 1987), 63–79.

[3] Which, of course is Harold Lasswell's very definition of *politics.* See Harold D. Lasswell, *Politics: Who Gets What When and How* (New York: McGraw-Hill, 1936).

TABLE 2–1   The Largest U.S. Industrial Corporations

Rank (by Assets)	Corporation	Assets ($ Billions)	Cumulative Percent*
1	General Electric	192.9	7.3
2	General Motors	191.0	14.6
3	Ford Motors	180.5	21.5
4	IBM	86.7	24.8
5	Exxon	85.0	28.0
6	Philip Morris	50.0	29.9
7	Chrysler	40.7	31.4
8	Mobil	40.6	33.0
9	Du Pont	38.9	34.5
10	Xerox	34.1	35.8
11	Chevron	34.0	37.0
12	RJR-Nabisco	32.0	38.3
13	Amoco	28.5	39.3
14	Shell Oil	27.0	40.4
15	Texaco	26.0	41.4
16	Dow Chemical	25.4	42.3
17	Atlantic Richfield	24.3	43.3
18	Procter & Gamble	24.0	44.2
19	Eastman Kodak	23.1	45.0
20	Pepsico	21.0	45.8
21	Textron	18.4	46.5
22	Hanson Industries	18.4	47.2
23	Weyerhaeuser	18.2	47.9
24	Boeing	18.1	48.6
25	Occidental	17.9	49.3
26	USX	17.3	50.0
27	Berkshire Hathaway	16.9	50.6
28	Tenneco	16.6	51.2
29	International Paper	16.5	51.9
30	United Technologies	15.9	52.5
31	American Brands	15.0	53.0
32	Caterpillar	13.9	53.6
33	McDonnell Douglas	13.7	54.1
34	Hewlett-Packard	13.7	54.6
35	Minnesota Mining & Mfg.	12.0	55.1
36	Johnson & Johnson	11.9	55.5
37	Phillips Petroleum	11.5	56.0
38	Deere	11.4	56.4
39	Digital Equipment	11.3	56.8
40	Merck	11.1	57.2
41	Coca-Cola	11.1	57.7
42	Alcoa	11.0	58.1
43	Georgia Pacific	10.9	58.5
44	Bristol Myers	10.8	58.9
45	Temple Inland	10.8	59.3
46	Allied Signal	10.8	59.7
47	Motorola	10.6	60.1
48	Coastal	10.6	60.5
49	Anheuser-Busch	10.5	60.9
50	Westinghouse	10.4	61.3
51	Sara Lee	10.0	61.7
52	Conagra	9.8	62.1
53	Rockwell	9.7	62.4
54	Pfizer	9.6	62.8
55	Baxter	9.5	63.2

TABLE 2–1 *(Continued)*

Rank (by Assets)	Corporation	Assets ($ Billions)	Cumulative Percent*
56	Unocal	9.5	63.5
57	Champion	9.4	63.9
58	J.E. Seagram	9.3	64.2
59	Ethyl	9.2	64.6
60	Monsanto	9.1	64.9
61	Amerada Hess	8.7	65.3
62	Eli Lilly	8.7	65.6
63	Goodyear	8.6	65.9
64	Intel	8.1	66.2
65	Coca-Cola Enterprises	8.0	66.5
66	Cooper Industries	7.6	66.8
67	Archer Daniels	7.5	67.1
68	Unisys	7.5	67.4
69	American Home	7.1	67.7
70	Hoechst	7.0	67.9
71	Abbott Laboratories	6.9	68.2
72	Reynolds Metal	6.9	68.5
73	Lockheed	6.8	68.7
74	Stone Container	6.7	69.0
75	Emerson	6.6	69.2
76	Pitney Bowes	6.5	69.5
77	James River	6.4	69.7
78	Scott Paper	6.3	70.0
79	LTV	6.2	70.2
80	Whirlpool	6.1	70.4
81	Sun Oil	6.1	70.7
82	Amax	6.0	70.9
83	Kimberly-Clark	6.0	71.1
84	Raytheon	6.0	71.3
85	H.J. Heinz	5.9	71.6
86	Ashland Oil	5.7	71.8
87	PPG	5.7	72.0
88	W.R. Grace	5.6	72.2
89	TRW	5.5	72.4
90	Colgate Palmolive	5.4	72.6
91	American Cyanamid	5.4	72.8
92	Black & Decker	5.4	73.0
93	Borden	5.3	73.2
94	Texas Instruments	5.2	73.4
95	CPC International	5.2	73.6
96	Owens Illinois	5.2	73.8
97	Ralston Purina	5.2	74.0
98	Bethlehem Steel	5.1	74.2
99	Miles	5.0	74.4
100	Union Carbide	4.9	74.6

Total Industrial Assets: $2,630 billion

Total Number of Industrial Corporations: 202,000

SOURCES: Derived from data in *Fortune*, April 19, 1993, pp. 184–203; also *Statistical Abstract of the United States 1992*, pp. 540–41.

*In this table and in Tables 2–3 and 2–4, cumulative percent refers to the total percentage of the nation's assets in the category (for example, industrial corporations) at a specific ranking. Thus, in this table the first ten corporations (through Xerox) account for 35.8 percent of the nation's industrial assets. Corporate figures are for 1992; total asset figures are for 1990.

TABLE 2–2   The Largest U.S. Utilities and Communications Companies

Rank (by Assets)	Company	Assets ($ Billions)
1	AT&T	57.2
2	GTE	42.0
3	BellSouth	31.5
4	Bell Atlantic	28.0
5	US West	27.9
6	NYNEX	27.7
7	Pacific Gas & Electric	24.2
8	Southwestern Bell	23.8
9	Ameritech	22.8
10	Pacific Telesis Group	22.5
11	Southern	20.0
12	Texas Utilities	19.4
13	SCECorp	19.1
14	Commonwealth Edison	18.0
15	Public Svc. Enterprise Group	14.8
16	Entergy	14.2
17	American Electric Power	14.2
18	Tele-Communications	13.1
19	Dominion Resources	12.6
20	Philadelphia Electric	12.6
21	Houston Industries	12.4
22	FDL Group	12.3
23	Centerior Energy	12.0
24	Consolidated Edison of New York	11.6
25	Pacificorp	11.3
26	Duke Power	10.8
27	Detroit Edison	10.4
28	Long Island Lighting	10.2
29	Central & South West	9.8
30	Northeast Utilities	9.8
31	Niagara Mohawk Power	8.6
32	Pennsylvania Power & Light	8.1
33	Ohio Edison	7.8
34	General Public Utilities	7.7
35	Carolina Power & Light	7.7
36	Baltimore Gas & Electric	7.3
37	Gulf States Utilities	6.9
38	CMS Energy	6.8
39	Columbia Gas System	6.5
40	Pinnacle West Capital	6.4
41	Panhandle Eastern	6.4
42	Potomac Electric Power	6.1
43	Union Electric	5.8
44	Western Resources	5.5
45	Oglethorpe Power	5.4
46	Florida Progress	5.3
47	Illinois Power	5.3
48	Consolidated Natural Gas	5.2
49	N.Y. State Electric & Gas	5.1
50	Allegheny Power System	5.0

SOURCE: Derived from data in *Fortune*, May 31, 1993, p. 224.

TABLE 2–3   The Largest U.S. Commercial Banks

Rank (by Assets)	Bank	Assets ($ Billions)	Cumulative Percent
1	Citicorp	213.7	6.2
2	BankAmerica	180.6	11.4
3	Chemical Banking	139.7	15.4
4	NationsBank	118.1	18.9
5	J.P. Morgan & Co.	102.9	21.8
6	Chase Manhattan	95.8	24.6
7	Bankers Trust New York	72.4	26.7
8	Banc One	61.4	28.5
9	Wells Fargo	52.5	30.0
10	PNC Bank	51.3	31.5
11	First Union	51.3	33.0
12	First Interstate Bancorp	50.8	34.4
13	First Chicago	49.2	35.9
14	Fleet Financial Group	46.9	37.2
15	Norwest	44.5	38.5
16	NBD Bancorp	40.9	39.7
17	Bank of New York	40.9	40.9
18	Barnett Banks	39.4	42.0
19	Republic New York	37.1	43.1
20	Suntrust	36.6	44.1
21	Wachovia	33.3	45.1
22	Bank of Boston	32.3	46.0
23	Mellon Bank	31.5	46.9
24	First Fidelity Bancorp	31.4	47.8
25	Keycorp	30.1	48.7
26	National City	28.9	49.6
27	Comerica	26.5	50.3
28	Shawmut	25.2	51.0
29	Society	24.9	51.8
30	Corestates Financial	23.6	52.4
31	First Bank System	23.5	53.1
32	Boatmen's Bancshares	23.3	53.8
33	National Westminster	22.7	54.5
34	Continental	22.4	55.1
35	U.S. Bancorp	20.7	55.7
36	First of America	20.1	56.3
37	Marine Midland	17.1	56.8
38	MNC Financial	16.9	57.3
39	Union Bank	16.8	57.8
40	State Street Boston	16.4	58.2
41	Northern Trust	14.9	58.7
42	Midlantic	14.4	59.1
43	Huntington Bancshares	13.8	59.5
44	UJB Financial	13.7	59.9
45	Firstar Corp	13.1	60.3
46	Harris Bankcorp	12.7	60.6
47	Southtrust	12.7	61.0
48	Bancorp Hawaii	12.7	61.4
49	Crestar Financial	12.6	61.7
50	Meridian Bancorp	12.2	62.1

Total Commercial Banking Assets: $3,458 billion

Total Number of Commercial Banks: 12,345

SOURCES: Derived from data in *Fortune*, May 31, 1993, p. 210; also *Statistical Abstract of the United States 1992*, pp. 490, 495.

TABLE 2–4   The Largest U.S. Life Insurance Companies

Rank (by Assets)	Corporation	Assets ($ Billions)	Cumulative Percent
1	Prudential of America	155.0	11.0
2	Metropolitan Life	118.1	19.4
3	Teachers Insurance & Annuity	61.8	23.8
4	Aetna Life	50.9	27.4
5	New York Life	46.9	30.7
6	Equitable Life Assurance	46.6	34.0
7	Connecticut General Life	44.1	37.2
8	Northwestern Mutual Life	39.7	40.0
9	John Hancock Mutual Life	39.1	42.8
10	Principal Mutual Life	35.1	45.3
11	Travelers	34.2	47.7
12	Massachusetts Mutual Life	31.1	49.9
13	Lincoln National Life	28.8	51.9
14	IDS Life	23.3	53.6
15	Hartford Life	20.8	55.1
16	Allstate Life	20.3	56.5
17	Nationwide Life	19.3	57.9
18	Variable Annuity Life	17.3	59.1
19	Mutual of New York	16.9	60.3
20	New England Mutual Life	16.4	61.5
21	State Farm Life	15.4	62.6
22	Aetna Life & Annuity	15.2	63.7
23	Jackson National Life	14.8	64.7
24	New York Life & Annuity	12.6	65.6
25	Pacific Mutual Life	11.5	66.4
26	Merrill Lynch Life Insurance	11.4	67.2
27	Continental Assurance	11.2	68.0
28	Connecticut Mutual Life	11.2	68.8
29	Phoenix Home Life Mutual	10.4	69.6
30	Equitable Variable Life	10.4	70.3
31	Provident Life & Accident	10.0	71.0
32	American Family Life Assurance	10.0	71.7
33	Transamerica Occidental Life	9.9	72.4
34	Transamerica Life & Annuity	9.6	73.1
35	Keyport Life	9.3	73.8
36	Unum Life	8.9	74.4
37	Guardian Life of America	7.9	75.0
38	American Life	7.8	75.5
39	Sun Life Assur. of Canada	7.5	76.0
40	Safeco Life Insurance	7.4	76.6
41	General American Life	7.1	77.1
42	National Home Life Assurance	6.9	77.6
43	Minnesota Mutual Life	6.8	78.0
44	State Mutual of America	6.7	78.5
45	Kemper Investors Life	6.5	79.0
46	Penn Mutual Life	6.2	79.4
47	Life Insurance Co. of Virginia	5.9	79.8
48	Western National Life	5.8	80.3
49	Sun Life of America	5.7	80.7
50	Franklin Life	5.6	81.1

Total Assets of Life Insurance Companies: $1,408 billion

Total Number of Life Insurance Companies: 2,200

SOURCES: Derived from data in *Fortune*, May 31, 1993, p. 218; also *Statistical Abstract of the United States 1992*, p. 514.

Concentration in *communications* and *utilities* is even greater than in industry. For many decades, this sector of the nation's economy was dominated by the American Telephone and Telegraph Company (AT&T)—the single largest private corporation in the world, prior to 1984. Following the federal court-ordered divestiture of its telephone operating companies, AT&T remains the largest communications company, with over $57 billion in assets. Its divested offsprings now occupy seven of the top ten positions on Table 2–2. (See also Chapter 6, AT&T: Evidence of Convergence.)

The financial world is also highly concentrated. Of 12,345 banks serving the nation, the 50 largest *banks* (see Table 2–3) control 62 percent of all banking assets. Five banks (Citicorp, BankAmerica, Chemical, NationsBank, and J.P. Morgan) control 22 percent of all banking assets. Giant bank mergers in the last decade have resulted in a greater concentration of banking assets than anytime in recent history. BankAmerica (formerly ranked number 3) merged with Security Pacific (formerly ranked number 6) to create a challenger to Citicorp's number 1 ranking. Two large New York banks, Chemical (formerly ranked number 4) and Manufacturers Hanover (formerly ranked number 7) merged to push once-dominant Chase Manhattan down in rankings. And banking in the southeastern United States was concentrated with the merger of NCNB (Charlotte, N.C.), C&S (Atlanta, Ga.), and Sovran (Norfolk, Va.) into NationsBank, currently ranked number 4.

In the *insurance* field, 50 companies (see Table 2–4) out of 2,200 control over 80 percent of all insurance assets. Two companies (Prudential and Metropolitan) control nearly 30 percent of all insurance assets.

Finally, in the field of *investment* banking, we have identified fifteen major Wall Street firms (see Table 2–5). These firms are in a central strategic position in the American economy. They decide whether, when, and under what terms American corporations (and state and local governments) can sell stocks, bonds,

---

TABLE 2–5   The Investment Firms

Bear, Stearns & Co.
Brown Brothers, Harriman & Co.
Dean Witter Reynolds Inc.
Dillon, Read & Company, Inc.
Donaldson, Lufkin & Jenrette
First Boston Corporation
Goldman, Sachs and Company
Kidder, Peabody and Company, Inc.
Lehman Brothers
Merrill Lynch
Morgan Stanley and Company, Inc.
Paine Webber Inc.
Salomon Brothers
Smith Barney Shearson Inc.
Lazard Frères and Company

---

and other securities. These firms "underwrite" the sale of new securities, usually joining together in a large syndicate to do so. Then they sell these stocks, bonds, and securities to their own individual and institutional client-investors.

THE MULTINATIONALS: WORLDWIDE BIG BUSINESS

The concentration of industrial power in a relatively few large institutions is not an exclusively American phenomenon. On the contrary, the trend toward corporate concentration of resources is worldwide. It is not only large American corporations which have expanded their markets throughout the world, invested in overseas plants and banks, and merged with foreign corporations. Large European and Japanese firms compete very effectively for world business. Just as American companies have greatly expanded investments abroad, so too have foreign companies sharply increased their business in the United States. The result is the emergence of truly supranational corporations, which not only trade worldwide but also build and operate plants in many nations.

The world's largest non-American corporations are listed in Table 2–6. Royal Dutch Shell (Netherlands) is the largest industrial corporation in the world, larger than its American competitor, Exxon. British Petroleum (BP) is

TABLE 2–6   The Multinationals: The World's Largest Non-American Corporations

Rank	Corporation	Business	Country
1	Royal Dutch Shell	Energy	Netherlands
2	Nippon Telegraph & Telephone	Telecommunications	Japan
3	Toyota Motor Corporation	Autos	Japan
4	Matsushita Electric	Appliances	Japan
5	Hitachi	Electronics	Japan
6	Daimler-Benz	Autos	Germany
7	Siemans	Electronics	Germany
8	British Petroleum	Energy	U.K.
9	Elf Aquitaine	Energy	France
10	Tokyo Electric	Utilities	Japan
11	Unilever	Food	Netherlands
12	British Telecommunications	Telecommunications	U.K.
13	Nestlé	Food	Switzerland
14	Alcatel Alsthom	Electronics	France
15	Nissan	Autos	Japan
16	Fiat	Autos	Italy
17	British Gas	Utilities	U.K.
18	Sony	Appliances	Japan
19	Mitsubishi	Trading	Japan
20	B.A.T.	Beverages	U.K.
21	Bayer	Drugs	Germany
22	BCE	Telecommunications	Canada
23	VEBA	Utilities	Germany
24	Imperial Chemicals	Chemicals	U.K.
25	Volkswagen	Autos	Germany

SOURCE: Derived from data in *Forbes*, July 20, 1992.

TABLE 2–7   The World's Largest Banks

Rank	Corporation	Country
1	Dai-Ichi Kangyo	Japan
2	Sumitomo	Japan
3	Fuji	Japan
4	Sanwa	Japan
5	Mitsubishi	Japan
6	Credit Agricole	France
7	Banque Nationale de Paris	France
8	Credit Lyonnais	France
9	Deutsche Bank	Germany
10	Barclays Bank	U.K.

SOURCE: *Institutional Investor*, July 1991.

roughly equivalent to Exxon. Toyota, Daimler-Benz, Nissan, Fiat, and Volkswagen all are smaller than America's GM, Ford, and Chrysler; but these foreign corporations sell more cars outside of the United States.

Foreign corporations sell their productions in the United States (oil, automobiles, chemicals, electrical products) and also buy American corporations, which become subsidiaries of the foreign multinationals. For example, Royal Dutch Shell owns Shell Oil; British Petroleum owns Standard Oil of Ohio; Tengelmann (Germany) owns A&P supermarkets; Nestlé owns the Libby, Stouffer, and Beech-Nut corporations; Unilever owns the Lever Brothers and Lipton companies; Bayer owns Miles and Cutter Laboratories (Bayer aspirin); and so on.

World banking is largely *outside* of the United States. America's largest bank, Citicorp, does not even appear on the list of the world's ten largest banks (see Table 2–7).

In brief, the central feature of the American and world economy is the concentration of resources in relatively few large corporations. Most of this concentration occurred many years ago. "The long-established norm of market structure and behavior is that of *oligopoly*, that is, the constrained rivalry of a few interdependent sellers who compete mainly by means of product differentiation."[4] In recent years concentration has continued to increase, although at a slower rate than early in the twentieth century. It is clear that society is *not* going to return to a small, romanticized, perhaps mythical, world of individual enterprise.

WHO CONTROLS THE CORPORATION?

In the formal, legal sense, the board of directors "controls" the modern corporation. The average number of board members in the 100 largest indus-

---

[4] Edward S. Herman, *Corporate Control, Corporate Power* (Cambridge, Mass.: Cambridge University Press, 1981), p. 1.

trial corporations is 15. However, "inside" directors—those who are also top management officers in the corporation—usually dominate board decision-making. Inside directors usually include the president and the top senior vice-presidents. About 40 percent of corporate directors are inside directors. Outside directors—persons who serve on the board but who take no direct part in managing the corporation—usually defer to the judgment of the inside officer-directors. About 60 percent of all directors are "outside" directors. Outside directors are chosen to serve on the board by the inside directors, usually the chairman and chief executive officer (CEO), who also decide on their pay and perks. Most outside directors are themselves current or retired chief executives of other large corporations; their loyalties tend to be with their fellow CEOs running the corporation. However, *all* directors have a legal responsibility to the owners (stockholders) of the corporation to protect their investment. All directors are formally elected by the stockholders, who cast their votes on the basis of one share equals one vote.

The millions of middle-class Americans who own corporate stock have virtually no influence over the decisions of directors. When confronted with mismanagement, these stockholders simply sell their stock, rather than try to challenge the powers of the directors. Indeed, most stockholders sign over "proxies" to top management so that top management may cast these proxy votes at the annual meetings of stockholders. Management itself usually selects its own "slate" for the board of directors and easily elects them with the help of proxies.

While a majority of large corporations are controlled by their own top management, some corporations are dominated by a small "control bloc" of stock owners in cooperation with top management. The stock of large corporations is widely distributed among the stock-owning public. This sometimes enables small "control blocs" of only 1 or 2 percent of the total stock of the corporation to hold a strategic position—electing its own directors and influencing corporate decisions. Thus, some outside directors may represent the interest of control blocs of stock on the board.

Another type of outside corporate director is one representing financial interests (banks, insurance companies, investment firms). These financial interests wish to oversee the use of their funds by the corporation. Sometimes part of the price of a large loan from a major bank or insurance company to an industrial corporation will include a seat on the board of directors of that corporation. Outside directors representing financial interests do not usually take a direct role in decision-making; they perform a general watch-dog role over their investment.

A few outside directors of large corporations represent public relations efforts by top management to improve the image of the corporation. For example, a few corporations have selected civil rights activists, blacks, women, and consumer activists for their boards. (When the Chrysler Corporation faced the prospect of bankruptcy, it ceded a seat on its board to the president of the United Automobile Workers in exchange for union acceptance of a less costly contract.) It may be true that these corporations really want the counsel of these people; however, one suspects that they also want to promote an image of social responsibility. It is doubtful that these particular people are influential in corporate decision-making.

Finally, there are the corporate directors—whether inside officers or outsiders—who represent family owners. Family ownership and domination of large corporations has not yet disappeared in America despite marked decline in family control of corporations over the last several decades.

Thus, corporate board members can be divided into types. The following percentage approximations of various types of corporate directors are estimated for the 1,475 members of the 100 largest industrial corporations:[5]

Insiders

Manager-directors	44%

Outsiders

Former managers	6
Financial representatives	8
Ownership representatives	13
Substantial business with corporation	11
Charitable, civic, or educational representatives	5
Other	<u>13</u>

Outsider total	56%

Managers usually triumph in the boardroom. The inside directors, although only a minority of most boards, usually vote as a solid, unified block under the direction of the president. Their block voting strength on the board is augmented by their greater depth of knowledge of the organization, its technology, and its business problems. Insiders work full time on corporate affairs, continuously communicating with each other. Outsiders have no such information or communication base.

Outside directors, with some exceptions, are "invited" to serve on boards by the managers. They are "guests" in the boardroom. They usually have a sense of loyalty to the president who put them on the board. They are passive on most management decisions. "No one likes to be the skunk at the garden party."[6] They may advise on special areas of competence; they may help coordinate decision-making with major suppliers or buyers; and by their presence on the board they may help assure the outside world that the organization is in good hands. The only important exceptions to these usually passive outside managers are those who still represent large stockholder interests.

A brief glimpse inside the boardrooms of Chase Manhattan, Du Pont, and IBM (see Table 2–8) gives some indication of the principle ties of the directors of these corporations. We have classified these directors as inside

---

[5] Estimates from materials presented in Herman, *Corporate Control, Corporate Power*, Chap. 2.
[6] *Business Week*, September 8, 1986, p. 60.

TABLE 2–8   Inside the Boardroom

AT CHASE MANHATTAN
(Directors of the Chase Manhattan Corporation, 1992)

Inside	Outside (Corporate)
Thomas G. Labrecque 　Chairman and Chief Executive Officer Arthur F. Ryan 　President and Chief Operating Officer Richard J. Boyle 　Vice Chairman Robert R. Douglass 　Vice Chairman	M. Anthony Burns 　Chairman & CEO, Ryder System James L. Ferguson 　Chairman & CEO, General Foods Edward S. Finkelstein 　Chairman & CEO, R.H. Macy Robert E. Floweree 　Retired Chairman, Georgia Pacific H. Lawrence Fuller
Outside (Public Interest)	Chairman & CEO, Amoco Oil Howard C. Kauffmann
Joan Ganz Cooney 　Chairman, Children's Television Workshop Richard W. Lyman 　Former President, Stanford University John H. McArthur 　Dean, Harvard School of Business David T. McLaughlin 　President, Aspen Institute	Retired President, Exxon Edmund T. Pratt, Jr. 　Chairman, Pfizer Henry B. Schacht 　Chairman & CEO, Cummins Engine A. Alfred Taubman 　President, Taubman Inc. Donald H. Trautlein 　Retired Chairman, Bethlehem Steel Kay R. Whitmore 　Chairman & CEO, Eastman Kodak

AT DU PONT
(Directors of the Du Pont Corporation, 1992)

Inside	Outside (Corporate)
Edgar S. Woolard, Jr. 　Chairman & CEO Constantine S. Nicandros 　Vice Chairman John A. Krol 　Vice Chairman	Edgar M. Bronfman 　Chairman & CEO, Seagram Company; 　President, World Jewish Congress Edgar M. Bronfman, Jr. 　President, Seagram Company Charles M. Harper
Family	Chairman & CEO, Conagra Inc. J.L. Weinberg
Edward B. du Pont	Chairman, Goldman, Sachs & Co.
Outside (Public Interest)	
Andrew F. Brimmer 　Brimmer & Company Louisa C. Duemling 　World Resources Institute Richard E. Heckart 　National Association of Manufacturers Howard W. Johnson 　Former President, M.I.T. Margaret P. MacKimm 　World Press Institute H. Rodney Sharp 　Longwood Foundation	

TABLE 2–8   (Continued)

AT IBM
(Directors of the IBM Corporation, 1992)

Inside	Outside (Corporate)
John F. Akers	Stephen D. Bechtel, Jr.
Chairman & CEO	Chairman, Bechtel Corporation
Jack D. Kuehler	James E. Burke
President	Former Chairman, Johnson & Johnson
John R. Opel	Thomas F. First, Jr.
Executive Comm.	Chairman, Hospital Corporation of America
Frank A. Metz, Jr.	Fritz Gerber
Senior Vice President	Chairman & CEO, Roche (drugs)
	Nicholas DeB. Katzenbach
Outside (Public Interest)	Former Attorney General of the U.S.;
Harold Brown	Chairman of American Bank Shares
Former Secretary of Defense	J. Richard Munro
Richard W. Lyman	Chairman, Time Warner
Former President, Stanford University	Thomas S. Murphy
John B. Slaughter	Chairman, Capital Cities–ABC
President, Occidental College	Edgar S. Woolard, Jr.
Nanneri O. Keohane	Chairman & CEO, Du Pont
President, Wellesley College	
Judith Richards Hope	
Attorney	

SOURCE: Based on data from *Moody's Industrial Manual, 1992.*

and outside; and we have classified outsiders as those who represent ties to other corporations and banks and those who we believe were appointed to their posts as representatives of the "public interest."

THE MANAGERS: CLIMBING THE CORPORATE LADDER

The top echelons of American corporate life are occupied primarily by people who have climbed the corporate ladder from relatively obscure and powerless bottom rungs. It is our rough estimate that less than 10 percent of the 1,475 presidents and directors of the top 100 corporations are heirs of wealthy families. The rest—the "managers"—owe their rise to power not to family connections, but to their own success in organizational life. Of course, these managers are overwhelmingly upper middle class and upper class in social origin, and most attended Ivy League colleges and universities. (The social origin and background of top elites are discussed in Chapter 7.) The rise of the manager is a recent phenomenon. As recently as 1950, we estimate that 30 percent of the top corporate elite were heirs of wealthy families. (Indeed, even since 1980, Henry Ford II stepped down as chairman of Ford Motors, and David Rockefeller retired as chairman of Chase Manhattan.) How can we explain the rise to power of the corporate manager?

Today the requirements of technology and planning have greatly increased the need in industry for specialized talent and skill in organization. Capital is something that a corporation can now supply to itself. Thus, there has been a shift in power in the American economy from capital to organized intelligence. This is reflected in the decline of individual- and family-controlled large corporations and in an increase in the percentage of large corporations controlled by management.

Following the Industrial Revolution in America in the late nineteenth century and well into the twentieth century, the nation's largest corporations were controlled by the tycoons who created them—Andrew Carnegie (Carnegie Steel, later United States Steel, and today USX); Andrew Mellon (Alcoa and Mellon banks); Henry Ford (Ford Motors); J.P. Morgan (J.P. Morgan); and, of course, John D. Rockefeller (Standard Oil Company, later broken into Exxon, Mobil, Chevron, Atlantic Richfield, and other large oil companies). But by the 1930s control of most large corporations had passed to professional managers. As early as 1932, Adolf Berle and Gardiner Means, in their classic book, *The Modern Corporation and Private Property*, described the separation of ownership from control. The theory of "managerialism" became the conventional wisdom about corporate governance.[7]

It was recognized early on that corporate managers might run their firms in ways that serve their own best interests rather than those of the owners; for example, paying themselves multimillion-dollar annual salaries and providing themselves with lavish corporate-paid lifestyles. But for decades, individual and institutional stockholders largely ignored this potential principal-agent problem. Stockholders' power was fragmented and dispersed; there was not much they could do, other than sell their stock, even if they knew that managers were taking personal advantage of their position. But perhaps a more important reason that managers were largely unchallenged was that the American economy prospered from the 1940s through the 1970s. (An investment in the average Fortune 500 stock in 1942 quadrupled in value, even after accounting for inflation, by 1972, even while paying yearly dividends of 6 percent.) Governance of the U.S. corporation seemed to be working well, rewarding both managers and owners.

Liberal economist John Kenneth Galbraith summarized the triumph of managerialism:

> Seventy years ago the corporation was the instrument of its owners and a projection of their personalities. The names of these principals—Carnegie, Rockefeller, Harriman, Mellon, Guggenheim, Ford—were well known across the land. They are still known, but for the art galleries and philanthropic foundations they established and their descendants who are in politics. The men who

---

[7] However, for some Marxists and others on the left, managerialism was denied, because it complicated the theory of class struggle in a capitalist society. They argued that great families retained "latent" power—power to be exercised when something goes seriously wrong. Some Marxists, however, accepted the managerial thesis and simply focused on managers as "the leading echelon of the capitalist class." See Paul A. Baran and Paul M. Sweezy, *Monopoly Capital* (Newark: Monthly Review Press, 1966).

now head the great corporations are unknown. Not for a generation did people outside Detroit in the automobile industry know the name of the current head of General Motors. In the manner of all men, he must produce identification when paying by check. So with Ford, Standard Oil, and General Dynamics. The men who now run the large corporations own no appreciable share of the enterprise. They are selected not by the stockholders but, in the common case, by a board of directors which narcissistically they selected themselves.[8]

How does one climb the corporate ladder? It is not easy, and most who begin the climb fall by the wayside at some point in their careers.

Just to be in the running, a career riser must discipline himself carefully. He must become a seasoned decision-maker. He must cultivate an aura of success and sustain his upward momentum on the executive ladder. He must be loyal to a fault, tolerably bright, fairly creative, politically agile, always tough, sometimes flexible, unfailingly sociable and, in the minds of his company's directors, seem superior to a dozen men who are almost as good. He must also be lucky.[9]

Today, more than ever before, getting to the top requires the skills of a "technocrat"—knowledge of bureaucratic organization, technical skills and information, extensive formal education (including postgraduate degrees), and proven ability to work within legal constraints and governmental regulations. Very few sons and no daughters are taking over the presidencies of large corporations owned by their families. Fewer than 10 of the nation's 500 largest corporations are headed by men whose families had previously run the corporation.[10] Top corporate management is drawn from the ranks of upper-middle-class, well-educated, white, male management, financial, and legal experts.

Perhaps the most significant change over the years has been the rising number of top corporate and governmental executives who have acquired graduate degrees. Today over half of the corporate presidents of the 500 largest corporations have advanced degrees, including M.B.A.s (masters of business administration), law degrees, and Ph.D.s. (See Chapter 7.)

An increasing number of top corporate leaders are coming out of finance and law, as opposed to production, operations, advertising, sales, engineering, or research. Lawyers and accountants now head two out of every five large corporations. This is further evidence that finance, taxation, and governmental regulation are the chief problems confronting large corporations. The problems of production, sales, engineering, and transportation have faded in relation to the pressing problems of money and power.

Getting to the top by climbing the ladder of the giant corporation is not only difficult, it is also risky. The chances of any one individual making it to the top are infinitesimal.

---

[8] John Kenneth Galbraith, *The New Industrial State* (Boston: Houghton Mifflin, 1967), p. 323.

[9] Howard Morgans, former president of Procter & Gamble, as quoted in "Proud to Be an Organization Man," *Forbes*, May 15, 1972, p. 241.

[10] Charles G. Burch, "A Group Profile of the Fortune 500 Chief Executives," *Fortune*, May 1976, p. 174. See also *Business Week*, October 23, 1987, p. 37.

Yet hundreds of thousands of executives willingly devote entire careers to working their way up through these giant corporations. On the lower rungs of the ladder, when they are in their 20s, all of them dream of reaching the top. As they advance into their 30s, and receive more responsibility and more money, the dream flowers brightly. Some time in their 40s and 50s, however, most realize they aren't going to make it. They are sorely disappointed, but it's too late to change. Comfortable and secure, they stay. Then each year there are perhaps a dozen or so—the lucky men who go all the way.[11]

CORPORATE COUNTER-REVOLUTIONS

Only a decade ago the top managers of large corporations were considered impregnable; nothing short of bankruptcy could dislodge them. Corporate managers ran the American economy, perpetuating themselves in office; they ruled without much interference from outside directors, stockholders, employees, or consumers. But beginning in the 1980s, new challenges to the imperial position of top management arose, most notably from: (1) a new activism by outside directors and large stockholders, checking the power of corporate chief executives and occasionally forcing their retirement; and (2) a rise in "hostile takeovers" led by corporate raiders who acquire corporate stock and voting power in order to force the ouster and replacement of existing management.

The new activism by outside directors and large stockholders, particularly institutional investors—pension funds, mutual funds, insurance companies, and banks—is largely attributable to slower economic growth in recent years and the failure of some American corporations to remain competitive in global markets.[12] Traditionally, poor economic performance by management resulted in the sale of the corporation's stock by institutional investors, who simply shifted their investment to more profitable corporations. The chief executives of poorly performing corporations might suffer some public embarrassment from falling prices of their companies' stock, perhaps even some shouted insults at annual stockholders' meetings, but their positions of power generally remained secure. However, as institutional stock ownership has grown to over half of all stockholding in the nation, top corporate managers have come face to face with more informed and aggressive representatives of owners.[13] Mutual and pension fund managers as well as managers of banks and insurance companies are more likely than small individual investors to take action against the managers of poorly performing corporations in which they have invested funds. Traditionally, fund managers routinely voted with management, but today they are taking a much more aggressive role in corporate governance. Because the funds now own so much stock, it is not always possible for them to "dump" it without suffering heavy losses,

---

[11] "Proud to Be an Organization Man," p. 244.

[12] See Margaret M. Blair, "Who's in Charge Here?" *Brookings Review* (Fall 1991), pp. 8–13.

[13] Institutional ownership of stock grew from 15 percent of all outstanding sharers of U.S. corporations in 1965, to 30 percent in 1980, to 50 percent in 1992. See *Fortune*, January 11, 1993, p. 36.

and fund managers have a legal responsibility to protect their own investors. Hence, these managers, acting on behalf of stockholders, are clipping the powers of the corporate chiefs and even on occasion getting some fired. According to *Fortune* magazine: "The fact is, the institutions' fingers are on the most celebrated CEO ousters."[14]

John F. Akers. Consider the rise and fall of John F. Akers, former chairman and chief executive officer of IBM, once America's premier corporation. Akers attended Yale University, majored in engineering, and served four years as a U.S. Navy pilot. He joined IBM in 1960 as a sales representative and rose rapidly up the corporate ladder, becoming a vice-president in 1982. But already IBM was facing tough competition from Japan and from newer, leaner, aggressive U.S. companies like Microsoft, Apple, and Wang. IBM continued to focus its business on large, expensive "mainframe" computers, while the market turned increasingly to smaller, cheaper desktop computers.

Akers was made president of IBM in 1983. He tried to steer "Big Blue" in new directions and to cut costs. Reorganizations and layoffs resulted in thousands of lost jobs in a company that once prided itself on employee morale. But the red ink continued to flow, and stockholders were crushed. IBM stock fell over 70 percent in value (from a 1987 high of $175 to a 1993 low of $48). While many individual and institutional stockholders were publicly critical of Akers, he defiantly held on to his job, claiming the backing of his board. But finally in early 1993, following a report of the corporation's record $5-billion annual loss for 1992, the IBM board forced Akers's resignation following an acrimonious meeting.[15] Prior to resignation Akers had been co-chairman of the Business Roundtable (see Chapter 5) and a director of the New York Times Company, Pepsico, the Metropolitan Museum of Art, the California Institute of Technology, and the United Way of America.

Louis V. Gerstner, Jr. Louis Gerstner made his career as a corporate "fixer"—a manager skilled at turning around the fortunes of depressed companies. So when the IBM board ousted Akers, it sought out Gerstner—an outsider who would bring new thinking to the stodgy corridors of Big Blue and resuscitate the sick giant.

Gerstner earned an engineering degree at Dartmouth before going on to Harvard Business School for his M.B.A. He began his career in 1965 as a corporate fixer with a leading management consulting firm—McKinsey & Company. In 1978 he accepted a senior management position with American Express and was named president six years later. He is credited with having introduced the glitzy gold card program that jacked up the company's revenues. In 1989, following one of the largest corporate mergers in history—R.J. Reynolds (tobacco) and Nabisco (foods) merged as RJR-Nabisco, cur-

---

[14] *Fortune*, January 11, 1993, p. 35.
[15] *Time*, February 8, 1993, p. 54.

rently the nation's twelfth-ranked industrial corporation—Gerstner was lured away from American Express to run the new food and tobacco giant. Its principal owners, the financial firm of Kohlberg, Kravis and Roberts, had funded the merger with billions in junk bonds, nearly sinking the new company with a huge debt load. But in four years, Gerstner cut costs, introduced new products, and reduced the debt load by half. He won the dubious reputation as one of the nation's toughest "slash and burn" CEOs, ruthlessly firing managers and selling off divisions that failed to produce profits.

The IBM board's public search for a new CEO generated an embarrassing squabble between insiders and outsiders. Insiders wanted someone with a technical background who was knowledgeable about the computer industry. Several well-known "techies" turned the job down; rescuing IBM may be the toughest job in corporate America. IBM's outside board member James E. Burke, former chairman of Johnson & Johnson (drugs), finally convinced the board to hire a nontechnical outsider to "bury the old culture" at IBM.[16] Gerstner was recruited from RJR-Nabisco to bring new life to America's largest computer manufacturer.

Other Ousters.   Slow growth and recession in 1991–92 resulted in the ouster of several other prominent corporate chieftains: Robert C. Stempel at General Motors, Paul Lego at Westinghouse, James Robinson at American Express, Kenneth Olsen at Digital Equipment, James Kefelman at Tenneco, Tom Barrett at Goodyear, and others.[17] Yet even though outside directors and institutional stockholders are more active than ever before, most top corporate managers remain firmly entrenched.

HOSTILE TAKEOVERS

The threat of hostile takeovers represents another challenge to management control of corporate America. A hostile takeover involves the purchase of enough stock in a publicly held corporation to force the ouster and replacement of existing corporate management. Indeed, the threat of a hostile takeover may be the dominant force in the behavior of top managers today. The rise of "corporate raiders" like T. Boone Pickens, who specializes in oil companies, and Carl Ichan, who ranges over all kinds of businesses, now threatens the secure and cozy life of the boardroom.

A hostile takeover begins with a corporate raider buying the stock of a corporation on the open market, usually with money borrowed for this purpose. The raider may wish to keep his early purchases secret for a while to avoid rapid rises in the price of the stock; but federal Securities and Exchange Commission rules require disclosure when a person acquires 5 percent of a

---

[16] *Business Week,* April 5, 1993, p. 20.

[17] See Thomas A. Stewart, "The King Is Dead," *Fortune,* January 11, 1993, pp. 34–40.

corporation's stock. The raider may then offer a takeover bid to existing management. Management may reject the bid outright or try to buy back the stock purchased by the raider at a higher price, that is, to offer the raider "greenmail." If the raider and management cannot reach agreement, the hostile takeover proceeds. The raider arranges to borrow additional money—perhaps several billion dollars—to make a purchase offer to the target corporation's stockholders, usually at a price higher than the current stock exchange price. Management may search for a "White Knight"—someone willing to offer even more money to purchase the corporation from its stockholders but who promises to keep the existing management. If the raider wins control of the corporation, he replaces management.

Following a successful takeover, the corporation is heavily laden with new debt. The raider may have borrowed billions to buy out shareholders. The investment firms that provide the loans to finance the corporation's purchase may issue "junk bonds" with high interest rates to attract investors to these risky ventures. The corporation must pay off these bonds with its own revenues. Additionally there may be many millions of dollars in bond-sale commissions and attorneys' fees to pay out. The raider may be forced to sell off parts of the corporation or some of its valuable assets in order to help pay off part of the debt. Thus, the target corporation itself must eventually bear the burden of the takeover battle.

Of course, the raider originally targets the corporation because its stock price is low compared to the value of its assets and/or its potential for future profits. The raider believes that the low price of the stock is a product of poor management performance. The raider hopes that with new management the corporation can improve its performance, pay off its debt, and produce greater profits. And the raider must convince the investment firms who provide the takeover money of the accuracy of his predictions.

Why does a corporation emerge as a target of a hostile takeover? Why have takeovers become so pervasive in the last decade? One explanation is inflation; the cost of replacing existing assets far exceeds the value placed on these assets. It is therefore cheaper to buy existing plants, buildings, machinery, inventories, and the like than to produce new ones. It is cheaper to buy known oil reserves held by oil companies than to search for new oil. Another explanation focuses on mismanagement by isolated, arrogant, lazy American management. Managers not only have allowed American industry to fall behind foreign competition, but they have also failed to put the assets of their corporations to their most productive use. Return on invested capital and world market shares have dwindled. The corporate raiders offer a way to "throw the rascals out" of the boardroom and reinvigorate American enterprise.

Government antitrust and tax policies combine to encourage mergers and takeovers. Tax policies contribute by allowing corporations to deduct from their taxable income the interest on loans used to acquire other companies.

Both the U.S. Department of Justice and the Federal Trade Commission are responsible for enforcing the nation's antitrust laws. These laws forbid "monopoly" and "combinations in restraint of trade" (Sherman Antitrust Act, 1887), "unfair method of competition" and "efforts to reduce competition" (Federal Trade Commission Act, 1914), and the acquisition by one corporation of another "where the effect of such acquisition is to substantially lessen competition" (Clayton Act, 1914). But the interpretations placed on these laws in recent years have given increasing attention to *world* market conditions. It is argued that increasing concentrations of corporate assets in the United States through mergers do *not* "substantially lessen competition" because these firms are competing in a world market against giant Japanese and European multinational corporations. Indeed, in such a world market, it is even argued that the U.S. government should *encourage* mergers of U.S. firms in order to strengthen them against foreign competition.

Still another explanation is greed. The banks and the Wall Street investment firms which finance hostile takeovers charge high fees and commissions on the transactions, and they levy excessive interest rates on the junk bonds. During the 1980s, banking "deregulation" encouraged traditionally conservative commercial banks to compete more intensely for profits. In order to maximize the "interest spread" between what the bank paid for money and what it charged borrowers, banks sought out high-risk loans on which high interest rates could be charged. Initially, banks turned to Third World foreign loans—Mexico, Brazil, Zaire, Argentina. But when these loans turned sour, the banks turned to junk bonds. "The American commercial bank is pinched by the shrinkage of its traditional sources of income and almost desperate to find borrowers willing to pay very high interest rates. And the raider who makes a hostile takeover bid is, of course, perfectly willing to promise very high interest rates; after all, he will not pay them—the company he is aiming to take over will, after it has succumbed."[18]

Are corporate takeovers good or bad for America? There is no easy answer to this important question. The raiders claim that their activities force improvements in efficiency and productivity. Even the potential threat of a takeover forces corporate managers to streamline their operations, eliminate waste, increase revenues, raise profits, and distribute profits to their shareholders rather than spend them on the comforts of management. The raiders argue that American management has grown soft, lazy, and self-satisfied; that, as a result, the American corporation has lost its competitive edge in the world marketplace.

Opponents of the corporate-takeover movement argue that fear of the raider forces management to focus on near-term profits at the expense of long-range research and development. Management must keep the current price of its stock high in order to deter a takeover attempt. Even worse, man-

[18] Peter Drucker, "Corporate Takeovers—What Is to Be Done?" *The Public Interest*, 82 (Winter 1986), 9.

agement often resorts to "poison pills" to deliberately weaken its own corporation to make it unattractive to raiders; it may increase its debt, buy other poorly performing corporations, devalue stockholders' voting powers, or provide itself with "golden parachutes" (rich severance benefits) in the event of ouster. The corporate raiders enrich the shareholders and speculators, but they do so at the expense of the industry itself.

The debt incurred in corporate takeovers is a concern to employees, consumers, and taxpayers. While the original stockholders are paid handsomely by the raider, the corporation must labor intensively to pay off the debt incurred. The corporation may be broken apart and its separate pieces sold, which may disrupt and demoralize employees. Consumers may be forced to pay higher prices. If the corporation cannot meet the high interest payments, bankruptcy threatens. The corporation's heavy interest payments are tax-deductible, thus depriving the U.S. Treasury of corporate tax revenues. And the diversion of American capital from productive investments to takeovers threatens to weaken national productivity.

THE CORPORATE RAIDERS

Carl Ichan.   This name generates fear in America's corporate boardrooms. The dreaded corporate raider has attacked such fortresses as TWA, Gulf + Western, American Can, Uniroyal, Goodrich, and Phillips Petroleum. Ichan graduated from Princeton University and then dropped out of medical school before starting his Wall Street career in investment banking. He founded Ichan and Company with a half-million dollars borrowed from his uncle. He began his corporate raiding in 1978 with a bid to take over the old, undervalued Tappan Company, maker of kitchen stoves. Over the years, he became skilled in identifying corporations whose assets were greater than the market value of their stock and then lining up the massive financial backing required to purchase the stock. Even when he fails to win control of a target corporation, Ichan usually reaps a large "greenmail" profit on the stock he has purchased.

In Ichan's opinion, the nation's top corporate managers have become a "new aristocracy." He sees himself as a champion of the rights of long-suffering stockholders. He deplores management's negligent and self-serving stewardship of America's industrial assets. Ichan truly believes that he is forcing American management to become more competitive, to eliminate waste and bureaucracy, to work harder, and become more productive. He ridicules what he calls the "corpocracy":

> Just like college, where the president of the fraternity is a real likable guy, the president or the CEO of the company is usually a likable guy . . .
>
> But they're not the cleverest, because clever guys, intelligent guys, are often abrasive and they're not that well-liked . . . what has happened in management is that the guys who got to the top are the guys that the board liked.

Top management, he claims, feathers its own nest at the expense of the stockholders, employees, and consumers.

> They're out on their jet planes with their wives going on safari and the company is going to the dogs, and then they'll give parties for themselves to celebrate how great they are.

> We can't have people on the dole. But when you have ten layers of bureaucracy in a corporation, isn't that the same as the dole? You can't have people walking around, all giving paperwork to other people . . . They're not producing for our society.

Ichan does not believe that the current style of corporate governance through a board of directors provides the necessary accountability for management.

> I was on the board of one company and really it's a frightening thing. . . . Here's what goes on. Literally, half the board is dozing off. The other half is reading *The Wall Street Journal.* And they put up slides and nobody can understand the slides and when it get dark they all doze off.

> [The CEO] was in control of that board. I mean nobody would say anything.

Ichan believes that only the *owners* of corporations can provide truly responsible leadership, because their own money is at stake. He believes America is losing its competitive edge in the world because management has grown lazy and self-satisfied.

> In the days when our country was the top industrial power—and we are really losing that edge today—my argument is that there was accountability. Because of ownership. The Andrew Carnegies and Mellons and other people who built us up made sure that there was accountability in the corporations they owned, because it was their money at stake.

So Ichan defends the role of the corporate raider in forcing America's corporate managers to perform better:

> The problem we have in our managerial society today is that there is no accountability because corporate democracy is a travesty. Except when a guy like Carl Ichan comes along or a few others and really holds them accountable, management really operates without any constraints.[19]

LEE IACOCCA: CELEBRITY CEO

The celebrity chairman of the Chrysler Corporation, Lee Iacocca, retired from his post in 1992 as the leading television spokesman for the American automobile industry. (After first announcing his retirement, he reportedly changed his mind and offered to stay on, only to have his board accept his resignation.) Iacocca's well-publicized career illustrates the splendors and pitfalls of life at the pinnacle of corporate power.

[19] Ichan as quoted in *Newsweek*, October 20, 1986, pp. 51–52.

No one climbed the corporate ladder to as much success and celebrity as Lido Anthony Iacocca.[20] His father Nicola emigrated from Italy and began a rent-a-car business in Allentown, Pennsylvania, in the 1920s. He sent his son to nearby Lehigh University to study mechanical engineering. Lido graduated in 1945, changed his name to Lee, and joined an executive training program at Ford Motors. Ford allowed him to accept a fellowship at Princeton, where he completed a master's degree in engineering before returning to Ford headquarters in Detroit.

At this time in Ford's corporate history, young Henry Ford II was trying to build a high-quality engineering department to change the reputation of the company for dull and unimaginative car designs. Ford recruited the nation's best young talent, the "Whiz Kids," including Robert McNamara (later secretary of defense) and Arjay Miller (later dean of Stanford's Business School). Iacocca was originally included in this gifted group, but he soon made a risky career decision to leave engineering for marketing. He left Ford headquarters for a job selling Ford trucks in Chester, Pennsylvania, not far from his home town. Detroit might never have heard from Iacocca again, except for the fact that he turned out to be the best car salesman in the nation's history.

Iacocca spent ten years in face-to-face sales work. He knew enough engineering to talk "nuts and bolts" to truck buyers. His first big success came in 1956 with a sales campaign slogan "56 in 56"—a monthly payment of $56 would buy a 1956 Ford. Iacocca's district sales office soared to the top in the nation. Ford vice-president Robert McNamara heard about it, ordered the campaign to be used nationwide, and called Iacocca back to Detroit.

Iacocca's skills in marketing have become legendary. On arriving in Detroit he pressed the company to develop a car that would appeal to the baby boom generation in high school and college in the early 1960s. McNamara wanted to stick with basic low-priced transportation, the Falcon, with an auto safety campaign. Iacocca argued with his mentor, "Safety doesn't sell," and urged the building of a new speedy convertible for the youth market.

Henry Ford II had been badly burned in the Edsel fiasco a few years earlier and was unwilling to devote capital to another new car concept. So Iacocca used parts and pieces of cars already in stock in designing what turned out to be the most successful Ford car since the original Model T—the Mustang. The Mustang was not really a new car from an engineering perspective, but Iacocca marketed it as a flashy, low-priced sporty car for America's youth. Later he topped his own success by introducing the Mark series of luxury cars, which became even more profitable than the Mustang.

Lee Iacocca's ambition, competitiveness, and skill in corporate politics created enemies as well as admirers. His detractors described him as a glorified car salesman who mercilessly drove his subordinates and frequently took credit for their accomplishments. Eventually Iacocca's ambition inspired sus-

[20] See Lee Iacocca, *Iacocca* (New York: Bantam Books, 1984).

picion in the boss himself, Henry Ford II. Iacocca became Ford president in 1970 after Henry Ford II abruptly fired Bunkie Knudson, whom Ford had earlier recruited from General Motors. But by 1975 the boss began to question Iacocca's leadership. Sales of the Mustang were fading, and the new Pinto was a disaster. Henry Ford denied Iacocca's $2 billion request to develop front-wheel-drive cars and ordered an investigation of his president's expense account. Finally, after a stormy exchange in 1978, Ford fired Iacocca. When Iacocca asked what he had done wrong, Ford snapped, "Nothing, I just don't like you."

Lee Iacocca later expressed his feelings about Henry Ford II in words that had to be bleeped out of a television documentary. But he also described his personal philosophy: "Don't get mad, get even." Three months after his dismissal from Ford, Lee Iacocca was named president of the Chrysler Corporation.

Chrysler had always been number three among the American automakers, following General Motors and Ford. When Iacocca took over, Chrysler was down to only 8 percent of the market. It had no small or fuel-efficient cars to compete in the new fuel-conscious market. Worst of all, Chrysler cars had a reputation for poor quality. Dealers were deserting the company in droves; Chrysler faced imminent bankruptcy.

The Chrysler turnaround, engineered by Lee Iacocca, is one of the most dramatic events in American corporate history. Iacocca moved decisively on many fronts to save the company—rolling back union wages, cutting inventories, slashing the work force by almost half, forcing suppliers to lower prices. By 1984 his drastic cutting placed the company in a position where it could make a profit on sales of 1.2 million cars versus the 2.3 million it needed in 1980. He placed union president Lane Kirkland on the Chrysler board of directors. He introduced new cars: first the front-wheel-drive K cars, later the first new convertibles to be produced by Detroit in over a decade, and still later a popular minivan. He revamped the company's quality-control procedures and introduced unprecedented guarantees to reclaim the confidence of Chrysler buyers. He purchased American Motors Corporation, producers of the Jeep line of vehicles, and doubled Chrysler's share of the truck market.

Iacocca became a national celebrity when he went on television to sell his cars and the "new" Chrysler Corporation. The advertising agency executives were at first skeptical, but they later realized that having a corporate president speak directly to the American people was the best way to restore confidence in the product. "People believe in him. He wasn't slick or made up. It was as if he had just come from the battlefield, which he had." Iacocca came across to the American public as just the man he was—brash, confident, tough-talking.

The most controversial aspect of Iacocca's efforts to save Chrysler was his federal "bail out" scheme. Iacocca asked the federal government for $1.2 billion in loan guarantees in 1979, after the nation's major banks had decided that the Chrysler Corporation was beyond help. Going hat-in-hand to Washington was a humiliating experience for the self-made champion of private enterprise. But Iacocca is a pragmatist: "U.S. aid for Central America. Hell, when I think of 'Central America' I think of Michigan, Ohio, Indiana." Very few people gave Chrysler much of a chance to survive even *with* federal assistance. In 1983, Iacocca paid back the federal loans—seven years ahead of schedule.

Iacocca is firmly established as the champion of smokestack America. He popularized the "Buy America" idea at the same time that he was importing more Japanese cars than any of his domestic rivals. Through the same marketing wizardry, he persuaded buyers to forgive Chrysler for tampering with odometers merely by apologizing in a massive ad campaign. Chrysler minivans became especially popular with American buyers and their sales helped revive the company. By the time Iacocca retired in 1992, he had begun to convince the American public that Chrysler was indeed building a better car than ever before, a car that was as high in quality as the Japanese imports. Indeed, for the first time in several decades, the Japanese share of the U.S. automobile market, which had risen to over 30 percent, began to decline. Detroit appeared to be on the verge of a historic turnaround, owing in part to Iacocca's vision and tenacity.

Iacocca's fame as a salesman, together with his reputation for battling foreign competition, prompted President Clinton to enlist the retired CEO in 1993 in the fight to pass NAFTA, the North American Free Trade Agreement.

THE INHERITORS: STARTING AT THE TOP

Unquestionably, the Rockefellers, Fords, du Ponts, Mellons, and other families still exercise considerable influence over America's corporate resources. However, research on family holdings in large corporations is not easy. Table 2–9 lists major family holdings of large corporations as revealed in a variety of sources. But it is not possible to tell from such a list whether a family really "controls" the operations of a corporation, or whether control has been passed on to the managers. It is possible for families who no longer hold active management positions in a corporation to exercise "latent" power— that is, to use their control blocs of stock as a restraint on management. Sometimes families interfere only when something goes seriously wrong. As late as 1967 *Fortune* suggested that 150 of the largest 500 industrial corporations were still controlled by one or more members of a single family.[21] However, even family-controlled corporations recruit professional managers from the ranks. Indeed, today all of the directors of Alcoa, Gulf, Exxon, Chase Manhattan, Du Pont, and other such corporations are professional managers recruited from outside the family.

[21] Robert Sheehan, "Family-Run Corporations: There Are More of Them Than You Think," *Fortune,* June 15, 1967, p. 179.

TABLE 2–9   Historic Family Ties to Corporations

Corporation	Family
E.I. du Pont de Nemours	du Pont
Ford Motor Co.	Ford
Aluminum Co. of America	Mellon
Carborundum Co.	Mellon
Gulf Oil Co.	Mellon, Scaife
Sun Oil Co.	Pew
Pittsburgh Plate Glass	Pitcairn
Exxon	Rockefeller
Mobil	Rockefeller
Standard Oil of California	Rockefeller
Sears, Roebuck & Co.	Rosenwald
Polaroid Corp.	Land
IBM	Watson, Fairchild
Dow Chemical Co.	Dow
Corning Glass Works	Houghton
International Paper Co.	Phipps
W.R. Grace & Co.	Grace, Phipps
Weyerhaeuser	Weyerhaeuser
Winn-Dixie, Inc.	Davis
Campbell Soup Company	Dorrance
H.J. Heinz Co.	Heinz
Firestone Tire & Rubber	Firestone
Columbia Broadcasting Co. (CBS)	Paley
Olin Chemical	Olin
Ralston Purina Co.	Danforth
Hilton Hotels	Hilton
Howard Johnson Co.	Johnson
Great Atlantic & Pacific Tea Co. (A&P)	Hartford
Woolco	Woolworth
McDonnell Douglas Aircraft	McDonnell
International Harvester	McCormick
Coca-Cola	Woodruff
Eli Lilly & Co.	Lilly
Duke Power Co.	Duke
Rockwell Mfg. Co.	Rockwell
Gerber Products Co.	Gerber
Deere & Company	Deere
Borden Co.	Borden

The Fords of Ford Motors.   Until 1980, Henry Ford II, grandson of the Ford Motor Company founder, served as chairman of the board. "The first thing you have to understand about the company is that Henry Ford is the boss. . . . He *is* the boss, he always was the boss since the first day I came in and he always will be the boss." These are the words of Arjay Miller, who spent twenty-three years climbing the rungs of Ford management to become president of the company, only to find that Henry Ford II actually ran things.

Miller eventually resigned to become dean of the Graduate School of Business at Stanford University.[22]

Henry Ford II grew up in a very narrow society; he was a member of a rich, insulated family that was dominated by his grandfather—known to be an exceedingly suspicious, prejudiced, and willful man. Young Ford attended Hotchkiss School and later Yale University. However, he failed to graduate in 1940 after admitting that he had cheated on a term paper. He enlisted in the U.S. Navy and served until his father died in 1943; President Roosevelt directed the secretary of the navy to release Ford to return to the family business.

Ford started in the automobile industry at the age of twenty-five as vice-president of Ford Motors, serving under his aged grandfather. A year later he took over the presidency. His initial decisions were to replace the one-person autocratic rule of the company with a modern management structure, recruiting bright, young management types (the famous Ford "Whiz Kids," including Robert S. McNamara, who later resigned as Ford president to become secretary of defense; Lee Iacocca; Arjay Miller; and Charles B. Thornton, later to become chairman of Litton Industries). He also initiated a modern labor relations program and ended the company's traditional hostility toward labor unions. As commonplace as these policies appear today, they were considered advanced, enlightened, and liberal for the Ford Motor Company at the time.

Over the years Ford proved himself a capable director of the company, despite some occasional and even colossal mistakes. (The Edsel fiasco cost the company over $300 million.) Ford worked long hours at the company headquarters in Detroit. He personally approved style changes in Ford cars and test-drove them himself. He was active on the board of the Ford Foundation and conscientiously reviewed research and grant proposals with other board members. His younger brothers, Benson and William Clay, eventually became Ford vice-presidents and board members. (William Clay Ford married the daughter of tire manufacturer Harvey S. Firestone, Jr., and purchased the Detroit Lions professional football team.)

Henry Ford II helped launch the National Urban Coalition and organized the National Alliance of Businessmen to provide more jobs for minorities. He was a prime mover in Detroit's urban renewal and redevelopment program, Renaissance Center. It was Ford himself who convinced his old rival, General Motors, as well as Amoco, Kmart, Parke-Davis, and Western International Hotels, to invest in the central city project. When cost overruns forced up the price of the project, Ford "arm-twisted" many Ford suppliers— U.S. Steel, Firestone, Budd Company—to come up with the additional funds.

Like many people born to wealth and power, Ford's personal style was far from that of the bland organizational person. He was frequently unpre-

---

[22] Quoted in Victor Lasky, *Never Complain, Never Explain* (New York: Richard Marek, 1981), p. 86.

dictable, sometimes abrasive, often profane; he expressed his opinions directly. His public and private actions were often controversial. (He divorced his wife of many years and married a beautiful, young Italian actress in 1965; in 1980, he divorced her to marry an American model.)

The Ford Foundation was created before the death of the elder Henry Ford. Originally, it supported charities in the Detroit area; its assets were primarily Ford stock. As the company prospered, the value of the foundation assets increased. In 1951, Henry Ford II asked Robert Hutchins, chancellor of the University of Chicago, to take over the foundation and make it a national force in civic affairs. Hutchins immediately funded some projects that "the Chairman" did not like; Hutchins was cut loose to become head of the Fund for the Republic, a smaller, Ford-funded foundation. The Ford Foundation supported moderate black civil rights organizations, including the Urban League, with Henry Ford II's approval. In 1966, McGeorge Bundy, Presidents Kennedy and Johnson's national security adviser, became the Ford Foundation head.

Bundy gradually sold off the Ford stock from the foundation assets. Bundy and Henry Ford clashed over the liberal programs of the Foundation. Finally, in 1976, Ford resigned from his directorship of the Ford Foundation. In his resignation letter, he pointedly advised the foundation to direct more attention to strengthening the capitalist system. "The Foundation is a creature of capitalism. . . . I'm just suggesting to the trustees and the staff that the system that makes the Foundation possible very probably is worth preserving."[23]

By 1980, Henry Ford II faced many troubles. The Pinto car had to be recalled for a faulty gas tank—the largest recall in auto history. Brother Benson Ford died of a heart attack. The break with Lee Iacocca was troublesome. Henry went through another divorce and remarriage. His nephew, Benson Ford, Jr., sued him over his father's will and demanded a seat on the Ford board, which Henry denied him. And in 1980, the Ford Motor Company lost $1.5 billion—the largest annual loss until then in the history of any American corporation. (Of course, General Motors lost money that year, and Chrysler would have gone bankrupt without favorable U.S. government loan guarantees.) Henry Ford II resigned as chairman of the board of Ford Motors.

The Ford family continues to hold a large bloc of Ford Motor stock. Henry Ford II's son, Edsel B. Ford, and his nephew, William Clay Ford, Jr., both became Ford Company executives. In 1980 Henry said that his son and nephew were still "a good ten years" away from top management. When Henry was reminded that he himself inherited the presidency at age twenty-six, he said only that "times have changed." But after Henry resigned as chairman, his brother William Clay Ford took a directorship and promptly saw to it that both Edsel B. and William Clay Ford, Jr., joined

---

[23] *Newsweek*, January 24, 1977, p. 69.

him on the board. With three family members on the board of directors, Ford Motors is perhaps the most family-controlled large corporation in America.

CHANGING OF THE GUARD

Top leadership in the corporate world changes slowly over time. A reasonably successful president or chairperson and chief executive officer can expect to run the corporation for eight to ten years. Management "climbers," those who have spent thirty years in the corporation, may become president or chairperson at age fifty-eight or sixty and may expect to serve to age sixty-five or sixty-seven. Of course, family "inheritors" may have much longer tenure at the top; Henry Ford II was the dominant figure at Ford Motors for over forty years.

Nonetheless, there is inevitably a "changing of the guard"—a succession to power—in the corporate world as elsewhere. In the last decade a generation of powerful corporate leaders stepped aside: Irving S. Shapiro of Du Pont, Thomas A. Murphy and later Roger Smith of General Motors, Reginald Jones of General Electric, J. Paul Austin of Coca-Cola, and Harold Geneen of ITT all announced their retirements. David Rockefeller retired as chairman of Chase Manhattan, Henry Ford II retired as chairman of Ford Motors, and Lee Iacocca retired from Chrysler.

Despite a few highly publicized firings, top corporate directors are well insulated in their positions. Turnover rates are far lower than in government. Only a really disastrous corporate performance can inspire a revolution against management.

Corporate leadership is very stable not only because turnover among managers and directors is low, but also because the nation's largest corporations are seldom displaced from their dominant positions in the marketplace. By and large, the nation's largest industrial corporations in the 1990s were the nation's largest industrial corporations in the 1940s (see Table 2–10). These large corporations, although not invulnerable, possess great power to protect and enlarge their positions over time. This power derives from various sources: obstacles to entry for new firms; their giant scale of operations and low marginal costs; worldwide access to raw materials and markets; ready access to money for expansion from their own profits and from large banks; and diversification which protects many of these giants from the vagaries of particular markets and allows them to shift resources to the most promising growth areas. Nonetheless, there are identifiable changes in the rankings of the largest industrial corporations. The growth of computer technology permitted IBM to emerge as an industrial giant; world surpluses of copper took their toll on America's great copper companies, Anaconda and Kennicott; world competition also contributed to the decline of the great steel companies—U.S. Steel (now USX), Bethlehem,

TABLE 2–10   Stability and Change among the Corporate Giants*

Rank	1940	Rank	1952	Rank	1970	Rank	1986	Rank	1992
1	Standard Oil of N.J. (Exxon)	1	Standard Oil of N.J. (Exxon)	1	Exxon	1	General Motors	1	G.E.
2	U.S. Steel	2	General Motors	2	General Motors	2	Exxon	2	General Motors
3	General Motors	3	U.S. Steel	3	Texaco	3	IBM	3	Ford
4	Socony Vacuum (Mobil)	4	Socony Vacuum (Mobil)	4	Ford	4	Ford	4	IBM
5	Du Pont	5	Standard Oil (Ind.)	5	Gulf Oil	5	Mobil	5	Exxon
6	Bethlehem Steel	6	Ford	6	IBM	6	G.E.	6	Philip Morris
7	Standard Oil (Ind.)	7	Texas Corp. (Texaco)	7	Mobil	7	AT&T	7	Chrysler
8	Ford	8	Du Pont	8	GTE	8	Chevron	8	Mobil
9	Texas Corp. (Texaco)	9	Gulf Oil	9	ITT	9	Texaco	9	Du Pont
10	Standard Oil (Calif.)	10	Bethlehem Steel	10	Standard Oil (Calif.)	10	Du Pont	10	Xerox
11	Anaconda Copper	11	G.E.	11	U.S. Steel	11	Shell	11	Chevron
12	Gulf Oil	12	Standard Oil (Calif.)	12	G.E.	12	Amoco	12	RJR-Nabisco
13	G.E.	13	Sears, Roebuck	13	Standard Oil (Ind.)	13	BP America	13	Amoco
14	International Harvester	14	Westinghouse	14	Chrysler	14	Atlantic Rich.	14	Shell
15	Republic Steel	15	International Harvester	15	Shell Oil	15	Chrysler	15	Texaco
16	Kennecott Copper	16	Union Carbide	16	Atlantic Rich.	16	USX	16	Dow Chemical
17	Shell Oil	17	Cities Service	17	Tenneco	17	Philip Morris	17	Atlantic Rich.
18	Union Carbide	18	Sinclair Oil	18	Western Electric	18	Tenneco	18	Procter & Gamble
19	Consolidated Oil	19	Phillips Petroleum	19	Du Pont	19	RJR-Nabisco	19	Eastman Kodak
20	American Tobacco	20	Chrysler	20	Union Carbide	20	Occidental	20	Pepsico

*Largest Industrial Corporations by Size of Assets, 1940, 1952, 1970, 1986, 1992.

and Republic. Yet overall, the industrial giants of fifty years ago are still the industrial giants of today.

THE LIMITS OF CORPORATE POWER

Elites do not like to acknowledge their own power. Kenneth Olsen, CEO of Digital Equipment, offered a typical elite response to the question of power: "I've got no power. All I can do is encourage people, motivate people to do things. I've got no power over them."[24] Why do elites say things like this? It is not merely modesty nor intent to deceive. "Power" in a democratic society has acquired a pejorative meaning—tyranny, arbitrariness, absolute rule. And this connotation conflicts with the requirements for successful corporate leadership today. Hence, corporate elites deny they have power, but they acknowledge that they have the principal responsibility for "how the company is run."

Yet top corporate elites feel more constrained today in the exercise of their authority than in the past. Many believe that the era of the all-powerful CEOs is over. No large corporation can be directed from the top in the fashion of William Paley's CBS, Armand Hammer's Occidental Petroleum, or Harold Geneen's ITT.

The greatest constraint on corporate power is the global market. Thirty years ago the American market was isolated; each sector of industry was a self-contained oligopoly with three to eight major manufacturers competing in a limited fashion. Top corporate elites were relatively unconstrained in deciding about products and prices, technologies and innovations, capital flows and investments. But today, global competition severely limits American corporate decision-making. The United States remains the world's largest market, but large shares of the U.S. market have been captured by foreign competition in nearly every industrial sector.

Top corporate elites believe their own power is more limited today than a few years ago. They believe other elites have gained in power relative to themselves. They acknowledge that labor unions have lost influence in American life, but they believe that institutional investors and bankers, Wall Street analysts, government regulators, and most of all, corporate raiders, are gaining power (see Table 2–11).

America's corporate elite has come under severe criticism for its failure to plan for the long term, to direct funds into research, and to develop strategies to confront global competition. It is charged with myopic concern with short-term profits, tomorrow's stock prices, and next quarter's earnings.

Elites agree that the criticism is justified, but they claim that their failure to focus on long-term growth strategies is a result of pressures from institutional investors, Wall Street analysts, and corporate raiders.

---

[24] Quoted in *Forbes*, May 30, 1988, p. 120. Inasmuch as Olsen was deposed as CEO by his board in 1992, his earlier disclaimer of power appears prophetic in retrospect.

TABLE 2–11   Pressures on the Corporate Elite

Compared with five years ago, would you say that the following individuals or institutions have gained influence over decisions in companies such as yours, lost influence, or kept their influence?

	Gained Influence	Lost Influence	Kept Influence	Not Sure
Institutions holding big stock blocs	47%	2%	42%	9%
Raiders and potential raiders	58	2	24	16
Investment bankers	46	13	36	5
Stock analysts	48	4	43	5
Government regulators	41	20	34	5
Environmentalists	37	14	40	9
Consumer groups	28	14	49	9
Labor unions	2	54	34	10

Let me read you a list of people, institutions, and other factors that might be the source of pressure on companies to focus on the short term, rather than on long-term growth. Tell me which three or four you believe exert the most pressure on companies to focus on the short term.

Banks holding debt	12%
Bond-rating services	14
Boards of directors	15
Financial press	34
Institutional shareholders	58
Investment bankers, takeover advisers	45
Securities analysts	65

SOURCE: Survey of 400 chief executives of corporations in the top 1,000, reported by *Business Week*, October 23, 1987, p. 28.

WHO OWNS AMERICA?

It is a very difficult task to learn exactly who "controls" a corporation. The concept of control may involve distinguishing between active and latent power where owners may intervene with management only when things go seriously astray. This latent power may be better understood as a constraint on management decision-making, similar to the constraints of government regulation or union activism. The concept of control may also involve distinctions between policy initiation and "veto power." Owners may exercise control over only a limited sphere of company activity (quantity of borrowing, dividend payouts, sale of assets, and so on). The concept of control may also involve a distinction between "financial" control and "operating" control. Owners may exercise prevailing influence over external financial functions (raising and supplying capital funds, buying and selling securities, merging and acquiring other corporations, and the like), while management exercises prevailing influence over the operating activities of the corporation (producing and selling automobiles, chemicals, or business machines).

The diffusion of ownership of the nation's largest corporations makes it possible to acquire power in the corporation by owning a very small percentage of the voting common stock. There is no specific percentage of ownership (under 50) which guarantees "control." Table 2–12 shows the five largest owners of each of the ten largest industrial corporations in 1981. Note that many of these largest owners own only 1 or 2 percent of the corporation's total common stock.

Who are these largest owners? Banks and their trust departments own nearly one quarter of the common stock in the Fortune 500 industrial corporations. While banks are owners of record, in many cases banks hold stock as trustees for other "ultimate" owners. It is not possible to trace all of the beneficiaries of banks' holdings. Banks often hold stock on behalf of employee stock-saving and profit-sharing plans (ESPs), as indicated on Table 2–12. Herman writes about ESPs: "I heavily discount bank power arising from the ESP trustee function. Because banks are dependent on management in all aspects of such plans, the ESP strengthens management control."[25]

Financial investment firms also hold about one quarter of the common stock of the nation's largest industrial corporations. Investment firms, like banks, very often hold these positions as trustees on behalf of other owners, and it is not possible to know who all of the ultimate owners may be. However, again we can identify ESPs as holders of about half of the positions under investment firms. Somewhat less important in ownership are the insurance companies and industrial corporations themselves. Foreign ownership is confined to a small number of corporations.

TABLE 2–12   **Strategic Ownership Positions in America's Largest Industrial Corporations, 1981**

Owners	Bloc Percentage
Exxon (outstanding shares: 453,205,000)	
Exxon Corporation	
Exxon Thrift Plan	2.09
Rockefeller Family	1.68
Chase Manhattan	1.03
Manufacturers Hanover	.98
SAROFIM & Co.	.96
General Motors (outstanding shares: 286,869,000)	
National Detroit Corp.	
GM ESP	13.65
du Pont Family	7.00
TIAA-CREF	1.46
J.P. Morgan & Co.	1.28
Prudential Insurance	1.23

[25] Herman, *Corporate Control, Corporate Power*, p. 24.

TABLE 2–12 *(Continued)*

Owners	Bloc Percentage
Mobil (outstanding shares: 212,143,000)	
Bankers Trust NY	
Mobil ESP	6.28
J.P. Morgan & Co.	2.29
Rockefeller Family	1.97
Internorth Inc.	1.41
Bancoklahoma	1.24
Standard Oil Indiana (outstanding shares: 292,335,000)	
First Chicago Corp.	
Standard Oil Indiana ESP	8.22
Blaustein Family	3.58
SAROFIM & Co.	1.60
Chase Manhattan	1.02
Mudd Family	.97
IBM (outstanding shares: 583,374,000)	
J.P. Morgan & Co.	2.35
Manufacturers Hanover	1.57
Bankers Trust NY	.99
Chase Manhattan	.98
TIAA-CREF	.97
Gulf Oil (outstanding shares: 195,033,000)	
Mellon Family	11.00
Mellon National Corp.	2.16
Prudential	1.83
TIAA-CREF	1.47
First Tulsa	1.09
Atlantic Richfield (outstanding shares: 236,244,000)	
Security Pacific	
Atlantic Richfield ESP	3.12
Citicorp	1.86
Manufacturers Hanover	1.72
Prudential	1.07
BankAmerica	1.03
Ford (outstanding shares: 177,262,000)	
Ford Family	40.40
Manufacturers National Corp.	
Ford ESP	17.48
Capital Group	1.86
Batterymarch Financial	1.11
Firestone (outstanding shares: 57,660,000)	
Firestone Family	22.00
Ameritrust Co.	14.39
Manufacturers Hanover	
Firestone ESP	6.48
Capital Group	3.34
Citicorp	1.65
Du Pont (outstanding shares: 144,718,000)	
du Pont Family	35.00
Delaware Trust	2.31
Capital Group	1.76
Prudential	1.48
Manufacturers Hanover	1.38

Family and individual ownership is still very impressive. Many of these family holdings are well known to students of American capitalism. The du Pont family holdings are more extensive and more valuable than any other. In 1981 the du Ponts owned large blocs in 24 of the Fortune 500 industrial corporations, positions worth a total of more than $5 billion. Their holdings included 35 percent of the Du Pont Corporation and 7 percent of General Motors. The Fords owned 40.4 percent of Ford Motors, and the Gettys owned 50.18 percent of Getty Oil.

THE SUPERRICH: DISTINGUISHING WEALTH FROM POWER

It is a mistake to equate *personal* wealth with economic power. Persons with relatively little personal wealth can exercise great power if they occupy positions that give them control of huge institutional resources. A president of a large corporation who came through the ranks of management may receive an income of only $1 million or $2 million a year, and possess a net worth of only $5 million or $6 million. Yet these amounts are small when you consider that this person may control a corporation with annual revenues of $2 *billion* and assets worth $10 *billion* or $20 *billion*. (The contrast is even greater in government, where $80,000-a-year bureaucrats manage government expenditures of $50 *billion* a year!) The important point is that personal wealth in America is insignificant in comparison to corporate and governmental wealth.

One must occupy top *positions* in large corporate *institutions* to exercise significant economic power. The mere possession of personal wealth, even a billion dollars, does not guarantee economic power. Indeed, among America's billionaires—individuals with personal wealth in excess of $1 *billion*—there are people such as widows, retirees, and other inheritors who have never played any role in the family business. There are also many "independent operators" who have acquired great wealth in, say, independent oil operations or land speculation, but who do not occupy high positions in the corporate world. Of course, there are many billionaires whose personal wealth has come to them through their personal ownership of corporate shares. Familiar names—Ford, Rockefeller, du Pont, Mellon—are liberally sprinkled among the nation's top personal wealth-holders. However, their personal wealth is a *byproduct* of their role, or their ancestor's role, in the corporate structure.

Socialist critics of America often fail to comprehend the insignificance of personal wealth in relation to corporate and governmental resources. They direct their rhetoric against inequality in personal income in the nation, when in fact the greatest inequities occur in the comparisons between corporate and government resources and the resources of individuals.

Let us illustrate our point: If the personal wealth of every one of America's billionaires was *completely confiscated* by government, the resulting

TABLE 2–13   Total Wealth of the 400 Richest Americans

	1982	1985	1988	1992
Total net worth ($ billions)	$ 92	$134	$220	$288
Median net worth ($ millions)	$150	$250	$375	$450
Number of billionaires	13	13	51	71

SOURCE: Derived from data in *Forbes*, October 21, 1992, p. 145.

revenue (about $288 billion) would amount to less than 20 *percent* of the federal budget for a *single year* (see Table 2–13).

The relationship between personal wealth and institutional power is described well by economist Adolf A. Berle:

> As of now, in the United States and in Western Europe, the rich man has little power merely because he is rich. . . . {He} amounts to little unless he connects himself with effective institutions. He must master past institutions or must create new ones. . . . However large his bank account, he can do nothing with it but consume. He can build or buy palaces, amuse himself at Mediterranean or Caribbean resorts, become a figure in Monte Carlo, Miami, or Las Vegas. He can amuse himself by collecting books or purchasing bonds. He can give libraries or laboratories to universities and have his name put on them. He can receive the pleasant but powerless recognition of decorations, honorary degrees, and even titles of nobility. None of these things entitle him to make decisions affecting other men or to give orders (outside his household) with any likelihood they will be fulfilled. . . .
>
> So, if he wishes a power position, he must find it outside his bank account. He can, it is true, use the bank account to buy into, or possibly create, an institution. He can buy control of a small corporation. (Few rich men are left who are capable of buying individual control of really large ones.) He can undertake the management of that corporation. Then he can derive power from the institution—if, and only if, he is capable of handling it. Whatever power he has comes from the corporation or other institutions, and from such intellectual or organizing skill as he may have—not from his wealth, which is largely irrelevant.[26]

Even if personal wealth is not the equivalent of economic power, the nation's top wealth-holders are worthy of study. (See Table 2–14.) They include at least two categories—old and established families whose wealth is inherited from large corporate enterprise, and newly rich individuals whose wealth is derived from "independent" oil operations, real estate speculation, fast foods and discount merchandising, or aerospace and computer industries. In 1918, the first year for which a reasonable estimate of the nation's wealthiest Americans is available, virtually all of the names on the list were newly rich, having acquired great wealth within a single generation. These were the great entrepreneurs of America's Industrial Revolution—Rockefeller, Carnegie, Frick, Harkness, Ford, Vanderbilt, Morgan, and so on.

[26] From Adolf A. Berle, *Power.* Copyright © 1967, 1968, 1969. Reprinted by permission of Harcourt Brace Jovanovich, Inc.

Only a few of the wealthiest Americans in the early twentieth century were inheritors: for example, the Astors, whose original fortune was made in the North American fur trade; and the du Ponts, who manufactured gun powder in Delaware even before the Revolutionary War. However, by the second half of the century, the great families of the Industrial Revolution had become the nation's established wealth-holders. Their wealth was tied to the large corporations and banks which their ancestors had founded.

It is widely believed that great personal wealth in America today is inherited and that opportunities to acquire great personal fortunes dried up after the Industrial Revolution. C. Wright Mills wrote that "Wealth not only tends to perpetuate itself, but . . . tends also to monopolize new opportunities for getting great wealth. . . . In none of the latest three generations has a majority of the very rich been composed of men who have risen."[27] But Mills and other Marxist critics of American society are *wrong!* All of the available evidence points to considerable social mobility among the wealthiest Americans.

It is true, of course, that great wealth, once accumulated, lingers for a generation or two after the death of the person who accumulated it. But in most families this wealth gradually dissipates over the generations, spreading more thinly among ever more heirs. Some families, like the Kennedys, dissipate great fortunes faster than others. Inheritance taxes play only a minor role in this process. The same energy and entrepreneurship that built the original family fortune is seldom found in later generations of a family. And claimants to portions of the family fortune multiply. (John D. Rockefeller had six grandchildren; the next generation had twenty-four fractious cousins, who so far have produced fifty-two offspring.) More important, this downward mobility is more than matched by the explosive upward strivings of new capitalist tycoons in each generation.

Today over half of America's top wealth-holders are self-made single-generation tycoons. On the lists of billionaires and centimillionaires, the names of self-made men and women outnumber heirs to family fortunes, and first- and second-generation immigrants abound. Moreover, in every successive list of top wealth-holders over the decades there are as many dropouts and newcomers as holdovers. It is true that America's great nineteenth-century industrial fortunes have held together remarkably well, despite inheritance taxes and family dispersions.[28] But in each generation, America produces a new crop of superrich entrepreneurs.

Representative of the newly rich in 1968 were the seven wealthiest Americans—J. Paul Getty and H.L. Hunt, whose fabulous fortunes were amassed in independent oil operations; Howard Hughes, whose fortune was made in the aerospace industry, as well as David Packard and William Hewlett; Edward H. Land, an inventor whose self-developing camera was the foundation of the Polaroid Corporation; and Daniel K. Ludwig, who wisely purchased war-surplus oil tankers in anticipation of U.S. dependence on foreign oil.

[27] C. Wright Mills, *The Power Elite* (New York: Oxford University Press, 1956), p. 105.

[28] See Michael Patrick Allen, *The Founding Fortunes* (New York: Dutton, 1987).

TABLE 2–14 America's Superrich

1918 "Wealthiest Americans"	1968 "Centimillionaires"	1987 "Billionaires"	1992 "Billionaires"
J.D. Rockefeller (oil)	J.P. Getty (oil)	S.M. Walton (retail)	W.H. Gates (computers)
H.C. Frick (coke, steel)	H. Hughes (aerospace)	J.W. Kluge (communications)	J.W. Kluge (communications)
A. Carnegie (steel)	H.L. Hunt (oil)	H. Ross Perot (computers)	S.M. Walton & family (retail)
G.W. Baker (banking)	E.H. Land (Polaroid)	D. Packard (aerospace)	W.E. Buffet (stock market)
W. Rockefeller (oil, RRs)	D.K. Ludwig (shipping)	S.I. Newhouse, Jr. (publishing)	S.I. Newhouse (publishing)
E.S. Harkness (oil)	Alisa M. Bruce (Mellon)	D.E. Newhouse (publishing)	D.E. Newhouse (publishing)
J.O. Armour (meat packing)	P. Mellon (Mellon)	Lester Crown (defense)	S.M. Redstone (theaters)
H. Ford (cars)	R.K. Mellon (Mellon)	K.R. Murdoch (publishing)	R.O. Perelman (finance)
W.K. Vanderbilt (RRs)	N.B. Hunt (oil)	W.E. Buffet (stock market)	Ted Arison (cruises)
Ed. H.R. Green (banking)	J.D. McArthur (insurance)	L.H. Wexner (retail)	P.G. Allen (computers)
Mrs. E.H. Harriman (RRs)	W.L. McKnight (3M)	J.A. Pritzker (real estate)	K.R. Murdoch (publishing)
V. Astor (real estate)	C.S. Mott (GM)	R.A. Pritzker (real estate)	R.M. DeVos (Amway)
J. Stillman (banking)	R.E. Smith (oil)	E.M. Bronfman (liquors)	J. Van Audel (Amway)
T.F. Ryan (transit, tobacco)	H.F. Ahmanson (banking)	Barbara C. Anthony (inherited)	H.L. Hillman (inherited)
D. Guggenheim (mining)	C. Allen, Jr. (banking)	Ann C. Chambers (publishing)	H. Ross Perot (computers)
C.M. Schwab (steel)	Mrs. W.V. Clark, Sr. (Avon)	Ted Arison (cruises)	E.M. Bronfman (liquors)
J.P. Morgan (banking)	J.T. Dorrance, Jr. (soup)	A.A. Taubman	F.M. Mars and family (candy)
Mrs. R. Sage (banking)	Mrs. A.I. du Pont (Du Pont)	H.L. Hillman (inherited)	Anne C. Chambers (publishing)
C.H. McCormick (farm machinery)	C.W. Englehard, Jr. (mining)	M.H. Davis (oil)	Ted Turner (communications)
J. Widener (transit)	S.M. Fairchild (cameras)	W.R. Hewlett (aerospace)	P.H. Knight (Nike)
A.C. James (mining, RRs)	L. Hess (oil)	Harry Helmsley (hotels)	L.H. Wexner (retail)
Nicholas F. Brady (transit)	W.R. Hewlett (aerospace)	P.F. Anschutz	D. Packard (aerospace)
J.H. Schiff (banking)	D. Packard (aerospace)	Anheuser Busch, Jr. (beer)	J.A. Pritzker (real estate)
J.B. Duke (tobacco)	A. Houghton (Corning Glass)	J.T. Dorrance, Jr. (soup)	S.R. Bass (oil)
G. Eastman (cameras)	J.P. Kennedy (investments)	M.J. Petrie (retail)	L.M. Bass (oil)
P.S. du Pont (gunpowder)	Eli Lilly (drugs)	E.M. Kauffman (drugs)	R.M. Bass (oil)
L.F. Swift (meat packing)	F.E. Mars (candy)	Ray Lee Hunt (oil)	E.P. Bass (oil)
J. Rosenwald (mail orders)	S.E. Newhouse (newspapers)	E.J. DeBartolo (real estate)	R.L. Hunt and family (oil)

Mrs. L. Lewis (oil)
H. Phipps (steel)

Marjorie M. Post (foods)
Mrs. J. Mauze (Rockefeller)
D. Rockefeller
J.D. Rockefeller
L. Rockefeller
N. Rockefeller
W. Rockefeller
Cordelia S. May (Mellon)
R.M. Scaife (Mellon)
D. Wallace (*Reader's Digest*)
Mrs. C. Payson (Whitney)
J.H. Whitney

W.H. Gates, III (computers)
D.L. Bren (real estate)
S.J. LeFrak (real estate)
R.M. Bass (oil)
E.L. Gaylord
F.E. Mars, Sr. (candy)
F.E. Mars, Jr. (candy)
J.F. Mars (candy)
J.M. Vogel
H.C. Simmons (investments)
Sol Goldman
Margaret H. Hill (Hunt oil)
Sid R. Bass (oil)
Lee M. Bass (oil)
L.A. Tisch (theaters, CBS)
P.R. Tisch (theaters, CBS)
David Rockefeller
L.N. Stern
C.H. Lindner, II
Roger Milliken
Joan B. Kroc (McDonald's)

E.C. Johnson and family (stock market)
S.C. Johnson (wax)
S.D. Bechtel, Jr. (construction)
L.A. Tisch (theaters, CBS)
M.H. Davis (oil)
G.P. Getty (oil)
D.L. Bren (real estate)
S.J. LeFrak (real estate)
W.B. Ziff, Jr. and family (publishing)
Lester Crown and family (inherited)
C.G. Koch (oil)
D.H. Koch (oil)
J.T. Dorrance III and family (Campbell Soup)
David Rockefeller and family (inherited, banking)
Kirk Kerkorian (casinos)
S.J. Heyman (investing)
S.A. Ballmer (computers)
Joan Kroc (McDonald's)
W.R. Hewlett (aerospace)
Milton Petrie (retail)
Paul Mellon (inherited, banking)
Estee Lauder and family (cosmetics)
Margaret Hunt Hill (oil)
M.M. Schwan (food)
M. Fribourg and family (grain)
Harry Helmsley (hotels)

Lists ranked in order of estimated wealth. Billionaires' list does not add to full 71 billionaires recognized by *Forbes* because of joint family entries.

SOURCES: 1918—*Forbes Magazine*, March 2, 1918, reprinted in *Forbes Magazine*, Fall 1983; 1968—*Fortune*, May 1968; 1987—*Forbes Magazine*, October, 1987; 1992—*Forbes Magazine*, October 1992.

TABLE 2–15   The Distribution of Family Income in America*

Quintiles	1929	1936	1944	1950	1956	1962	1972	1980	1990
Lowest	3.5	4.1	4.9	4.8	4.8	4.6	5.5	5.2	4.6
Second	9.0	9.2	10.9	10.9	11.3	10.9	12.0	11.6	10.8
Third	13.8	14.1	16.2	16.1	16.3	16.3	17.4	17.5	16.6
Fourth	19.3	20.9	22.2	22.1	22.3	22.7	23.5	24.1	23.8
Highest	54.4	51.7	45.8	46.1	45.3	45.5	41.6	41.5	44.3
Total	100.0	100.0	100.0	100.0	100.0	100.0	100.0	100.0	100.0
Top 5 percent	30.0	24.0	20.7	21.4	20.2	19.6	14.4	15.6	17.4

SOURCE: U.S. Bureau of the Census, *Current Population Reports*, Series P-60; data for early years from Edward C. Budd, *Inequality and Poverty* (New York: Norton, 1967).

* By quintiles and top 5 percent.

By 1987 additional new names on the roster of the superrich emerged from the burgeoning computer industry—William Gates, the "boy wonder" billionaire who dropped out of Harvard to found Microsoft; and Ross Perot, who founded his own software company, Electronic Data Systems. Other newly rich included the Bechtels, whose giant construction firm is the world's largest privately owned enterprise; Ray Kroc, who founded McDonald's; Forest Mars, the original creator of the Milky Way bar and other candies; the Bass brothers, independent oil operators (see Chapter 8); and Sam Walton, who opened his first Wal-Mart Store in rural Arkansas in 1962. And by 1992 new self-made billionaire Ted Turner (see Chapter 5) and cosmetics empress Estee Lauder had made the top list.

America offers *opportunity*, not income equality. Inequality is and has always been a significant component of the American social structure. The top fifth of income recipients in America accounts for over 40 percent of all income in the nation, while the bottom fifth accounts for only about 5 percent (see Table 2–15). Since the pre–World War II years, the income share of the top 5 percent of families has declined dramatically from 30 to 17 percent. However, the bottom fifth of the population still receives a very small share of the national income.

Inequality increased in America in the 1980s. While the increase is slight by historical standards, and the United States remains one of the most equalitarian nations in the world, nonetheless, this increase reverses the historical tendencies toward greater equality. Various theories have been put forward to explain this reversal: the decline of the manufacturing sector of the economy with its relatively high-paying jobs; a rise in the number of two-wage-earning families, which makes single-headed households relatively less affluent; and demographic trends which include larger proportions of the aged as well as larger proportions of female-headed families. The popular notion that miserly government welfare and social insurance payment caused the increase in inequality is untrue; aggregate government transfer payments did not decline in the 1980s. Nor is there any evidence that income taxation has any significant effect on the distribution of income. Before-tax and after-tax income distribution are nearly identical.

SUMMARY

In later chapters, we examine interlocking, recruitment, conflict, and consensus, as well as corporate involvement in national policy-making, in greater detail. Now, however, let us summarize our initial observations of corporate management as one of the key elites in the institutional structure of American society.

Economic power in America is highly concentrated. A small number of corporations control almost three quarters of the nation's industrial assets; one half of all assets in communications and utilities; almost two thirds of all banking assets; and more than three quarters of all insurance assets. This concentration of economic power is increasing gradually over time, as the nation's largest corporations gain ever-larger shares of total corporate assets.

Power over corporate assets rests in the hands of about 4,300 officers and directors. These managers, not the stockholders or the employees, decide major policy questions, choose the people who will carry out these decisions, and even select their own replacements. However, most of these officers and directors have climbed the corporate ladder to their posts. They owe their rise to power to their skills in organizational life and to their successful coping with the new demands for expertise in management, finance, technology, and planning. Individual capitalists are no longer essential in the formation of capital assets. Most industrial capital is raised either within the corporation itself or from institutional borrowing.

Corporate boardrooms are inhabited by "inside" directors (top officers of the corporation, including the CEO) and "outside" directors (often current or retired CEOs of other corporations). Outside directors may also represent financial institutions with a large stake in the corporation, and they may represent family owners. Virtually all large corporations also appoint a few notable "public interest" representatives to their boards. But corporate decision-making is usually dominated by the inside manager-directors rather than the outside directors.

In recent years challenges to managerial control of the corporation have arisen from (1) a new activism by outside directors and large stockholders, and (2) the threat of hostile takeovers often led by corporate "raiders." Slow growth and global competition have inspired outside directors and large stockholders to oust some prominent corporate chieftains. Corporate raiders claim to reinvigorate American enterprise and competition by ousting poorly performing managers and reorganizing corporate assets to maximize their value. But critics claim that takeover activity wastes capital resources, demoralizes managers and workers, and burdens corporations with excessive debts.

Corporate ownership is largely institutional—banks, investment firms, employee stock ownership trusts. But family holdings are still important. The Rockefellers, du Ponts, Mellons, and other great entrepreneurial families still exercise power over corporate resources. But a majority of the directors of family-dominated firms have been brought in from outside the family.

Personal wealth is insignificant in relation to corporate (or governmental) wealth. It is necessary for individuals to achieve top corporate positions in order to exercise significant economic power.

3 The Governing Circles

If there ever was a time when the powers of government were limited—when government did no more than secure law and order, protect individual liberty and property, enforce contracts, and defend against foreign invasion— that time has long passed. Today it is commonplace to observe that governmental institutions intervene in every aspect of our lives—from the "cradle to the grave." Government in America has the primary responsibility for providing insurance against old age, death, dependency, disability, and unemployment; for organizing the nation's health-care system; for providing education at the elementary, secondary, collegiate, and postgraduate levels; for providing public highways and regulating water, rail, and air transportation; for providing police and fire protection; for providing sanitation services and sewage disposal; for financing research in medicine, science, and technology; for delivering the mail; for exploring outer space; for maintaining parks and recreation; for providing housing and adequate food for the poor; for providing job training and manpower programs; for cleaning the air and water; for rebuilding central cities; for maintaining full employment and a stable money supply; for regulating business practices and labor relations; for eliminating racial and sexual discrimination. Indeed, the list of government responsibilities seems endless, yet each year we manage to find additional tasks for government to do.

THE CONCENTRATION OF GOVERNMENTAL POWER

Governments do many things that cannot be measured in terms of dollars and cents. Nonetheless, government expenditures are the best available measure of the dimensions of government activity. Such expenditures in the United States amount to about 35 percent of the gross national product. This is an increase from about 8 percent of the GNP at the beginning of the century. The largest governmental cost is "income maintenance"—social security, welfare, and related social services. Medical care is the second largest governmental cost, followed by education.

Of course, the observation that government expenditures now account for over one third of the nation's GNP actually understates the great power of government over every aspect of our lives. Government regulatory activity cannot be measured in government expenditures. Indeed, large segments of the economy come under direct federal regulation, notably transportation and utilities; yet these are officially classified as private industries and are not counted in the governmental proportion of the GNP.

Concentration of governmental resources is also evidenced in the proportion of *federal* expenditures in relation to *state* and *local* government expenditures. There are 86,743 separate governmental units operating in the United States today (U.S. government—1; state governments—50; counties—3,043; municipalities—19,296; townships—16,666; school districts—14,586; special districts—33,131).[1] But only one of these, the U.S. government, accounts for nearly *two thirds* of all governmental expenditures. This means that approximately 23 percent of the GNP is accounted for by federal expenditures alone.

We have defined our governmental elite as the top executive, congressional, military, and judicial officers of the *federal* government; the President and Vice-President; secretaries, undersecretaries, and assistant secretaries of executive departments; senior White House presidential advisers; congressional committee chairpersons and ranking minority members; congressional majority and minority party leaders in the House and Senate; Supreme Court Justices; and members of the Federal Reserve Board and the Council of Economic Advisers.

The governmental elite is composed of both *elected politicians*—whose principal talent is running for office—and *appointed executives*—most of whom have had some experience and competence in running public or private organizations. In the pages that follow, we describe both elected politicians and governmental executives, their backgrounds and educations, and how they came to their positions of power.

THE POLITICIANS: AMBITION AND OFFICE-SEEKING

Ambition is the driving force in politics. Politics attracts people for whom power and celebrity are more rewarding than money, leisure, or privacy. "Political office today flows to those who want it enough to spend the time and energy mastering its pursuit. It flows in the direction of ambition—and talent."[2]

Political ambition is the most distinguishing characteristic of elected officeholders. The people who run for and win public office are not necessarily the most intelligent, best informed, wealthiest, or most successful business

---

[1] U.S. Bureau of the Census, *Census of Governments 1992* (Washington, DC: Government Printing Office, 1993).

[2] Alan Ehrenhalt, *The United States of Ambition: Politicians' Power and Pursuit of Office* (New York: Random House, 1991), p. 22.

or professional people. At all levels of the political system, from presidential candidates, members of Congress, governors and state legislators, to city councils and school board members, it is the most politically ambitious people who are willing to sacrifice time, family and private life, and energy and effort for the power and celebrity that comes with public office.

Most politicians publicly deny that personal ambition is their real motivation for seeking public office. Rather they describe their motives in highly idealistic terms—"civic duty," "service to community," "reform the government," "protect the environment," "bring about change." These responses reflect the norms of our political culture. People are not supposed to enter politics to satisfy *personal* ambitions but rather to achieve *public* purposes. Many politicians do not really recognize their own drive for power—the drive to shape the world according to their own beliefs and values. Often they do not realize how much they crave celebrity—the public attention, deference, name recognition, and social status that accompanies public office. But if there were no personal rewards in politics, almost no one would run for office.

The talent required is that of political entrepreneurship—the ability to sell oneself to others as a candidate, to raise money from contributions, to organize people to work on one's behalf, to communicate and publicize oneself through the media. Perhaps the most important personal qualification is the willingness to work long and hard; to live, eat, and breathe politics every day. Occasionally people win high office who really do not like political campaigning; they view it as a torture they must endure in order to gain office and exercise power. But most successful politicians are people who really *like* politics—the meetings, appearances, speeches, interviews, hand-shaking— and really enjoy interacting with other people.

Politics is becoming increasingly professionalized. "Citizen-statesmen"—people with business or professional careers who get into politics part-time or for short periods of time—are being driven out of political life by career politicians—people who enter politics early in life as a full-time occupation and expect to make it their career. Politically ambitious young people seek out internships and staff positions with members of Congress, with congressional committees, in state legislators' or governors' offices, or mayors' or council chambers. Others volunteer to work in political campaigns. Many find political mentors, as they learn how to organize campaigns, contact financial contributors, and deal with the media. By their early thirties, they are ready to run for local office or the state legislature. Rather than challenge a strong incumbent, they may wait for an open seat to be created by retirement, reapportionment, or its holder seeking another office. Or they may make an initial attempt against a strong incumbent of the opposition party in order to gain experience and win the appreciation of their own party's supporters for a good effort. Over time, running for and holding elective office becomes their career. They work harder at it than anyone else, in part because they have no real private sector career to return to in case of defeat.

The prevalence of lawyers in politics is an American tradition. Among the nation's Founders—the fifty-five delegates to the Constitutional Convention in 1787—some twenty-five were lawyers. The political dominance of lawyers is even greater today, with lawyers filling nearly two thirds of U.S. Senate seats and nearly half of the seats in the U.S. House of Representatives.

It is sometimes argued that lawyers dominate in politics because of the parallel skills required in law and politics. Lawyering is the representation of clients; a lawyer employs similar skills whether representing clients in private practice or representing constituents in Congress. Lawyers are trained to deal with statutory law, so they may at least know how to find United States Code (the codified laws of the United States government) in a law library when they arrive in Congress to make or amend these laws.

But it is more likely that the people attracted to politics decide to go to law school, fully aware of the tradition of lawyers in American politics. Moreover, political officeholding, at the state and local level as well as in the national government, can help a struggling lawyer's private practice through free public advertising and opportunities to make contacts with potential clients. Finally, there are many special opportunities for lawyers to acquire public office in "lawyers only" posts in federal, state, and local government as judges and prosecuting attorneys. The lawyer-politician is not usually a top professional lawyer. (We will examine the "superlawyers"—the nation's legal elite—in Chapter 5). Instead, the typical lawyer-politician uses his or her law career as a means of support—one that is compatible with political office seeking and officeholding.

A significant number of top politicians have inherited great wealth. The Roosevelts, Rockefellers, Kennedys, Bushes, and others have used their wealth and family connections to support their political careers. However, it is important to note that *a majority of the nation's top politicians have climbed the ladder from relative obscurity to political success.* Many have acquired some wealth in the process, but most political leaders started their climb from very middle-class circumstances. Only two of the last nine presidents (John F. Kennedy and George Bush) were born to great wealth. Thus, as in the corporate world, we find more "climbers" than "inheritors" at the top in the world of politics.

RONALD REAGAN: THE QUICK-STUDY COWBOY

Ronald Wilson Reagan was always a "quick study"—he learned his acting lines easily and well. He made fifty-four movies over a period of twenty-seven years. He never won an Oscar; he was never even nominated for one. His best role was the legendary Notre Dame halfback, George Gipp ("win one for the Gipper") in the movie *Knute Rockne, All-American,* with Pat O'Brien in the title role. But Ronald Reagan was a steady, hard-working professional. He showed up on time, knew his lines, and took direction easily. He was comfortable—even modest—in front of the camera. The Hollywood crowd thought he was a square—no drugs, booze, or high living. He was a liberal and a Democrat, and in 1947 he was elected president of the Screen Actors Guild, a post he held through six terms.

Reagan's boyhood in small towns of the Midwest—Tampico, Dixon, and Eureka, Illinois—was far removed from the glitter of Hollywood or the power of Washington. Reagan "climbed" the ladder of success: he was the child of a failed, alcoholic shoe salesman; he washed dishes at tiny, threadbare Eureka College; he won a partial athletic scholarship (football and swimming); he graduated in 1932 in the middle of the Great Depression; and he struggled for five years as sports announcer (beginning at five dollars per game) for radio station WHO in Des Moines, Iowa. Later, when WHO sent "Dutch" Reagan to California to cover spring training for the Chicago Cubs, Reagan contacted an agent who arranged a screen test for him. The test was shown to Jack Warner, resident tycoon at Warner Brothers, and another grade-B movie actor was signed to a studio contract.

Reagan was never a true "star" like Humphrey Bogart or James Cagney or Errol Flynn. He served in the Army Air Corps in World War II making training films, and his acting career faded after the war. His marriage to actress Jane Wyman (who won the best-actress Oscar for her work in *Johnny Belinda*) also faded. The good acting roles went to other actors, and new stars—Brando, Newman, Holden—replaced the old. By 1957, Reagan was playing opposite a chimpanzee in *Bedtime for Bonzo*. He met and married an aspiring young actress, Nancy Davis, who was to stick by him in the lean years, all the way to the presidency.

Turning fifty, Reagan was rescued from obscurity by Ralph J. Cordiner, president of General Electric. G.E. was putting together a weekly network television show, *G.E. Theatre*, and Reagan was offered the job as host. Reagan believed that a television show would be the end of his Hollywood career, but he had little choice. Fortunately, *G.E. Theatre* turned out to be an Emmy Award–winning venture; it held a prime Sunday evening spot for seven years before being replaced by one of Reagan's own favorites, *Bonanza*.

More important, Reagan began making public appearances and pro-business speeches across the country on behalf of General Electric. Hollywood receded into the background as Reagan collected a vast array of three-by-five index cards filled with examples of federal bureaucracy run amok, social welfare programs wasting money and ruining lives, and the ever-increasing threat of socialism to America's free enterprise system. Reagan's early liberalism gave way to staunch conservatism.

Several new-money southern California millionaires decided that Reagan had a more promising future than merely speaking at Chamber of Commerce meetings. When *G.E. Theatre* was finally canceled and Reagan was hosting *Death Valley Days* at a lower salary, his wealthy admirers came to his rescue. In 1964, Reagan was in debt; he had failed to invest his money when he was in Hollywood, and he owed back income taxes to the U.S. government. A group headed by Justin Dart (Dart Industries, Rexall Drugs, Kraft

Foods); Holmes Tuttle (a Los Angeles Ford dealer); William French Smith (a wealthy Los Angeles attorney and later attorney general of the United States); and A.C. (Cy) Rubel (chairman of Union Oil Co.) formed the Ronald Reagan Trust Fund to take over his personal finances and free him to concentrate on a political career. His first political venture was the production of a film to assist Republican presidential candidate Barry Goldwater in 1964. Reagan made the perfect pitch; the money rolled in, but Goldwater was overwhelmingly rejected at the polls. Nonetheless, Reagan won the hearts of conservatives throughout the country, who recognized a new and highly gifted media politician.

Two years later, Ronald Reagan took on the incumbent governor of California, Edmund G. "Pat" Brown (the father of later Governor Jerry Brown), who had defeated Richard Nixon for the post in 1962. It was Reagan's first try for public office. Like so many other politicians, Brown underestimated Reagan's appeal. Reagan buried him with nearly a million-vote margin. As California's governor, Reagan was willing to compromise; he was never angry or bitter; if he could not reduce the size of government, he was satisfied to slow its growth. He delegated responsibility and relied on his staff. He did not read books; he wanted one-page summaries of major issues. He worked in a relaxed manner; he built his Rancho del Cielo on weekends. Reagan was reelected in 1970 by another million-vote margin.

The camera is a tool of both of Ronald Reagan's trades—actor and politician. Newspaper journalists could never understand Reagan's success. Reporters wrote up his commonplace phrases and time-worn slogans—the simple messages on the old and yellowed three-by-five cards. The printed words were lifeless and uninspiring. Journalists missed Reagan's true appeal as a comfortable, pleasant, reassuring man of traditional American values.

The political landscape is littered with candidates who underestimated Reagan—the supposedly lightweight, "too-old" actor. President Carter hoped Reagan would win the Republican nomination in 1980, because Carter's aides thought Reagan would be the easiest person to beat! In the general election, however, Reagan skillfully turned his age from a liability to an asset. In 1980, the "good old days" never looked better. Reagan spoke of traditional values; he knew that America could be "great again." Carter mistakenly tried to portray Reagan as an unstable warmonger. But Reagan's polished style and charm—his appearance as a kindly, older, soft-spoken, western rancher—deflected Carter's attack. In the presidential debate, Reagan was the master of the stage; he was relaxed, smiling, even joking. He never said anything of great importance. He merely asked, "Are you better off now than you were five years ago?" Simple, yet highly effective.

Just as Reagan's opponents underestimated his abilities as a campaigner, they also underestimated his skills as President. Yet with polished personal appeals to Democrats and Republicans in Congress and successful national television appeals, Reagan rolled over his congressional opponents. He reduced proposed government spending and later pushed through the largest tax cut in the nation's history. In slowing the growth of social welfare programs, rebuilding national defenses, and cutting federal income taxes, Reagan changed the course of government more than any President since Franklin D. Roosevelt.[3]

The nation's oldest President could have retired to the ranch after his first term, secure in the knowledge that he had achieved most of his major goals. First Lady Nancy Reagan worried about the stresses on her husband and remembered the nearly successful assassination attempt. But Reagan himself seemed to thrive on the challenges of the job. He worked fewer hours than any other modern President, vacationed more, and kept himself in better physical condition.

During his campaign for reelection, the "Great Communicator" stumbled only once on the road to his landslide reelection. In the first of two televised debates with Walter Mondale, Reagan looked like a heavyweight champ who had gone soft against a hungrier challenger. Reagan appeared confused and out of touch as he stumbled over statistics and frequently lost his train of thought. Indeed, his performance was so bad that it raised an issue which Mondale was afraid to raise directly—the President's age. But in the second debate, almost as if he had set a trap for Mondale, the President regained his old mastery of the medium. When questioned whether he might be too old for the job, he answered, "I want you to know that I will not make age an issue in this campaign. I am not going to exploit for political purposes my opponent's youth and inexperience." Even Mondale had to laugh, along with millions of viewers. Mondale may have won a debate on the issues, but Reagan reassured his fans that he was still champion of the one-liner.

Reagan's romantic nature—personally worrying over the fate of individual hostages—and his hands-*off* leadership style, eventually led to his only serious mistake—the Iran-Contra scandal. Despite the advice of the experienced heavyweights in his Cabinet, Secretary of State George Schultz and Secretary of Defense Caspar Weinberger, Reagan set in motion the trading of arms to Iran for the release of hostages. He personally encouraged support for the "Contras," the democratic resistance in Communist Nicaragua, but he did not personally approve of the diversion of arms "profits" by Lt. Col. Oliver North.

Reagan's popularity tumbled during the various Iran-Contra investigations. But over time, the general public appeared to forgive the popular President, and by November 1988, Reagan had recovered in the opinion polls. Over eight years he had come to view his Vice-President, George Bush, as both a personal friend and the legitimate heir to the Reagan legacy. Reagan campaigned hard for Bush and took great satisfaction in Bush's election. Upon leaving office Ronald Reagan enjoyed the highest approval rating of any modern President.

---

[3] See John L. Palmer and Isabel V. Sawhill, eds., *The Reagan Record* (Washington: Urban Institute, 1984).

TED KENNEDY: INHERITING A POLITICAL DYNASTY

The Kennedy dynasty began with the flamboyant career of Joseph P. Kennedy, a son of a prosperous Irish saloon-keeper and ward boss in Boston. Joseph Kennedy attended Boston Latin School and Harvard, receiving his B.A. in 1912. He started his career in banking, moved into stock market operations, dabbled in shipbuilding, formed movie-making companies (RKO and later Paramount), and married the daughter of the mayor of Boston. "Old Joe" made the major part of his fortune in stock market manipulations. With his associate, William Randolph Hearst, Kennedy provided key financial backing for the 1932 presidential campaign of Franklin D. Roosevelt. FDR later made Kennedy head of the Securities and Exchange Commission. But making a market speculator head of a commission that was designed to protect investors caused such public outcry that Kennedy was forced to resign after one year. FDR then appointed Kennedy head of the Maritime Commission, but rumors of extravagant subsidies to shipbuilding friends forced his resignation after only two months on the job. In 1937, FDR appointed him ambassador to England. His diplomatic career lasted three years and ended over differences with FDR regarding U.S. assistance to the Allies. Old Joe is said to have advised FDR of the likelihood of German victory and the advantages of placating Hitler.

Joseph P. Kennedy, Sr. was the father of nine children. (Joseph P., Jr. was killed as a World War II Navy pilot; President John F. Kennedy was assassinated; Senator Robert F. Kennedy was assassinated; Kathleen died in a plane crash; Rosemary is living in an institution for the mentally retarded; Eunice is married to Sargent Shriver, former director of the Peace Corps and the War on Poverty and replacement for Senator Thomas Eagleton as the Democratic vice-presidential nominee in 1972; Patricia, formerly married to actor Peter Lawford; Jean, wife of Stephen Smith; and the youngest, Edward M. "Ted" Kennedy.)

Although born to great wealth and accustomed to an upper-class style of living (he received his first communion from Pope Pius XII), Ted Kennedy acquired the sense of competition fostered in the large Kennedy household. In 1951, suspended from Harvard for cheating on a Spanish examination, he joined the Army and served two years in Germany. He was readmitted to Harvard, where he played on the Harvard football team and graduated in 1956.

Despite his family background, Harvard Law School rejected Ted Kennedy's application for admission. He enrolled instead in the University of Virginia Law School and completed his law degree in 1959. Following graduation and work on his brother's 1960 presidential campaign, he was appointed assistant district attorney for Suffolk County, Massachusetts.

When he was just thirty years old, the minimum age for a U.S. senator, he announced his candidacy for the Massachusetts Senate seat formerly held by his brother, who was then President. In the Democratic primary he faced

Edward J. McCormack, nephew of the then Speaker of the House, John W. McCormack. During a televised debate, McCormack said to Kennedy, "You never worked for a living. You never held elective office. You lack the qualifications and maturity of judgment. . . . If your name were not Kennedy, your candidacy would be a joke." But Kennedy won overwhelmingly and went on to defeat the Republican candidate, George Cabot Lodge. (George Cabot Lodge was the son of U.S. Ambassador to South Vietnam and former U.S. Senator Henry Cabot Lodge, Jr. In 1916, Kennedy's grandfather, Boston Mayor John F. Fitzgerald, had been defeated in a race for the same Senate seat by Lodge's great-grandfather, Senator Henry Cabot Lodge.)

Kennedy performed better in the Senate than many had expected. He cultivated Senate friends, appeared at fund-raising dinners, and informed himself about several important policy fields. He worked hard learning about national health problems and problems of the elderly. In 1969 he was elected Senate Democratic whip by his colleagues.

His personal life, however, was marred by accident, tragedy, and scandal. He nearly died in a 1964 plane crash in which he suffered a broken back. An athletic and handsome six foot two inches, Kennedy was frequently the object of romantic gossip at Washington cocktail parties. On July 19, 1969, a young woman, Mary Jo Kopechne, died when the car Kennedy was driving plunged off a narrow bridge on Chappaquiddick Island after a late-night party. Missing for ten hours after the accident, Kennedy later made a dramatic national television appearance, saying that the tragedy had been an accident and that he had been too confused to report the tragedy until the next day. The official inquest has been kept secret, and many feel that there are still unresolved discrepancies in Kennedy's story.[4] Kennedy pled guilty to the minor charge of leaving the scene of an accident. Senate Democrats removed Kennedy from his position as majority whip. But the national news media never pressed the Chappaquiddick incident and continued favorable reporting of the still charismatic senator.

Kennedy deliberately avoided the Democratic presidential nomination in both 1972 and 1976. His advisers argued that the public's memory of Chappaquiddick was still too fresh for Kennedy to enter a campaign battle in which the issue of his personal life would certainly be raised. However, in late 1979, with Jimmy Carter standing at a near all-time low for Presidents in the opinion polls, Kennedy announced his presidential candidacy. Most observers thought that Kennedy was unbeatable, but Carter was temporarily saved by the Iranian seizure of American embassy employees in Iran as hostages. Shortly thereafter, Soviet troops invaded neighboring Afghanistan. Support for the President was equated with support for America, and Carter benefited from a "rally round the flag" effect. The media focus was on the President, and the international news simply obliterated the Kennedy campaign. But Ted Kennedy reestablished his leadership of liberal Democrats

---

[4] See Robert Sherrill, "Chappaquiddick + 5," *New York Times Magazine,* July 14, 1974.

and polished his own charismatic image with a dramatic and inspiring speech at the 1980 Democratic National Convention. It was clearly Ted Kennedy's finest public performance.

Kennedy avoided subsequent presidential races, citing family affairs as his reason. And indeed, his family situation might have caused him political problems had he chosen to run. He was divorced from his wife, Joan, and many stories were published in women's magazines portraying her as a victim of Ted's heavy drinking and "womanizing." At the same time, he felt responsible for the many sons and daughters of his deceased brother Robert as well as his own children. Several of these "third-generation" Kennedys suffered serious personal problems;[5] David Anthony Kennedy dropped out of Harvard and died a drug-related death in a Miami motel in 1984. Nephew William Kennedy Smith was found not guilty of rape charges in a nationally televised trial in 1992; the charges arose following a late-night visit to a Palm Beach bar with his Uncle Ted.

Clearly, Ted Kennedy is an inheritor rather than a climber in the world of politics. His success rests upon his image and style more than upon his substantive contributions to public policy. He was elected to the Senate solely because he was a Kennedy, an inheritor of a famous political image. The image survived tragedy and scandal, and he remains the recognized leader of the liberal wing of the Democratic party. Perhaps he is prepared now to help pave the way for the next generation of the family political dynasty.

Joseph P. Kennedy II, son of the late Senator Robert F. Kennedy, leads the third generation of Kennedys. (There were twenty-six children born to John F. Kennedy, Robert F. Kennedy, Patricia Kennedy Lawford, Eunice Kennedy Shriver, and Edward M. Kennedy.) In 1986 young Joe inherited the Boston congressional seat of his Uncle Jack, when the venerable House Speaker Thomas P. "Tip" O'Neill conveniently retired. Joe had struggled through various private prep schools and dropped out of M.I.T. and the University of California at Berkeley, before finally getting a degree from the University of Massachusetts. He floundered for several years after graduation; he was the driver in a Jeep accident that crippled a passenger. Later he headed a nonprofit company to deliver heating oil to poor Bostonians. But when he announced his candidacy for Congress, the Kennedy name made him the instant frontrunner, the focus of media attention, and the recipient of heavy campaign contributions.

GEORGE BUSH: PATRICIAN PRESIDENT

Try as he may, George Bush could never shed his upper-class "preppy" image. His personal mannerisms, his diction and dress, his Episcopalian morality, all belied his efforts to portray himself as a cowboy and "kick-ass" Texan.

---

[5] See Peter Collier and David Horowitz, *The Kennedys: An American Dream* (New York: Summit, 1984).

George Bush was another inheritor in politics. His father, U.S. Senator Prescott Bush, was the managing partner in the great Wall Street investment firm of Brown Brothers, Harriman & Co. (see Table 2–5), as well as chairman of the board of Yale Corporation, which governs Yale University, and Republican U.S. senator from Connecticut from 1962 to 1972. George Herbert Walker Bush was born in 1924 and spent his boyhood in upper-class Greenwich, Connecticut. He attended the Greenwich Country Day School before entering Phillips Academy in Andover, Massachusetts, where he was captain of the soccer team and president of his senior class.

At age seventeen, in the dark days of World War II, George Bush set aside his admission to Yale in order to join the Navy. His worried father asked President Roosevelt to ignore the age requirements and allow George to be commissioned as an ensign in flight school. As the youngest pilot in the U.S. Navy, Bush was assigned to the light aircraft carrier U.S.S. *San Jacinto* in 1943. He flew fifty-eight combat missions. He was awarded the Distinguished Flying Cross and three Air Medals for action in the Pacific. His torpedo bomber was shot down, his two crewmen were killed, and he was rescued at sea by a submarine. He returned home on leave to marry Barbara Pierce, daughter of the publisher of *Redbook* and *McCall's* magazines. He spent the rest of the war training Navy pilots.

George Bush entered Yale in September of 1945. He captained the baseball team and graduated in three years, Phi Beta Kappa in economics. His father wanted him to join Brown Brothers, Harriman in New York, but at twenty-five George wanted to strike out on his own. "On his own" turned out to be a job as vice-president of Dresser Industries, a Texas oil-drilling equipment firm of which his father was a director. George Bush quickly became very successful in the Texas oil business. He formed several oil companies with financing from his uncle, Herbert Walker: Bush-Overby, Zapata Petroleum, and Zapata Offshore Oil. He served as a director of the First International Bank of Houston and London as well as of Eli Lilly, Texas Gulf, and Purolator. By the early 1960s Bush was a multimillionaire Texas oilman still in his thirties. Having conquered the world of business, he turned to politics.

Bush did not have the same easy success in politics that he enjoyed in business. Bush served a term as chairman of the Republican party in Harris County (Houston), and then in 1964 he plunged into a campaign to unseat Ralph Yarborough, U.S. senator from Texas and ally of President Lyndon Johnson. Bush fell victim to the Johnson landslide in that year but captured a larger share of the vote than any previous Republican candidate in Texas. In 1966, Bush returned to the political fray to win election to Congress from a wealthy suburban Houston district. After serving two terms in the House, he set out again in 1970 to defeat Ralph Yarborough and win a Senate seat. But Yarborough was upset in the Democratic primary by another wealthy oilman, conservative Democrat Lloyd Bentsen. The Bush-Bentsen race was hard fought and expensive for both sides; Bush was edged out in a very close election. The unsuccessful Senate race cost Bush his safe seat in the House.

President Richard Nixon named Bush to the post of United Nations ambassador in 1970, where he served for two years. Following Nixon's reelection, the President named Bush as chairman of the Republican National Committee, a job which became very difficult as the Watergate scandal mushroomed. But most of the Watergate evils occurred under the Committee to Reelect the President (CREEP—an organization which was separate from the Republican National Committee), and George Bush was successful in keeping the regular Republican organization free of scandal and his own name untarnished. A grateful President Gerald Ford asked Bush to pick his own post in the new administration, and Bush chose the newly created ambassadorship to the People's Republic of China. In 1975 President Ford asked him to return from China to head the Central Intelligence Agency.

George Bush inherited the support of the Eastern Establishment wing of the Republican party. These internationalist Wall Street Republicans had formed the foundation of Eisenhower's administration and had been led for many years thereafter by Nelson Rockefeller. Following Gerald Ford's defeat at the hands of Jimmy Carter, Bush began his own bid for the presidency. He hoped to combine his Eastern Brahmin support with his Texas oil friends, thus bringing together the new wealth of the Sunbelt and the old wealth of the East. He recruited his friend, Houston attorney James A. Baker, Ford's campaign manager, as his own and conducted a vigorous nationwide campaign. But Ronald Reagan had spent years building his political base among the southern and western Sunbelt Republicans. Following a Nashua debate in which Bush looked stiff and inflexible and Reagan relaxed and amiable, Bush narrowly lost the 1980 New Hampshire presidential primary. Although Bush went on to win primaries in Massachusetts, Connecticut, and Pennsylvania, he was "stunned" again by Reagan's victory in Bush's home state of Texas. Despite his many years in Texas, George Bush was unable to escape his Eastern preppy background to win the hearts of Texans. At the Republican National Convention, Ronald Reagan turned to George Bush as his vice-presidential running mate to balance the Reagan ticket with his foreign policy experience and appeal to Republican moderates.

George Bush was a supremely loyal Vice-President. He steadfastly refused to differ with his President—even when he was being skewered by the media for the Iranian arms-for-hostages dealings. Indeed, George Bush was portrayed as a terminal second-banana with no principles or passions of his own, forever to be overshadowed by Ronald Reagan. *Newsweek* magazine even devoted its cover to branding Bush as a "wimp."[6]

The remaking of Bush's image began at the Republican National Convention in 1988. His World War II–Navy fighter pilot photos and film of his dramatic rescue from the water by a submarine helped overcome the wimp image. His support for President Reagan, even during the Iran-Contra scandal, was recast as a test of his loyalty to a popular President under fire. In

[6] *Newsweek*, October 19, 1987.

his acceptance speech, an astonishingly new and telegenic George Bush emerged—warm, relaxed, authoritative, even presidential.

Andover teaches its boys to fight hard to win. George Bush was prepared to do what was necessary to defeat the Democratic challenger, Massachusetts Governor Michael Dukakis. The media campaign strategy called for a series of hard-hitting "attack" videos linking Dukakis to unpopular liberal policy positions. The Bush team succeeded in creating an image of Dukakis as an unpatriotic liberal who furloughed murderers, befouled harbors, spurned the American flag, and belonged to an organization (the ACLU) that defended child pornography. Even before the first televised debate, Dukakis's lead in the polls had evaporated.

In the end, George Bush's loyalty to his President paid off. Ronald Reagan recovered his popularity in his final year. Eight years of peace and prosperity were rewarded at the polls. Bush was perceived as the legitimate heir to the Reagan legacy, both in the primary elections where he swept away his Republican challengers, and in the general election where Michael Dukakis failed to convince Americans that their well-being was a temporary illusion.

George Bush's presidential performance was schizophrenic—strength, perseverance, and victory in foreign and military affairs, and weakness, vacillation, and defeat on domestic matters. He became President at a turning point in world history—the collapse of communism in Eastern Europe, the end of the Soviet-led Warsaw Pact anti-Western military alliance, and the disintegration of the Soviet Union itself. He was given the opportunity to declare Western victory in the decades-long Cold War and to lay the foundation for a "new world order" in which the United States occupied the predominant global position. His finest hour was his resolute performance in the Persian Gulf. He assembled a worldwide political coalition, including the Soviet Union, China, and Western and Arab nations, against Saddam Hussein's invasion and occupation of Kuwait. He wisely left the strategic planning and implementation of military operations to a highly capable team—Defense Secretary Richard Cheney, Joint Chiefs of Staff Chairman Colin Powell, and field commander General Norman Schwarzkopf. He avoided the mistakes of Vietnam—gradual escalation of force, prolonged operations, accumulating casualties, muddled negotiations, moratoriums of bombings, political interference in military operations. He sought a rapid, decisive military victory with the use of overwhelming force. He resisted efforts to stall the attack or engage in endless negotiations or allow intermediaries to compromise the outcome. He sought to limit casualties among Americans and coalition forces and perhaps ended the war too soon. But his overall performance as Commander-in-Chief earned him the highest public approval rating ever attained by an American President.

By contrast, in the domestic policy arena, George Bush was a failure. He came into office with no clear policy agenda, publicly referring to "the vision thing" as a public relations gimmick rather than a policy guide for the nation.

He lacked his predecessor Ronald Reagan's ideological commitments. He was never able to use his Gulf War popularity to seize the initiative in domestic affairs. He offered few domestic policy ideas to Congress; his only legislative successes were in gathering enough votes to sustain his vetoes of bills he opposed. But on key issues he collapsed in the face of congressional pressure. He campaigned on as firm a promise as any candidate could make on taxes: "Read my lips! No new taxes!" Yet in his second year in office he agreed to support an increase in income-tax rates. He took a strong rhetorical stand against "quotas" in civil rights legislation, yet later signed a bill almost identical to an earlier one he had vetoed. And when recession struck the nation's economy, he responded with too little too late, leaving the impression that he was "out of touch" with the concerns of the American people.

Bush's public approval ratings plummeted throughout the spring of 1992. Although the economy began a slow recovery, the media focused on the nation's economic ills. Ross Perot detached millions of middle-class voters from Bush by turning the spotlight on the government's huge deficits. Democrat Bill Clinton dodged attacks on his own character and captured the image of change. Bush's reelection campaign was in shambles; James Baker left his post as secretary of state to try to rescue his old friend. But Bush turned in a lackluster performance in the first two presidential debates, and a final mini-surge in his campaign fell short. The nation clearly wanted change as 62 percent of the voters chose either Clinton or Perot over Bush. The voters did not so much express confidence in Clinton as dissatisfaction with Bush and his neglect of their domestic discontents.

BILL CLINTON: THE FRUITS OF POLITICAL AMBITION

Bill Clinton is "a political robot who's been running for president all of his life."[7] Born Billy Blythe in rural Hope, Arkansas, three months after his father's death in an automobile accident, young Bill learned that persistence and tenacity were the keys to success and acclaim. His strength was always his ability to mold himself into what others expected him to be.

Young Bill held so many class offices in high school that the principal told him he wasn't allowed to take on any more. He assumed his stepfather's name at age fifteen, even though he would later talk about the older man's alcoholism and abuse. He won first place in the state band's saxophone section, but his sights were set on politics, not music. As a delegate to Boys' Nation, he won a handshake from President John F. Kennedy in 1963. He chose to study international relations at private, prestigious Georgetown University in Washington. No sooner had Clinton arrived at the capital, he called on his state's U.S. senator, William J. Fulbright, chairman of the Senate Foreign Relations Committee, presenting his job recommendations from

---

[7] *U.S. News and World Report,* March 30, 1992, p. 28.

home-town politicians. Fulbright took the young college student under his wing as a legislative aide. Clinton soon began reflecting his new mentor's opposition to the Vietnam War.

Fulbright himself had been a Rhodes scholar at Oxford, and when Clinton graduated with his international affairs degree from Georgetown, Fulbright recommended Clinton for the same honor. At Oxford Clinton never finished a degree, but he cultivated friendships that would later enhance his public career. In London he helped organize anti–Vietnam War demonstrations, even while he worried that his antiwar activities might some-day come back to haunt his political ambitions. When he received a draft notice, he promptly enrolled in the ROTC program at the University of Arkansas, making himself temporarily ineligible for the draft. Later, draft calls were cut back as President Richard Nixon de-escalated the war, and a lot-tery system was instituted. Clinton drew a high number making him unlikely to be drafted. Soon after, he wrote to the ROTC withdrawing his name, "Thank you for saving me from the draft. . . ," acknowledging that his real plans were to go to Yale Law School, which he entered in 1970. He continued to be active in the antiwar movement while in law school; he was George McGovern's Texas campaign manager in 1972. He met his future wife, Hillary Rodham, a classmate at Yale Law School, daughter of a wealthy Chicago fam-ily, and a graduate of Wellesley.

Upon graduation from Yale Law School, Clinton turned down offers to return to Washington as a congressional staff aide. He was anxious to launch his own political career, and he knew that the road to elective office ran through his home state. He accepted a short-term post teaching law at the University of Arkansas, but within a year he was running for a seat in Congress. Trying to capitalize on the Watergate scandal, he challenged a vet-eran Republican congressman. As a young law professor with long 60s-style hair, a Yale and Oxford background, and liberal friends coming from Washington to help in the campaign, including Hillary Rodham, he could have lost by a wide margin in conservative Arkansas. But instead, he came within a few votes of defeating a strong incumbent, in part as a result of the Watergate scandal that swept many Democrats into Congress in 1974, and in part a result of his own tireless campaigning.

Clinton's strong showing in the congressional race won him political recognition statewide. When the state's elected attorney general decided to run for Congress in 1976, Clinton mounted a successful campaign to replace him. After winning the Democratic primary, Clinton was unopposed in the general election, giving him time to manage Jimmy Carter's campaign in Arkansas. With his sights set on higher office, he used the Arkansas attorney general post to establish a reputation as a consumer advocate battling the big utility companies. In 1978, when Governor David Pryor left office to run for the U.S. Senate, Clinton jumped into the open gubernatorial contest. His rel-atively easy victory (he won 60 percent of the vote in a five-man Democratic primary, and 63 percent of the vote in the general election) made him the nation's youngest governor at age thirty-two. Viewing himself as a vanguard of a new generation, he set about pushing a broad program of liberal reform for Arkansas, increasing taxes and expenditures. But as a Yale-educated Rhodes scholar, he created an image of an arrogant, isolated, crusading, liberal politician, out of touch with his more conservative Arkansas constituency. And it did not help that Jimmy Carter chose to send thousands of Cuban refugees to Fort Chaffee in Arkansas during Clinton's first term in office. Clinton was defeated in his 1980 reelection bid by a conservative Republican banker.

Clinton's defeat "forever influenced the way he approached government and politics."[8] He proceeded to remold himself into a political moderate, calling for "workfare" to replace welfare, supporting the death penalty, and working to create a favorable business climate in Arkansas. He cut his hair and his wife began using her married name, so as not to offend social conservatives. He told his state's voters that he had been humbled by his earlier loss and he promised "to listen to the people." He was elected governor once again in 1982, winning 42 percent of the vote in a five-man Democratic primary and 54 percent against the Republican governor in the general election. He would go on to win two more two-year terms by more substantial margins.

By most accounts, Bill Clinton became a successful governor. He focused his energies on two areas—economic development and education. He raised taxes for education and forced both students and teachers to take competency tests. He declared himself an environmentalist but granted concessions to his state's giant chicken industry in the interest of the economy. His many compromises and accommodations led to his "slick Willie" label by the *Arkansas Democrat Gazette.*

Michael Dukakis's disastrous defeat in 1988 reinforced Bill Clinton's view that only a moderate Democrat could succeed in winning the presidency. Just as he had shaped his image to better fit his Arkansas constituents, he molded his national image as a "new" Democrat—concerned with economic growth, favoring workfare over welfare, tough on crime, and willing to stand up to traditional core Democratic interest groups—labor unions, minorities, and government employees. He served for a while as chairman of the centrist Democratic Leadership Conference (DLC), denounced by Jesse Jackson as "Democrat for the Leisure Class." He used the DLC as a platform to promote a winning Democratic presidential profile—a moderate, pro-business, pro-investment Democrat capable of winning back the support of the white middle class. He espoused "neo-liberal" ideas about government's role in promoting and "investing" in American industry, and he began winning constituents among Wall Street and business interests. He perfected his down-home "aw shucks" Elvis-style mannerisms. He sought to control his motor-mouth delivery of programmatic facts and figures. (In his long-winded 1988 Democratic convention speech, he had drawn cheers with the words "In conclusion.") He honed his skills as an organizer and fund-raiser. He promised everything to everybody: "We can be pro-growth and pro-environment, we can be pro-business and pro-labor, we can make government work again by making it more aggressive and leaner and more effective at the same time, and we can be pro-family and pro-choice."[9]

Success in politics is often a product of good fortune. Few would have predicted in 1991 that George Bush's all-time high presidential popularity after the Gulf War would plummet with the onset of an economic recession. Indeed, the real heavyweights in the Democratic party—Mario Cuomo, Bill Bradley, Richard Gephardt, Lloyd Bentsen, Jesse Jackson—all decided early not to try to challenge the popular incumbent President. But Bill Clinton had little to lose; in fact, a good run at the presidency in 1992 might gain him national prominence and a real chance to capture the office in 1996. Yet as the recession lengthened into 1992 and Bush's popularity drastically declined, Clinton's teenage dreams of becoming President took on real meaning.

Early in the Democratic primaries, Bill Clinton almost lost the prize he had sought for a lifetime when Genifer Flowers held a nationally televised press conference to expose a long-term affair with the governor. Rumors of marital infidelity had shadowed Clinton for many years. The same problem had driven Gary Hart out of the presidential race in 1988. But a tenacious Bill Clinton decided to confront the "bimbo" issue head-on early in the campaign. So when Don Hewitt, liberal producer of *60 Minutes,* offered Clinton a Sunday night prime-time interview just after the Superbowl, the candidate accepted. With Hillary at his side, Clinton told a huge nationwide audience that his marriage had survived shaky moments but it was rock solid now. While never specifically acknowledging adultery, he went further than any presidential candidate had ever gone in describing his personal life. He correctly calculated that the public was increasingly disgusted with the media's focus on sexual scandal.

But Clinton had more difficulty confronting the charge of draft dodging during the Vietnam War. When the story broke just before the New Hampshire primary, Clinton was evasive. First he said he had never received a draft notice before pledging to join the ROTC at the University of Arkansas, but later he was forced to acknowledge that he had. His letter of withdrawal from the ROTC thanking the commander for "saving me from the draft" and not spoiling "my political viability" was embarrassing. How could a man who dodged the draft serve as Commander-in-Chief and perhaps order troops into combat? The draft issue hurt Clinton in New Hampshire, and Bush would later use it in the general election campaign.

Clinton's campaign strategy was to hammer home, over and over again, a single theme: The economy is in bad shape and the nation demands change. Yet in early 1992 the most powerful voice for economic change in the nation was that of Ross Perot. Clinton was running *third* in the polls, trailing

---

[9] *Time,* November 2, 1992, p. 33.

both President Bush and the independent billionaire. Yet Perot was focusing the nation's attention on the economy and the need for change, detaching millions of middle-class voters from Bush, and sending the President's popularity ratings into a nose dive.

With the prospect of a three-man race looming, some Clinton strategists urged their candidate to jettison his moderate image in favor of cultivating the core liberal constituencies of the Democrat party in order to eke out a plurality victory. But Clinton rejected this advice and insisted on sticking with the original game plan—moderation and change. Indeed, in addressing a meeting of Jesse Jackson's Rainbow Coalition, Clinton denounced the words of black rap singer "Sister Souljah" and thereby demonstrated his independence from the special interests, including African Americans.

The Democratic convention was a celebration of Clinton's good fortune and sound political judgment. When the temperamental Perot unexpectedly withdrew from the race, millions of his disillusioned supporters were set adrift at precisely the moment that Clinton was broadcasting his message of change to national audiences. Perot's moderate, middle-class, independent supporters flocked to Clinton's banner. They had lost confidence in Bush's handling of the economy and were prepared to overlook Clinton's character flaws. The choice of Al Gore as running mate, a man of presidential stature in his own right, seemed to demonstrate Clinton's good judgment and self-confidence. It also balanced the ticket with a Vietnam War veteran and committed family man. By the end of the Democratic convention, Clinton had soared to a twenty-point lead in the polls.

Clinton went into the debates with two simple goals—to keep the focus of the campaign on the economy and the need for change, and to avoid making any mistakes. Bush had a much more challenging task—to refocus the campaign on Clinton's character and somehow overcome his huge lead in the polls. But in the first debate Clinton nimbly deflected Bush's attack on his organizing of antiwar demonstrations: "Your father was right to stand up to Joe McCarthy. You were wrong to attack my patriotism." Bush was awkward and uncomfortable in the attack mode; Clinton was boyish and knowledgeable. Ross Perot clearly "won" the battle of sound bites in the first debate. But what mattered most was Clinton had achieved his goals, while Bush had failed to hit the home run he so badly needed.

In the final days of the campaign the Clinton team had to guard against overconfidence. Bush had finally hit his stride with a fierce attack on Clinton's character. Could "Slick Willie"—a taxer, a spender, a liberal, a draft dodger, an antiwar demonstrator, and a liar—be trusted to run the country? While Bush's theme was negative and failed to give voters a reason to vote *for* the President, it began eroding Clinton's support after the third debate. But just as Bush appeared to be narrowing the gap, the media undercut the theme by rehashing old news about Bush's role in the Iran-Contra affair. The Clinton team wanted the election to be a referendum on the economy, not on their candidate's character. In the end that is what they got.

The voter's anxieties about the economy determined the election outcome. While Clinton emerged only five percentage points ahead of Bush in the popular vote, the nation's desire for change was clearly evident in the combined votes for Clinton and Perot. Fully 62 percent of the voters chose to vote against their incumbent President. Clinton prevailed in one of the toughest political campaigns in American history because he skillfully presented himself to the voters as an agent of change. Voter turnout rose for the first time since John F. Kennedy ran in 1960. Clinton was swept into office not so much by people's confidence in him as by their disgust with the way things were.

Clinton's first months in office demonstrated once again the distinction between the skills required in running for office and those required in running the government. In his first hundred days, Clinton lost public approval faster than any previous President. He stumbled over a series of poorly chosen issues, from homosexuals in the military to an "economic stimulus" package that Republican successfully labeled as "pork barrel" and defeated in the Senate. His media relations gaffes included a $200 fashion haircut that delayed air traffic. But Bill Clinton always showed remarkable powers of political recovery throughout his career (he likes to label himself "the comeback kid"), and his narrow victories in passing the budget and approving NAFTA once again proved that.

ASPIRING POLITICOS

For people of great ambition in American politics, there is only one goal—President of the United States. Aspiring political leaders will cultivate a style and an image that encourage others to think of them as "presidential timber," and they will prepare themselves to seize the opportunity when it arises. Both Edward M. Kennedy and George Bush were inheritors in the world of politics; they were blessed with personal wealth, Ivy League educations, and family connections to help establish their careers. But most others are climbers in the political world—people of relatively modest backgrounds who have devoted themselves to the quest for the presidency.

Mario Cuomo. No American politician can inspire so much passion among his followers, or so much fear among his enemies, as Mario Matthew Cuomo. He casts a giant shadow over the presidential ambitions of all of his fellow Democrats. His speeches can stir audiences as no other orator in recent times. Many political strategists agree that he could have won the Democratic presidential nomination in 1988 and given George Bush a much tougher race than Michael Dukakis. Yet Cuomo remained darkly brooding on the sidelines. "This is not the year," he said. "It doesn't feel right."

Few in national politics have climbed so far from such humble beginnings as Mario Cuomo. His father immigrated from Salerno, Sicily, in the 1920s and sold goods from a pushcart in the borough of Queens in New York

City. Later, he opened an Italian grocery store where young Mario and his brothers and sisters worked long hours each day. Cuomo attended Catholic schools in Queens and won a scholarship to the local St. John's University. He briefly tried semiprofessional baseball, playing one summer with the Brunswick Georgia Pirates. But he stayed at St. John's for both his bachelors and law degrees. Cuomo believes that his working-class Italian background and nonprestigious educational credentials kept him out of the big New York law firms. Instead he joined a Brooklyn firm and began working his way up through the political machinery of the New York Democratic party. His old St. John's Law School friend, Governor Hugh Carey of New York, offered him the post of secretary of state in 1975. From that post Cuomo entered the New York City mayor's race in 1977 against six rivals seeking to run the near-bankrupt metropolis. In a bitter run-off election, Cuomo lost to Ed Koch, who would later restore the city to solvency and become its longest serving mayor. In 1978 Cuomo won election as Governor Carey's lieutenant governor, but their political partnership soon dissolved in petty squabbling. In 1982 Carey announced that he would not seek a third term and endorsed Mayor Koch for the governorship.

Cuomo was an underdog against the popular mayor in the governor's race. But Koch's devotion to his beloved city of New York got him in trouble upstate. (Koch publicly described life outside of New York City as "sterile" and a "joke.") Again Cuomo and Koch waged a bitter personal campaign against each other for the votes of Democrats. Cuomo squeaked out a close victory over Koch, only to face a strong Republican opponent, drugstore magnate Lewis E. Lehrman. Lehrman castigated Cuomo for sending his own children to Catholic schools yet supporting publicly funded abortions and opposing tuition tax credits for parochial schools. Cuomo barely survived the attacks in the heavily Democratic state and won only a narrow victory over Lehrman.

As governor, Cuomo combined liberal rhetoric with conservative administration to win both the hearts and minds of New Yorkers. He kept his liberal support with national speeches portraying himself as a champion of ethnics, minorities, and the poor. Yet he won moderate and conservative support with tax cuts, deficit reductions, spending restraint, and tougher criminal penalties. He reinvigorated traditional liberal themes by appealing to the symbols of family, community, and opportunity in America. He won reelection in 1986 by the largest margin (65 percent) in the state's history. His popularity faded somewhat over time, but he was reelected in 1990 with 53 percent of the vote.

Cuomo is frequently combative and occasionally arrogant in dealing with his critics, including the press. He is extremely sensitive, even hot tempered, in dealing with perceived ethnic slurs. He does not accept criticism gracefully. People react emotionally to Cuomo's inspirational messages about family, helping others, and living out the American dream. He rarely troubles his audiences with specifics. In short, he would make a formidable presidential candidate.

Few politicians have ever publicly pondered and procrastinated over their own political fate as has Mario Cuomo. Both in 1988 and 1992 Cuomo was the recognized heavyweight among potential Democratic presidential contenders. He regularly perched atop the early Democratic preference polls, and he appeared to enjoy the view, often toying with the media in their persistent questioning about his presidential ambitions. Yet in the end he always pulled away, leaving commentators to speculate about the "Hamlet on the Hudson" who could not bring himself to a final decision. Most observers believed he could have won the Democratic nomination and the presidency in 1992, had he actively sought it. His announcement that he would not be a candidate cleared the way for Bill Clinton. Cuomo publicly wished for the life of a Supreme Court Justice, but when Clinton offered it to him, he declined.

Al Gore. Vice-President Al Gore stands silent and rigid behind the President so often that he could easily be mistaken for a Secret Service agent. Yet Gore's stoic performance as loyal prop for the President is the traditional vice-presidential role. Al Gore is no lightweight; he brings impressive presidential credentials to his office.

Young Al was born into a political dynasty. His father, Albert Gore, Sr., served four years in the House and eighteen years in the Senate as a strong supporter of FDR's New Deal and the Tennessee Valley Authority that served his state and region. Young Al grew up in Washington, attended a prestigious private prep school, St. Alban's, and went on to Harvard. Apparently he set his sights on the presidency early in his career; his senior honors thesis was entitled "The Impact of Television on the Conduct of the Presidency." Like his father, Gore opposed the Vietnam War; yet when drafted in 1970, he accepted induction and served as an Army newspaper reporter in Saigon.

When he returned home, he took a job as a reporter for the Nashville newspaper, the *Tennessean*. At the same time he became a land developer with his Tanglewood Home Builders Company as well as a livestock and tobacco farmer. A devout Baptist, Gore briefly studied religion at Vanderbilt University before entering the law school. Upon obtaining his law degree in 1976, he immediately jumped into the Democratic primary race for a Tennessee congressional seat. At age twenty-eight, he relied primarily on his father's name to defeat an experienced Democratic state legislator and go on to win the general election over token Republican opposition in the traditionally Democratic district.

Like many younger Democrats of the era, Gore sought to expand his traditional liberalism by developing a reputation in environmental issues as well as nuclear arms control. He also remained in close contact with his constituents, returning to Tennessee virtually every weekend and practicing "homestyle" politics. Indeed on some high-profile issues, including federal funding of abortions, Gore abandoned his liberalism to reflect his constituents' views. His wife "Tipper" improved her husband's standing among social conservatives by leading a national effort to label obscene recordings.

When Howard Baker, the Republican leader in the U.S. Senate, announced that he would not seek reelection in 1984, Gore quickly established himself as the leading Democratic contender to capture his Tennessee Senate seat. With his famous name, four congressional terms serving constituents, and growing personal stature in his state, Gore swept to victory. In the Senate, Gore switched his focus of activity from arms control, where Reagan-Bush successes captured the issue for the GOP, to the environment. He fervently embraced a whole series of environmental causes and even published a book on the topic.

In the 1988 Democratic presidential primaries, Al Gore's "southern strategy" relied on winning a mother lode of delegates in the early Super Tuesday southern state primaries and using the momentum of victory to sweep into the later big state primaries. But Jesse Jackson undercut Gore in the South, and Michael Dukakis bested him in the North. Gore bowed out of the 1988 race gracefully. Perhaps the biggest mistake of Gore's political career was his decision not to run again for President in 1992. Early Democratic preference polls showed him running behind only New York Governor Mario Cuomo; Bill Clinton was hardly recognized by voters outside of Arkansas. But like other Democratic heavyweights, Gore put his White House aspirations on hold; Bush's popularity following victory in the Gulf War appeared unassailable. Gore's decision helped create the vacuum that Bill Clinton leaped to fill.

Traditionally, Democratic presidential candidates sought to "balance" the national ticket by selecting vice-presidential running mates from different regions of the country, from different generations, and from different ideological wings of the party. But in 1992 Bill Clinton wisely sought a new kind of balance. Beset by charges of marital infidelity and draft evasion, Clinton saw the advantage of selecting a devout family man and Vietnam veteran. And Gore's established presidential stature contrasted sharply with the popular image of Bush's running mate, Dan Quayle. Clinton's selection of Al Gore put two southern "baby boomers" on the same ticket, but it convinced many voters that Clinton was wise enough to select a Vice-President who was indeed qualified to become the President.

Jack Kemp. Jack Kemp's "game plan" for politics was to "get first downs, and the touchdowns will come up and hit you in the face." A former quarterback for the Buffalo Bills and the AFL's Most Valuable Player in 1965 made a great many political "first downs" since first winning election to Congress in 1970. But in 1988 he went for the "long bomb"—a presidential primary campaign to take the Republican nomination away from George Bush—but failed to put points on the board. He served loyally in Bush's Cabinet as secretary of Housing and Urban Development, winning an unusual reputation for a top Republican as a champion of blacks, Hispanics, and blue-collar workers. His populist brand of conservatism makes him a leading contender for the GOP presidential nomination.

Kemp grew up in Los Angeles, where his father owned a small trucking firm. Kemp admits to being "totally tunnel-visioned" about his early goal in life—"to play football." Assigned in junior high school to write an essay on a great invention, he wrote on the forward pass. Kemp chose smaller Occidental College, rather than USC or UCLA, to ensure that he would get a lot of playing time. He was only an average student, majoring in physical education. But as an outstanding quarterback, he was drafted by the Detroit Lions. He spent thirteen years with various professional teams, but his best years were with the Buffalo Bills in 1963, 1964, and 1965, when he led the team to three consecutive Eastern division titles and two AFL championships. Kemp compiled a number of AFL records and served as co-founder and president of the AFL Players Association. But by 1970, he had accumulated two broken ankles, two broken shoulders, a broken knee, and eleven concussions. When he quit, the Buffalo Bills permanently retired his jersey number.

Kemp moved directly from the playing field to the political arena. Buffalo Republicans urged him to run for a suburban congressional seat held by the Democrats. Kemp's high name recognition and his success as the home-team quarterback helped him win a narrow victory over the incumbent. In later elections, his margin of victory soared to over 75 percent of the vote.

In his first years in Washington, Kemp was regarded as an "ex-jock" and a "lightweight." Kemp took advantage of these years by informing himself about a wide range of social, economic, military, and foreign policy issues. Kemp was especially impressed with the ideas of Arthur B. Laffer, an economist at the University of Southern California. Laffer argued that high federal tax rates had reached a point of diminishing returns. Taxes were so high that they were undermining incentives to produce and save; lowering tax rates might actually increase federal revenues if more people were encouraged to work and save.

Kemp became the leading congressional spokesman for the new "supply-side" economics. "If you tax something, you get less of it. If you subsidize something, you get more of it. In America we tax work, growth, investment, employment, savings, and productivity. We subsidize nonworking, consumption, welfare, and debt." In 1978, Kemp, together with Republican Senator William V. Roth of Delaware, proposed an across-the-board slash in income taxes by 30 percent in three years. This "Kemp-Roth" tax bill was at first ridiculed in Establishment circles. (The Brookings Institution called it "the most irresponsible financial policy ever suggested in U.S. history.") But in 1980 it was incorporated into the Republican platform. When Ronald Reagan captured the White House, his first priority was economic recovery, and Jack Kemp's tax plan became a key part of the President's program. The 1981 Reagan tax cuts included a 25-percent reduction in personal income taxes over three years, only a slight modification of Kemp's original plan. Jack Kemp became a recognized leader in the Congress.

Jack Kemp's presidential hopes rested on his ability to unify the conservative wing of the Republican party on behalf of his candidacy; to portray

George Bush as an upper-class, Eastern-Establishment, Republican moderate; and to capture the hearts of the Reagan voters in both the primary and general elections. Kemp's populist brand of conservatism certainly appealed to the ideological right more than Bush or Dole centrism. But the Rev. Pat Robertson entered the race to claim the religious right; Pierre S. du Pont, governor of Delaware, claimed the intellectual conservatives; and the Reagan loyalists decided that George Bush was indeed the true heir to the Reagan legacy. Jack Kemp's bid for the presidency collapsed shortly after the first New Hampshire primary.

Kemp gave up his sure congressional seat to make his presidential bid, and his loss left him out of public office for the first time since his quarterbacking days. He was obliged to seek a Cabinet post from his primary opponent. In the spirit of party unity, Bush agreed; but the post given Kemp—secretary of Housing and Urban Development—was not a highly visible or influential one. Nonetheless, Kemp seized the opportunity to push new initiatives to "empower" public housing residents to evict drug dealers and take over management and eventually ownership of their projects. He urged Congress to establish tax-free "enterprise zones" to encourage economic development in the nation's ravaged inner cities. But despite Kemp's efforts, President Bush never succeeded in developing a domestic program that could win support in Congress.

Kemp's blue-collar conservatism, his energy and initiative, and his appeal to many traditional Democratic voters may provide him the opportunity to rebuild the Reagan coalition and lead the GOP back to power.

EXECUTIVE DECISION-MAKERS: THE SERIOUS PEOPLE

The politician is a professional office-seeker. The politician knows how to run for office—but not necessarily how to run the government. After victory at the polls, the prudent politician turns to "serious" people to run the government.[10] The corporate and governmental experience and educational credentials of

---

[10] Pultizer Prize–winning writer David Halberstam reports a revealing conversation between newly elected President John F. Kennedy and Robert A. Lovett in December 1960, a month before Kennedy was to take office: "On the threshold of great power and great office, the young man seemed to have everything. He was handsome, rich, charming, candid . . . [But] he had spent the last five years, he said ruefully, running for office, and he did not know any real public officials, people to run a government, *serious men*. The only ones he knew, he admitted, were politicians. . . . Politicians *did* need men to serve, to run the government." Robert Lovett was "the very embodiment of the Establishment." His father had been chairman of the board of Union Pacific Railroad and a partner of the great railroad tycoon, E.H. Harriman. Lovett urged Kennedy to listen to the advice of Lovett's partner and former governor of New York and ambassador to the Soviet Union, Averell Harriman; to see "Jack McCloy at Chase" (then chairman of the board of Chase Manhattan), and "Doug Dillon too" (to become Kennedy's secretary of the treasury); to look up a "young fellow over at Rockefeller, Dean Rusk" (to become Kennedy's secretary of state); and to get "this young man at Ford, Robert McNamara" (to become Kennedy's secretary of defense). Kennedy gratefully accepted the advice: he turned to these "serious men" to run the government. David Halberstam, *The Best and Brightest* (New York: Random House, 1969), pp. 3–4.

these "serious" decision-makers greatly exceed those of most members of Congress or other elected officials. When presidents turn from the task of *running for office* to the task of *running a government*, they are obliged to recruit higher quality leadership than is typically found among political officeholders.

The responsibility for the initiation of national programs and policies falls primarily upon the top White House staff and the heads of executive departments. Generally, Congress merely responds to policy proposals initiated by the executive branch. The President and his key advisers and administrators have a strong incentive to fulfill their responsibility for decision-making. In the eyes of the American public, they are responsible for everything that happens in the nation, regardless of whether they have the authority or capacity to do anything about it. There is a general expectation that every administration, even one committed to a "caretaker" role, will put forth some sort of policy program.

The President and Vice-President, White House presidential advisers and ambassadors-at-large, Cabinet secretaries, undersecretaries, and assistant secretaries constitute our executive elite. Let us take a brief look at the careers of some of the people who have served in key Cabinet positions in recent presidential administrations.

SECRETARIES OF STATE

John Foster Dulles. (1953–60). Senior partner of Sullivan & Cromwell, and member of the board of directors of the Bank of New York, Fifth Avenue Bank, American Bank Note Co., International Nickel Co. of Canada, Babcock and Wilson Corp., Shenandoah Corp., United Cigar Stores, American Cotton Oil Co., United Railroad of St. Louis, and European Textile Corp. He was a trustee of the New York Public Library, Union Theological Seminary, the Rockefeller Foundation, and the Carnegie Endowment for International Peace; also a delegate to the World Council of Churches.

Dean Rusk. (1961–68). President of the Rockefeller Foundation.

William P. Rogers. (1969–73). U.S. attorney general during Eisenhower administration; senior partner in Royall, Koegal, Rogers and Wells (one of the twenty largest Wall Street law firms).

Henry Kissinger. (1973–77). Special assistant to the president for national security affairs; former Harvard professor of international affairs, and project director for Rockefeller Brothers Fund and for the Council on Foreign Relations.

Cyrus Vance. (1977–80). Senior partner in the New York law firm of Simpson, Thacher & Bartlett. A member of the board of directors of IBM and Pan American World Airways; a trustee of Yale University, the Rockefeller Foundation, and the Council on Foreign Relations; former secretary of the army under President Lyndon Johnson.

Alexander M. Haig, Jr. (1981–82). President of United Technologies Corporation, and former four-star general, U.S. Army. He was former Supreme Allied Commander, NATO forces in Europe; former assistant to the President under Richard Nixon; former deputy assistant to the President for national security under Henry Kissinger; former deputy commandant, U.S. Military Academy at West Point; former deputy secretary of defense.

George P. Shultz.   (1982–89). President of the Bechtel Corporation. Former secretary of the treasury, former secretary of labor, and former director of Office of Management and Budget under President Richard Nixon. Earned Ph.D. in economics from M.I.T. Former dean of the school of business, University of Chicago. Former director of General Motors, Borg-Warner, and Dillon, Read & Co.

James A. Baker III.   (1989–92). Houston attorney and oil man who previously served as secretary of the treasury and White House chief of staff in the Reagan administration.

SECRETARIES OF TREASURY

George M. Humphrey.   (1953–57). Former chairman of the board of directors of the M.A. Hanna Co.; member of board of directors of National Steel Corp., Consolidated Coal Co. of Canada, and Dominion Sugar Co.; trustee of M.I.T.

Robert B. Anderson.   (1957–61). Secretary of the navy, 1953–54; deputy secretary of defense, 1945–55; member of board of directors of Goodyear Tire and Rubber Co. and Pan American World Airways; member of the executive board of the Boy Scouts of America.

Douglas Dillon.   (1961–63). Chairman of the board of Dillon, Read & Co. (one of Wall Street's largest investment firms); member of New York Stock Exchange; director of U.S. and Foreign Securities Corp. and U.S. International Securities Corp.; member of board of governors of New York Hospital and the Metropolitan Museum of Art.

David Kennedy.   (1969–71). President and chairman of the board of Continental Illinois Bank and Trust Co.; director of International Harvester Co., Commonwealth Edison, Pullman Co., Abbott Laboratories, Swift and Co., U.S. Gypsum, and Communications Satellite Corp.; trustee of the University of Chicago, the Brookings Institution, the Committee for Economic Development, and George Washington University.

John B. Connally.   (1971–72). Secretary of the navy, governor of Texas, administrative assistant to Lyndon B. Johnson; attorney for Murcheson Brothers Investment (Dallas); former director of New York Central Railroad.

George P. Shultz.   (1972–74). Secretary of labor and director of the Office of Management and Budget; former dean of the University of Chicago Graduate School of Business; former director of Borg-Warner Corp., General American Transportation Co., and Stein, Roe & Farnham (investments).

William E. Simon.   (1974–77). Director of Federal Energy Office, and former deputy secretary of the treasury; formerly a senior partner of Salomon Brothers (one of Wall Street's largest investment firms specializing in municipal bond trading).

Warner Michael Blumenthal.   (1977–79). President of the Bendix Corporation; former vice-president of Crown Cork Co.; trustee of Princeton University and the Council on Foreign Relations.

G. William Miller.   (1979–81). Chairman and chief executive officer of Textron Corporation. Former partner in Cravath, Swaine & Moore (one of the nation's twenty-five largest and most prestigious law firms); a former director of Allied

Chemical and Federated Department Stores; former chairman of the Federal Reserve Board.

Donald T. Regan. (1981–85). Chairman of the board and chief executive officer of Merrill Lynch & Co. Inc. (the nation's largest investment firm); former vice-chairman of the New York Stock Exchange; trustee of the University of Pennsylvania and the Committee for Economic Development; member of the policy committee of the Business Roundtable.

James A. Baker III. (1985–89). Wealthy Houston attorney whose father owned Texas Commerce Bank. Former undersecretary of commerce in the Ford administration and campaign chairman for George Bush's unsuccessful presidential race in 1980. President Reagan's White House chief of staff in his first term.

Nicholas Brady. (1989–93). Former chairman of Dillon, Read & Co.; a director of Purolator, NCR, Georgia International, ASA, and Media General.

SECRETARIES OF DEFENSE

Charles E. Wilson. (1953–57). President and chairman of the board of directors of General Motors.

Neil H. McElroy. (1957–59). President and chairman of the board of directors of Procter & Gamble; member of the board of directors of General Electric, Chrysler Corp., and Equitable Life Assurance Co.; member of the board of trustees of Harvard University, the National Safety Council, and the National Industrial Conference.

Thomas S. Gates. (1959–60). Secretary of the navy, 1957–59; chairman of the board and chief executive officer, Morgan Guaranty Trust Co.; member of the board of directors of General Electric, Bethlehem Steel, Scott Paper Co., Campbell Soup Co., Insurance Co. of North America, Cities Service, SmithKline and French (pharmaceuticals), and the University of Pennsylvania.

Robert S. McNamara. (1961–67). President and chairman of the board of directors of the Ford Motor Co.; member of the board of directors of Scott Paper Co.; president of the World Bank, 1967–81.

Clark Clifford. (1967–69). Senior partner of Clifford & Miller (Washington law firm); member of board of directors of the National Bank of Washington and the Sheridan Hotel Corp.; special counsel to the President, 1949–50; member of the board of trustees of Washington University in St. Louis.

Melvin Laird. (1969–73). Wisconsin Republican congressman, and former chairman of Republican conference in the House of Representatives.

James R. Schlesinger. (1973–77). Director, Central Intelligence Agency; former chairman of Atomic Energy Commission; formerly assistant director of the Office of Management and Budget; economics professor; and research associate of the RAND Corp.

Harold Brown. (1977–81). President of the California Institute of Technology. A member of the board of directors of International Business Machines (IBM) and the Times-Mirror Corp. Former secretary of the air force under President Lyndon Johnson, and U.S. representative to the SALT I talks under President Richard Nixon.

Caspar W. Weinberger. (1981–89). Vice-president and director of the Bechtel

Corporation, the world's largest privately owned corporation. A member of the board of directors of Pepsico and Quaker Oats Co. Former secretary of Health, Education, and Welfare under President Richard Nixon; former director of the Office of Management and Budget; former chairman of the Federal Trade Commission. A former San Francisco attorney and California state legislator.

Richard B. Cheney. (1989–93). Congressman and chairman of the House Republican Conference; assistant to the President, Gerald Ford; chairman of the Cost of Living Council; director of Office of Economic Opportunity under President Richard Nixon. Attorney.

FRIENDS OF BILL AND HILLARY

If the Clinton administration "looks like America," then America has become a nation of lawyers and lobbyists.

Unlike his predecessors in the White House, Bill Clinton never had any experience outside of politics and government. His world has been confined to office seeking and office holding. So it should come as no surprise that almost all of the top jobs in the Clinton administration are filled by lawyers, lobbyists, politicians, and bureaucrats. Among Clinton's top advisers, only his chief of staff, home-town friend Thomas McLarty, and his secretary of energy, Hazel O'Leary, were recruited from the business world. Nor is there any significant military experience represented on Clinton's top team, although several members are veterans. (See Table 3–1.)

Clinton's pledge to bring to Washington an administration that "looks like America" presumably meant more minorities and women appointed to Cabinet-level positions. Clinton's initial Cabinet team includes three women—Attorney General Janet Reno, HHS Secretary Donna Shalala, and Energy Secretary Hazel O'Leary. Three African Americans also serve in the Clinton Cabinet—Commerce Secretary Ron Brown, Agricultural Secretary Mike Espy, and Veterans Affairs Secretary Jesse Brown. And two Hispanics head Cabinet departments—HUD Secretary Henry Cisneros and Transportation Secretary Frederico Pena. Thus, the Clinton Cabinet is slightly more diverse than that of his most recent predecessor.[11]

But like all previous administrations, the friends of Bill and Hillary are drawn overwhelmingly from among the most privileged, best educated, well connected, upper- and upper-middle-class segments of America. There is very little "diversity" in the educational and social backgrounds of top Clinton advisers. Eight out of eighteen (44 percent) received their educations, either

---

[11] Bush had two women in top posts (Transportation Secretary Elizabeth Dole and Special Trade Representative Carla Hills), one African American (HHS Secretary Louis Sullivan), and two Hispanics (Interior Secretary Manual Lujan and Education Secretary Lauro Cavazus). Comparisons across administrations depend in part on the definition given to "Cabinet-level" post in each administration. Inclusion of Clinton's Special Trade Representative, lawyer-lobbyist Mickey Kantor, adds little diversity to the top team, but UN Ambassador Madeleine K. Albright and CEA Chair Laura Tyson presumably do so, as does the EPA administration's Carol M. Browner, whose post has been promised elevation to the Cabinet.

TABLE 3-1 The Washington Insiders: The Clinton Administration

Name and Position	Experience/Occupation	Education	Career Highlights
Albert Gore, Jr. Vice-President	Newspaper reporter, real estate developer, lawyer.	Harvard, B.A., 1969; Vanderbilt, LL.B., 1976	U.S. Army, Vietnam, 1969–71; U.S. representative, 1977–85; U.S. senator, 1985–92.
Warren M. Christopher Secretary of State	Lawyer, government official.	U. of Southern Calif., B.S., 1945; Stanford U., LL.B., 1949.	U.S. Naval Reserve, 1943–46; U.S. deputy attorney general, 1967–69; deputy secretary of state, 1977–81.
Lloyd Bentsen Secretary of Treasury	Lawyer, financial executive.	U. of Texas, LL.B., 1942.	Army Air Corps, 1942–45; Hidalgo County judge, 1947–48; U.S. House, 1948–55; U.S. Senate, 1971–93; Democratic nominee for Vice-President, 1988.
Les Aspin Secretary of Defense	Economics professor.	Yale U., B.A., 1960; Oxford U., M.A., 1962; Massachusetts Institute of Technology, Ph.D., 1965.	U.S. Army, 1966–68; elected to the House in 1970; chairman of the House Armed Services Committee, 1985–92.
Janet Reno Attorney General	Lawyer, state attorney.	Cornell, B.A., 1960; Harvard, LL.B, 1963.	Miami law practice, 1963–71; staff director, judiciary committee, Florida House of Reps., 1971–72; assistant state attorney, 1973–78; state attorney, 1978–93; Dade County.
Ronald H. Brown Secretary of Commerce	Lawyer, party chair, lobbyist.	Middlebury College, B.A., 1962; Univ. of St. John's, J.D., 1970.	National Urban League, 1969–79; deputy national campaign manager Kennedy for President, 1979–80; staff director, Sen. Edward M. Kennedy, D-Mass and chief counsel for Senate Judiciary Committee, 1981; partner, Patton, Boggs & Blow, 1981–92; convention manager for Rev. Jesse Jackson, 1988; senior political adviser Dukakis/Bentsen campaign, 1988; chairman, the Democratic National Committee, 1989–92.

TABLE 3–1 *(Continued)*

Name and Position	Education	Experience/Occupation	Career Highlights
Henry G. Cisneros Secretary of Housing and Urban Development	Texas A & M Univ., M.A., 1970; John F. Kennedy School of Govt., M.A., 1973; George Washington Univ., doctor of public administration, 1975.	Public official.	Member of the San Antonio City Council, 1975–81; assistant to the secretary of Health, Education and Welfare, 1971–72; mayor of San Antonio, 1981–89.
Robert B. Reich Secretary of Labor	Dartmouth College; Yale Law School, J.D.; and Oxford Univ.	Lawyer, lecturer, author.	Public policy lecturer, Harvard University; planning director at the Federal Trade Commission under Carter administration; assistant solicitor general, Justice Department under Ford administration.
Federico F. Pena Secretary of Transportation	Univ. of Texas–Austin, B.A., 1969; J.D., 1972.	Lawyer, public official.	Member of Colorado General Assembly, 1979–83; House Democratic leader, 1981; mayor of Denver, 1983–91.
Bruce Babbitt Secretary of Interior	University of Notre Dame, B.S., 1960; U. of Newcastle, England, M.A., 1962; Harvard Law School, LL.B., 1965.	Lawyer, public official, lobbyist.	Arizona attorney general, 1975–78; Arizona governor, 1978–87; ran for presidency in 1988; president of the League of Conservation Voters.
Donna E. Shalala Secretary of Health and Human Services	Western College, A.B., 1962; Syracuse Univ., Ph.D., 1970.	University administrator, professor.	Professor of politics and education, Teachers College, Columbia Univ., 1972–79; assistant secretary, HUD, 1977–80; president, Hunter College, 1980–88; chancellor, Univ. of Wisconsin, Madison, 1988–92.
Richard W. Riley Secretary of Education	Furman Univ., B.A., 1954; U. of South Carolina Law School, LL.D., 1959.	Lawyer, public official.	U.S. Navy, 1954–56; South Carolina House, 1963–67; South Carolina Senate, 1967–77; governor of South Carolina, 1979–87.

Name / Position	Education	Profession	Biography
Mike Espy Secretary of Agriculture	Howard U., B.A., 1975; Santa Clara U., J.D., 1978.	Lawyer, businessman, public official.	Mississippi assistant secretary of state, 1980–84; assistant attorney general, 1984–85; elected to the House in 1986.
Hazel R. O'Leary Secretary of Energy	Fisk College, B.A., 1959; Rutgers University School of Law, J.D., 1966.	Lawyer, energy company executive.	Was to have been promoted to president of Northern States Power's Natural Gas Utility in January 1993; worked in Washington as vice president of O'Leary Associates, an energy consulting firm; served in the Carter and Ford administrations as a utility regulator.
Jesse Brown Secretary of Veterans Affairs	Chicago City College.	Veterans advocate, lobbyist.	Marine Corps, 1963–65, wounded in 1965; Disabled American Veterans, 1967–92.
W. Anthony Lake National Security Adviser	Harvard U., B.A., 1961; Woodrow Wilson School of Public and International Affairs, Princeton U., Ph.D., 1974.	Professor, government official.	U.S. vice consul in Saigon, Vietnam, 1963; U.S. vice consul in Hue, Vietnam, 1964–65; special assistant to Henry A. Kissinger, 1969–70; director, International Voluntary Services, 1974–76; Director of Policy Planning, State Dept, 1977–81; professor of international relations, Mount Holyoke College, 1981–92.
Thomas F. McLarty III Chief of Staff	Univ. of Arkansas, B.A., 1968.	Gas company executive.	Founder McLarty Leasing, 1969–79; Arkansas state rep., 1970–72; chairman, Arkansas Dem. Committee, 1974–76; treasurer of Gov. Bill Clinton's 1978 campaign; president Arkla Inc., 1984–88; chairman, CEO Arkla Inc., 1985–92.
Leon E. Panetta Director, Office of Management and Budget	U. of Santa Clara, B.A., 1960; J.D., 1963.	Lawyer, public official.	U.S. Army, 1963–65; elected to the House, 1976; chairman of the House Budget Committee, 1989–92.

TABLE 3–2   Profile of Administration Leadership

	Truman through Carter	Reagan	Bush	Clinton
Education				
Advanced degree	69%	68%	80%	89%
Law degree	40	26	40	67
Ivy League degree	48	58	50	50
Ph.D.	19	16	25	22
No college degree	0	0	0	0
Women	4%	5%	10%	17%
Blacks	4%	5%	5%	17%
Occupations				
Law	28%	11%	40%	5%
Business	28	32	55	5
Government	16	16	5	67
Education	19	16	25	11
Military	3	5	10	0

SOURCE: For Truman through Carter, see Phillip H. Burch, Jr., *Elites in American History*, Vol. 3

graduate or undergraduate, at just three of the nation's most prestigious private universities: Harvard, Yale, and Stanford. Sixteen of the eighteen (89 percent) hold *advanced* degrees. Law degrees predominate; twelve of eighteen (67 percent) are lawyers. Four (22 percent) hold Ph.D. degrees: Aspin in economics, Cisneros and Shalala in public administration, and Lake in international affairs.

The profusion of lawyers on the Clinton team exceeds any previous presidential administration. However, even though two thirds of Clinton's top appointees are educated in law, few of these people have actually practiced law for any extended period of their careers. Only Attorney General Janet Reno can really be said to have devoted her career to law. All of the other lawyers devoted their careers principally to elected or appointed governmental office.

While experience in the private sector is limited, Clinton's team can boast of a wealth of experience in government—in both elected offices and bureaucratic posts. Indeed only Chief of Staff McLarty has no previous experience in government. Nine of the eighteen Cabinet-level posts (50 percent) are filled with people who have won high *elected* office sometime in their careers: Gore and Bentsen served in the U.S. Senate; Aspin, Espy, and Panetta served in the House of Representatives; Babbitt and Riley were governors; Cisneros and Pena were big-city mayors. The rest served in bureaucratic positions. Donna Shalala was chancellor of the University of Wisconsin; Janet Reno was the state attorney for Miami's Dade County, a post to which she was initially appointed and subsequently elected and reelected.

Overall, the Clinton administration is clearly distinguishable from previous administrations in its heavy reliance on politicians and bureaucrats, its oversupply of lawyers, and its absence of experience in business and the military (see Table 3–2).

LEADERS OF THE CLINTON TEAM

A brief examination of the backgrounds of some of the key figures in the Clinton administration suggests a contrast between strong, liberal, and activist domestic policy leaders and relatively weak, passive, and impotent foreign and defense policy people.

Warren Christopher. In his presidential campaign Clinton sought to focus on domestic issues and gave less priority to international affairs. His selection of the lackluster, former Carter administration lawyer and bureaucrat, Warren Christopher, as secretary of state is consistent with his professed desire to de-emphasize foreign policy. Christopher is a prominent California attorney (with the influential Los Angeles firm, O'Melveny & Myers) who has been in and out of Washington posts for several decades. His principal experience was serving as deputy secretary of state under President Jimmy Carter, a post that involved him in various foreign policy setbacks in the 1970s—the Soviet invasion of Afghanistan, U.S. withdrawal from the 1980 Olympics, the loss of the Panama Canal, the seizure of power in Nicaragua by the anti-American Sandinista regime, and the Iranian seizure of American embassy personnel in Tehran as hostages. Christopher was assigned the job of securing the release of the hostages, a task that required over a year of negotiations and billions in ransom payments and did not produce freedom for the captives until Ronald Reagan's inauguration. As a private attorney in the 1980s, Christopher represented American energy companies in negotiations with Arab nations.

Anthony Lake. Clinton's choice of a relatively obscure Mount Holyoke College professor of international relations for the post of national security adviser also reflects the President's desire to keep foreign and defense policy issues off the front pages. Lake is another "Carter retread" on the Clinton team, having served as director of the State Department's policy-planning staff in the Carter administration. Upon completing a Ph.D. in international relations at Princeton, Lake joined the Foreign Service and was sent to Vietnam in 1962. He was an early hawk, encouraging Presidents Kennedy and Johnson to commit U.S. military forces to the Vietnam War. Henry Kissinger brought him to Washington on the staff of the National Security Council in 1969. But after public opinion began to turn against the war, Lake, like many early war supporters, reversed his position and resigned his post in 1970, calling his decision "painful." He returned to Washington in 1977 under

President Carter, heading the State Department's internal "think tank"—the policy-planning staff. He was an architect of Carter's "human rights" approach to foreign policy. Lake taught international relations during the Reagan-Bush years, and then Clinton recruited him as a campaign adviser on foreign policy. As national security adviser to President Clinton, Lake has remained in the background, avoiding talk shows and other public appearances.

Les Aspin. Perhaps it was inevitable that the end of the Cold War would bring about a shift of focus in Washington from defense and foreign policy concerns to domestic issues. Secretary of Defense Les Aspin is the only recognized political heavyweight on Clinton's international relations team, and Aspin's principal task is to oversee the cutback of U.S. military forces. Aspin is an Oxford University Rhodes scholar with a Ph.D. in economics from M.I.T. He apprenticed in Washington in various staff jobs and served his Army ROTC obligation as a Pentagon economist. He returned to Wisconsin and taught briefly at Marquette University before launching a political career. He ran unsuccessfully for Wisconsin state treasurer in 1968 but won election to Congress in 1970 by a scant twenty votes in a recount. A liberal maverick in his early congressional years, Aspin delighted in publicizing Pentagon gaffes—from ridiculous cost overruns to officer dining-room extravagances. His ability to embarrass the brass made him a favorite among anti-defense liberals to take over the chairmanship of the House Armed Forces Committee. But once in power, Aspin became a responsible overseer of national defense, urging his fellow Democrats to do more than just oppose defense spending and to develop positive defense programs of their own during the Reagan-Bush years. Aspin was an influential supporter of President Bush's decision to go to war in the Persian Gulf. He developed his own post–Cold War defense strategy and challenged his counterpart in the Senate, Armed Forces Committee Chairman Sam Nunn, for congressional leadership in defense matters. He lobbied hard with Clinton to get the job as secretary of defense, but even before sitting down at this Pentagon desk, Aspin was obliged to try to repair relations between a Commander-in-Chief perceived to be anti-military and the military services he commands.

Lloyd Bentsen. Clinton's key economic policy appointments—Treasury Secretary Lloyd Bentsen and Budget Director Leon Panetta—bring extensive Washington political experience to the administration. Lloyd Bentsen was first elected to Congress when Clinton was two years old (1948). Bentsen is the son of a wealthy, self-made Rio Grande Valley rancher, cattleman, and banker, "Big Lloyd." Lloyd Jr. graduated from the University of Texas Law School, enlisted in the Army Air Corps, and flew combat missions in Europe in World War II, winning the Distinguished Flying Cross and returning home as a colonel. He promptly won a county judicial election, and then in 1948 at age twenty-seven, he became the youngest member of

Congress. He served three terms in the House but became bored with life as a young congressman. He returned to Texas, and with $7 million from his father he formed Consolidation Life Insurance Company, and later Lincoln Consolidated, a holding company which acquired businesses, banks, oil fields, and ranches. He acquired a number of prestigious corporate director- ships, including the Lockheed Corporation. Having conquered the world of business, he returned to politics in 1970, defeating incumbent liberal U.S. Senator Ralph Yarborough in the Democratic primary, and then trouncing fellow oil man Republican Congressman George Bush in the general elec- tion. In the Senate the elegantly dressed, baritone-voiced Bentsen used his power as chairman of the tax-writing Finance Committee to secure so many tax breaks for the oil industry that he earned the title "Loophole Lloyd." But he charmed the nation with his polished performance as vice-presidential running mate with Michael Dukakis in 1988; polls showed him with higher favorable ratings than either presidential candidate. And he overpowered Dan Quayle in their television debate. By 1992 Bentsen appeared ready to retire from the Senate and to crown his career with the Treasury post. Liberals were uncomfortable with the choice of Bentsen, but his appointment added stature to the Clinton team, as well as knowledge of Congress.

Leon Panetta. Leon Panetta's appointment as budget director also worried liberals for whom deficit reduction takes low priority to new spend- ing programs. Panetta and his deputy, former Brookings Institution econo- mist Alice Rivlin, are known as budget "hawks"—determined to cut govern- ment spending and bring the huge annual deficits under control. After law school and a stint in the Army, Panetta went to Washington as a congressional staffer and rose to director of the U.S. Office of Civil Rights before returning to his home in California. He was elected to Congress in 1976 and served six- teen years in the House, eventually chairing the Budget Committee before accepting his White House post. An effective budget director must be able to say "No" and make it stick. Panetta is reported to be a tough and knowledge- able insider with a passion for slashing the budget deficit. But within the Clinton administration, he faces strong opposition from more liberal spenders, including the powerful First Lady.

Hillary Rodham Clinton. Hillary Clinton is not the first politically pow- erful First Lady with strong ties to liberal interest groups. That distinction belongs to Eleanor Roosevelt, but in her era the power of the First Lady was exercised in a more subtle fashion. As chair of the president's health-care task force, Hillary Rodham Clinton possesses official responsibility for a key area of national policy-making. But Hillary's influence extends well beyond the health-care field to virtually all areas of presidential responsibility, earning her the label "co-president."

Hillary Rodham grew up in suburban Chicago, the daughter of a wealthy businessman who sent his daughter to prestigious private Wellesley

College. A "Goldwater Girl" in high school, Hillary quickly reversed political direction to become a leader in radical and antiwar politics on campus. A 1969 honors graduate with a counterculture image—horn-rimmed glasses, long straggling hair, no makeup—she was chosen by her classmates to give a commencement speech—a largely inarticulate rambling about "more immediate, ecstatic, and penetrating modes of living." (Years later her views would coalesce around the New Age writings of leftist Jewish thinker Michael Learner, who coined the phrase *the politics of meaning.*) At Yale Law School, she met a long-haired, bearded Rhodes scholar from Arkansas, Bill Clinton, who was even more politically ambitious than Hillary. Both Bill and Hillary received their law degrees in 1973, but Bill returned to Arkansas to build a career in state politics, while Hillary went to Washington as an attorney, first for the liberal lobbying group the Children's Defense Fund, and later for the staff of the House Judiciary Committee seeking to impeach President Nixon.

Hillary and other Yale grads traveled to Arkansas to help Bill run unsuccessfully for Congress in 1974. Hillary decided to stay with Bill in Little Rock; they married before his next campaign, a successful run for state attorney general in 1976. Hillary remained Hillary Rodham, even as her husband went on to the governorship in 1978. She taught briefly at the University of Arkansas Law School and eventually joined Little Rock's influential Rose law firm. She kept her Washington ties with the Children's Defense Fund. She also became a director of Wal-Mart Stores, TCBY Enterprises, the LaFarge Corporation, and the federal government's Legal Services Corporation. Her husband's 1980 defeat for reelection as governor was blamed on his liberal leanings; in his 1982 comeback Bill cut his hair and repackaged himself as a moderate and centrist. Hillary cooperated by becoming Mrs. Bill Clinton, shedding her hornrims for contacts, blonding her hair, and echoing her husband's more moderate line. These tactics helped propel them back into the governor's mansion.

Hillary was far from the traditional governor's wife. She chaired the governor's task force on education and drew up his key educational reform package. She became a full partner in the Rose law firm, regularly earning over $200,000 a year (while Bill earned only $35,000 as Arkansas governor). She won national recognition as one of the "100 most influential lawyers in the United States" according to the American National Law Journal. She chaired the American Bar Association's Commission on Women and the Profession.

Hillary's support for Bill's presidential ambitions was absolutely crucial to this success. Married life in the governor's mansion was at best "rocky," as Bill and Hillary would later acknowledge on national television. Rumors of Bill's "womanizing" had long circulated in Little Rock, and they broke into the national news early in the presidential race when Genifer Flowers held a press conference describing a long-term affair with the governor and playing tapes of their telephone conversations. Similar charges had destroyed the promising presidential candidacy of Gary Hart four years earlier. The focus was on Hillary in an interview on *60 Minutes*. In a very convincing performance, Hillary stood by her man, acknowledging that their marriage had been "shaky" but it was "rock solid" now.

Hillary's prominent role in the Clinton presidency is no surprise to those who followed her career. Her social consciousness, upper-class liberalism, and "burning desire to make the world better for everybody" were evident in her early radical critique of the "prevailing acquisitive and competitive corporate life" in America.[12] Her "politics of meaning" combine a progressive social agenda with a strong dose of moralism. Reportedly very influential in all aspects of the Clinton presidency, including appointments, she also undertook the leadership of the President's Task Force on Health Care Reform. Her knowledgeable performance as the principal lobbyist in Congress on behalf of the President's comprehensive health care plan was widely praised.[13] Following her testimony before a Senate committee hearing on the proposal, Senator John H. Chafee (R.RI) reported: "There's no question who's in charge of the administration's health-care plan."[14]

Friends of Hillary.   Hillary's liberal influence is supported by the academics in the Clinton administration, notably Robert Reich, secretary of labor; Ira Magaziner, presidential adviser on health care; and Donna Shalala, secretary of Health and Human Services. Both Reich and Magaziner were Oxford University Rhodes scholars together with Bill Clinton. Reich went on to Yale Law School, worked at the Federal Trade Commission in the Carter years, and then built an impressive academic record at the John F. Kennedy School of Government at Harvard. He published numerous books and articles touting neoliberal "industrial policy" ideas; he relabeled government spending programs in education, training, research, and infrastructure as "investment." He is the principal Cabinet exponent of increased government spending. Magaziner founded a very successful business and public-policy consulting firm with clients such as General Electric, Corning Glass, and Volvo. With activists from Brown University, Magaziner tried unsuccessfully to get the state of Rhode Island to turn itself into a "greenhouse" for hi-tech industry. As executive director of the health-care task force, Magaziner worked directly with Hillary Clinton on the formidable task of establishing a new national health-care system. It was rumored in Washington that Donna Shalala was less than pleased to see health-care reform removed from her direct supervision as secretary of Health and Human Services. Shalala served in the Peace Corps in Iran, taught urban affairs at Columbia University, and

---

[12] *New York Times Magazine,* May 23, 1993, p. 64.

[13] Hillary is not the first First Lady to testify before Congress on behalf of her husband's programs. That distinction belongs to Eleanor Roosevelt (to whom Hillary is often compared), who testified in hearings on migrant workers in 1940. Rosalynn Carter testified on behalf of mental health programs in 1979.

[14] *Congressional Quarterly Weekly Report,* October 2, 1993, p. 2643.

went to work in the Carter administration as an assistant secretary in Department of Housing and Urban Development. In 1980, she was tapped to be president of Hunter College, part of the City University of New York, and in 1988 she became chancellor of the University of Wisconsin, where she won fame (or notoriety) for instituting politically correct speech codes.

THE CONGRESSIONAL ESTABLISHMENT

Although policy initiatives are usually developed outside Congress, Congress is no mere "rubber stamp." Key members of Congress do play an independent role in national decision-making; thus, key congressional leaders must be included in any operational definition of a national elite.

Many important government decisions, particularly in foreign and military affairs, are made without any direct participation by Congress. The President, with the support of top people in the administration, can commit the nation to foreign policies and military actions that Congress can neither foresee, prevent, nor reverse. Often congressional leaders are told of major foreign policy decisions or military actions only a few minutes before they are announced on national television.

Congress is more influential in domestic affairs and budgetary decisions than in foreign or military policy. Executive agencies must go to Congress for needed legislation and appropriations. Congressional committees can exercise power in domestic affairs by giving or withholding the appropriations and the legislation wanted by these executive agencies. Committees are also important communication links between governmental and nongovernmental elites; they serve as bridges between the executive bureaucracies and the major nongovernmental elites in American society.

Political scientists have commented extensively on the structure of power *within* the Congress. They generally describe a hierarchical structure in both houses of the Congress—a "congressional establishment"—which largely determines what the Congress will do. The congressional establishment has survived periodic efforts at decentralization. It is composed of the speaker of the House and president pro tempore of the Senate; House and Senate majority and minority leaders and whips; and committee chairpersons and ranking minority members of House and Senate standing committees (see Table 3–3). Party leadership roles in the House and Senate are major sources of power in Washington. The Speaker of the House and the majority and minority leaders of the House and Senate direct the business of Congress. Although they share this task with the standing committee chairpersons, these leaders are generally "first among equals" in their relationships with committee chairpersons. But the committee system also creates powerful congressional figures, the chairpersons of the most powerful standing committees—particularly the Senate Foreign Relations, Appropriations, and Finance committees, and the House Rules, Appropriations, and Ways and Means committees.

TABLE 3–3 The Congressional Establishment, 1993–95

Senate Leadership	House Leadership

President Pro Tempore: Robert C. Byrd, W.Va.

Majority Leader: George J. Mitchell, Me.
Majority Whip: Wendell H. Ford, Ky.
Minority Leader: Robert Dole, Kan.
Minority Whip: Alan K. Simpson, Wyo.

Speaker of the House: Thomas S. Foley, Wash.

Majority Leader: Richard A. Gephardt, Mo.
Majority Whip: David E. Bonior, Mich.
Minority Leader: Robert H. Michel, Ill.
Minority Whip: Newt Gingrich, Ga.

Senate Committee Leaders

Agriculture, Nutrition and Forestry: Patrick J. Leahy, Vt.; *Richard G. Lugar, Ind.*
Appropriations: Robert C. Byrd, W. Va.; *Mark O. Hatfield, Oreg.*
Armed Services: Sam Nunn, Ga.; *Strom Thurmond, S.C.*
Banking, Housing and Urban Affairs: Donald W. Riegle Jr., Mich.; *Al D'Amato, N.Y.*
Budget: Jim Sasser, Tenn.; *Pete V. Domenici, N.M.*
Commerce, Science and Transportation: Ernest F. Hollings, S.C.; *John C. Danforth, Mo.*
Energy and Natural Resources: J. Bennett Johnson, La.; *Malcolm Wallop, Wyo.*
Environment and Public Works: Max Bacucus, Mont.; *John H. Chafee, R.I.*
Finance: Daniel P. Moynihan, N.Y.; *Bob Packwood, Oreg.*
Foreign Relations: Claiborne Pell, R.I.; *Jesse Helms, N.C.*
Governmental Affairs: John Glenn, Ohio; *William V. Roth Jr., Del.*
Indian Affairs: Daniel K. Inouye, Hawaii; *John McCain, Ariz.*
Judiciary: Joseph R. Biden Jr., Del.; *Oren G. Hatch, UT.*
Labor and Human Resources: Edward M. Kennedy, Mass.; *Nancy L. Kassebaum, Kan.*
Rules and Administration: Wendell H. Ford, Ky.; *Ted Stevens, Ark.*
Select Ethics: Howell Heflin, Ala.; *Warren B. Rudman, N.H.*
Selecting Intelligence: David L. Boren, Okla.; Dennis DeConcini, Ariz.; *John W. Warner, Va.; William S. Cohen, Me.*
Small Business: Dale Bumpers, Ark.; *Larry Pressler, S.D.*
Special Aging: David Pryor, Ark.; *William S. Cohen, Me.*
Veterans' Affairs: John D. Rockefeller, W.Va.; *Frank H. Murkowski, Ark.*

House Committee Leaders

Agriculture: E. "Kika" de la Garza, Tex.; *Pat Roberts, Kan.*
Appropriations: William Natcher, Ky.; *Joseph M. McDade, Pa.*
Armed Services: Ronald Dellums, Calif.; *Floyd Spence, S.C.*
Banking, Finance, and Urban Affairs: Henry B. Gonzalez, Tex.; *Jim Leach, Ia.*
Budget: Martin Sabo, Minn.; *John Kasich, Ohio*
District of Columbia: Pete Stark, Calif.; *Thomas J. Billey, Va.*
Education and Labor: William D. Ford, Mich.; *Bill Gooding, Pa.*
Energy and Commerce: John D. Dingell, Mich.; *Carlos Moorhead, Calif.*
Foreign Affairs: Lee V. Hamilton, Ind.; *Benjamin Gilman, N.Y.*
Government Operations: John Conyers Jr., Mich.; *William F. Clinger, Pa.*
House Administration: Charlie Rose, N.C.; *Bill Thomas, Calif.*
Judiciary: Jack Brooks, Tex.; *Hamilton Fish, Jr., N.Y.*
Merchant Marine and Fisheries: Gerry Studds, Mass.; *Jack Fields, Tex.*
Natural Resources: George Miller, Calif.; *Don Young, Ark.*
Post Office and Civil Service: William L. Clay, Mo.; *John T. Myers, Ind.*
Public Works and Transportation: Norman Mineta, Calif.; *Bud Shuster, Pa.*
Rules: Joe Moakley, Mass.; *Gerald Solomon, N.Y.*
Science, Space and Technology: George E. Brown, Calif.; *Robert S. Walker, Pa.*
Select Intelligence: Dan Glickman, Kan.; *Larry Combest, Tex.*
Small Business: John J. LaFalce, N.Y.; *Jan Myers, Kan.*
Standards of Official Conduct: Jim McDermott, Wash.; *Fred Grandy, Ia.*
Veterans' Affairs: G.V. "Sunny" Montgomery, Miss.; *Bob Stump, Ariz.*
Ways and Means: Dan Rostenkowski, Ill.; *Bill Archer, Tex.*

Majority Democrats are set in regular type, minority Republicans in italics.

Viewed within the broader context of a *national elite*, congressional lead-ers appear "folksy," parochial, and localistic. Because of the local constituency of members of Congress, they are predisposed to concern themselves with local interests. Members of Congress are part of local elite structures "back home"; they retain their local businesses and law practices, club member-ships, and religious affiliations. Members of Congress represent many small segments of the nation rather than the nation as a whole. Even top congres-sional leaders from safe districts, with many years of seniority, cannot com-pletely shed their local interests. Their claim to *national* leadership must be safely hedged by attention to their local constituents. Consider, for example, the parochial backgrounds of the following top congressional leaders.

Thomas S. Foley.   After two successive House Speakers (Thomas P. "Tip" O'Neill and Jim Wright) whose hard-ball politics engendered conflict and partisanship, the elevation of the tall, soft-spoken Tom Foley to the speakership was initially welcomed in the House of Representatives. Unlike his predecessors, Foley was well-liked and highly respected by both Democrats and Republicans. While he was expected to advance the Democratic party program in the House, he was also expected to uphold the integrity of the House of Representatives.

Foley's father was a Washington State superior court judge and a close political associate of the state's senior U.S. Senator, Henry M. "Scoop" Jackson. Young Tom Foley completed his B.A. and law degrees at the University of Washington, served briefly as an assistant state attorney, and then went to Washington to serve on Senator Jackson's staff. In 1964, after only three years in the capitol, the Democratic state committee asked Foley to run against a long-term incumbent Republican in a conservative district which included the city of Spokane.

Foley was only expected to gain campaign experience and fill out the Democratic slate, but to everyone's surprise he squeaked out a narrow victory over the heavily favored incumbent. Foley's victory was generally attributed to the coattail effects of President Lyndon B. Johnson's landslide election. But in subsequent congressional elections, Foley held on to his seat by close mar-gins. In 1978 he won with only 48 percent of the vote in a three-way contest. In recent years, however, he has won by large margins.

Foley's experience as a Democrat representing a conservative district may help explain his success in the Congress as a conciliator. He gradually built a reputation within the institution as a man who understood and respected his opponents' point of view. When the reform-minded, post-Watergate Democrats flooded Congress in 1974, they elected Foley chair-man of the Agricultural Committee; at the time he was the youngest person ever to chair a major committee. By most accounts, Foley was a strong yet cautious chairman. He was elected Democratic whip in 1981 and moved up to house majority leader in 1985 when Speaker "Tip" O'Neill retired and for-mer Majority Leader Jim Wright became Speaker. Wright's abrasive style infuriated most Republicans and alienated many Democrats. When the House Ethics Committee brought charges against him regarding his personal financial affairs, Wright had very little personal support to fall back on. Tom Foley publicly supported his embattled Speaker and did nothing to assist in his downfall. Yet the presence of the respected, telegenic Foley as next in line for the speakership doubtlessly contributed to the movement to oust Wright.

Foley's first task as House Speaker was to try to restore public confidence in the Congress itself—a task made very difficult by a series of revelations about congressional pay raises, the House Bank scandal, and other perks and privileges flowing to House members. Foley stumbled badly in initially trying to withhold information from the media regarding the names of the House check kiters; the tactic only intensified media coverage and produced discontent in the House over Foley's leadership. But he managed to survive the crisis and suppress a mini-revolt of moderate and conservative Democrats against his leadership.

Foley's principal task today is to shepherd President Clinton's legislature program through the House. During the Reagan and Bush years, Foley was effective in blocking Republican presidential initiatives. But with a Democratic President, Foley must prove that his skills go beyond creating "gridlock" in Washington. He must produce positive legislative results, not only to polish the image of the Democratic party but also to restore public confidence in the Congress itself.

Robert H. Michel. As the House minority leader, Bob Michel's job is to prevent the Democratic leadership from steamrolling over the Republican members. The son of a French immigrant factory worker, Michel attended tiny Bradley University. He began his career in politics fresh out of college as an administrative assistant to Congressman Harold H. Velde. When Velde retired in 1956, Michel, with several years' experience as a congressional aide, decided to run for the office himself. He won in a close race and has represented the city of Peoria in Congress since 1957. One of his constituents was Senate Republican leader Everett Dirksen, who helped him on Capital Hill. Dirksen's son-in-law, Howard H. Baker, who also became a Senate Republican leader, became a close friend. The wives of Baker and Michel attended college together.

Early in his career, Michel was appointed to a seat on the powerful House Appropriations Committee. Over the years, Michel was described as "a party man" who almost always voted with the Republican majority. He was described as "a plodder rather than a thinker." The *Congressional Quarterly* described him as in the "Mr. Nice Guy tradition—unpretentious, self-effacing, Rotary Club glad-hander with a gee-whiz vocabulary and a rambling speaking style."[15] In 1980, long-time Republican House leader John Rhodes

---

[15] Congressional Quarterly *Weekly Report,* December 3, 1988, p. 3436.

voluntarily stepped down. Michel, the party workhorse, found himself in a struggle for Republican leadership with Guy Vander Jagt of Michigan, a moderate with an impressive speaking style. Michel won, even though Vander Jagt was better known throughout the nation. Michel immediately set to work to win over conservative friends in the Democratic party. He was very effective during President Reagan's first term in combining Republican and conservative Democratic votes to win support for tax and spending cuts, frequently embarrassing Democratic Speaker Thomas P. "Tip" O'Neill. But in Reagan's second term, the loss of Republican House seats combined with the Iran-Contra scandal's adverse impact on Reagan's popularity undermined Michel's power.

In recent years Michel's power has been diluted by the rise of Georgia Republican Newt Gingrich as a spokesman for younger, more aggressive conservative Republican House members. Gingrich is a more effective speaker than Michel and better able to grab the media spotlight. But Michel appears to have developed a working relationship with his more flamboyant minority whip. Both moderate and conservative Republican House members must stick together to have any influence at all when both the White House and Capital Hill are controlled by Democrats.

George Mitchell.   The rise of George Mitchell to majority leader of the U.S. Senate was very rapid by historic standards. First elected to the Senate in 1980, Mitchell quickly established himself as a soft-spoken, serious leader of liberal Democrats. The collapse of the crusty old Democratic Senate leadership of Robert Byrd in 1988 left a power vacuum that Mitchell skillfully exploited. His career defies the conventional wisdom that Senate leadership requires a long institutional apprenticeship.

Mitchell graduated from Maine's Bowdoin College with a degree in history, served two years in the U.S. Army in Europe, and went to Georgetown University for his law degree. He served a brief stint as a Justice Department attorney before attaching his star to Maine Senator Edward S. Muskie. He was Muskie's top congressional aide and campaign manager for both his vice-presidential bid in 1968 and his disastrous presidential effort in 1972. Returning to Portland, Maine, as a lawyer, Mitchell spent most of his time building a personal political following as Democratic state party chairman and national committeeman. He easily won the Democratic nomination for governor in 1974, but despite Democratic post-Watergate sweeps elsewhere, he was upset by the only Independent candidate to win a governorship in modern times, James Longley. President Carter appointed Mitchell U.S. attorney for Maine in 1977 and made him a federal judge in 1979. When Muskie resigned from the U.S. Senate to become Carter's secretary of state, Mitchell was appointed to Muskie's seat. With the advantage of incumbency, he won election to the seat with 61 percent of the vote in 1982.

Early in his Senate career, Mitchell organized Senate liberals to oppose Majority Leader Robert Byrd, a staunch defender of West Virginia coal industry, on the issue of acid rain. He led liberals in their opposition to lower income-tax rates in the Tax Reform Act of 1986. By 1988 liberals dissatisfied with Robert Byrd had been joined by many others who believed Byrd's rustic television image was hurting the Democratic party's cause nationally. Senator Daniel Inouye was in line for the leadership post, but Inoyue was embarrassed by the fine performance of Lt. Col. Oliver North in the nationally televised Iran-Contra hearings. The only Democrat to effectively counter the Marine hero was George Mitchell. Mitchell went on to win the secret ballot vote of his Democratic Senate colleagues for the post of majority leader.

Mitchell's task in the Clinton years, like that of his counterpart Tom Foley in the House, is to move the President's program through the Congress. But unlike the House, Senate rules and traditions require the majority to give much greater deference to the views of individual members. Mitchell must negotiate with more conservative Senate Democrats to hold his majority together. And he must deal with a Republican minority in the Senate that, when unified, can filibuster a bill to death and prevent the majority from closing off debate. (Sixty votes are required to cut off debate in the Senate; in the 1993–95 session, Democrats held only 56 seats following a GOP victory in Texas for Lloyd Bentsen's vacated seat.) Indeed, Mitchell's first embarrassment in the Clinton years was his failure to overcome a Republican filibuster halting the President's "economic stimulus package." Republican Leader Bob Dole effectively labeled it a "Democratic pork barrel" and inflicted the first major congressional defeat on the Democratic majority and the White House. For twelve years under Republican Presidents Mitchell had honed his skills in stalling presidential initiatives. Now he must learn a new role—the more difficult one of expediting the president's legislation.

Bob Dole.   Few national leaders have had as difficult an early start in life as Bob Dole. But today, as Senate Republican leader, he has emerged as President Clinton's principal political opponent in Washington.

Dole left the small family farm in Kansas to join the Army during World War II and suffered serious wounds in Italy. He was nearly blown apart by mortar and machine-gun fire and was left for dead on the battlefield for twenty-four hours. Later he was paralyzed from the neck down; he spent three years in the hospital recovering from wounds, and even today he cannot use his right arm. He married his physical therapist and completed a law degree at tiny Washburn Municipal University in Topeka in 1952. But even before he finished law school, Dole won a seat in the Kansas legislature at the age of twenty-six, and he has not been out of public office since. He was district attorney for Russell County, Kansas, for four terms, and then a Kansas congressman for four terms. In 1968 he was elected to the U.S. Senate and has been reelected by large margins ever since. He divorced his first wife in 1972 and married Elizabeth Hanford Dole, a member of the

Federal Trade Commission, in 1975. She later became secretary of transportation in the Reagan administration and now heads the American Red Cross. In 1976 Dole was Gerald Ford's running mate on the unsuccessful Republican ticket. It was in that vice-presidential campaign that Dole appeared to be a "hatchet man" compared to the boy scout image of his opponent, Walter Mondale. Dole is perhaps one of the wittiest elected officials in Washington, but on television his quips often seem bitter and caustic. Dole is generally a moderate on policy issues; he supports big spending programs for his farm constituents as well as for veterans and handicapped persons. As chairman of the Senate Finance Committee, Dole helped to shepherd Reagan's tax cuts through Congress. When Republican leader Howard Baker retired from the Senate, Dole emerged the winner in a heated fight for the leadership post.

Dole's presidential ambitions looked bright very early in 1988. Bush had been labeled a "wimp" by the media, and even though he led in the opinion polls his support was considered "soft." Dole's hopes to beat the Vice-President depended on an early win in the Iowa caucuses, followed by an upset victory in the New Hampshire primary. Dole won Iowa on the strength of his long-standing support for farmers, but he was ambushed by slick Bush TV ads in New Hampshire attacking his willingness to raise taxes to reduce the deficit. Dole was personally embittered; he frequently contrasted his own hard scramble in life to Bush's upper-class ease.

As minority leader during the Bush White House years, Dole was notably unsuccessful in overcoming "gridlock" in Washington. It was hardly Dole's fault that very little was accomplished by Congress: Bush set forth no major domestic legislative program, and Democrats controlled both the House and Senate.

Today Bob Dole is the Republican party's principal spokesman. As Senate Republican leader, he must lead the opposition to Clinton programs, both in the Senate and in the national news media. And Dole has been effective in both forums in voicing opposition to the "tax and spend" policies of the Democratic administration. Indeed, the new focus on Dole as Clinton's major antagonist has led to renewed speculation about the senator's presidential ambitions.

THE JUDGES

Nine people—none of whom is elected and all of whom serve for life—possess ultimate authority over all the other institutions of government. The Supreme Court of the United States has the authority to void the acts of popularly elected Presidents and Congresses. There is no appeal from their decision about what is the "supreme law of the land," except perhaps to undertake the difficult task of amending the Constitution itself. Only the good judgment of the Justices—their sense of "judicial self-restraint"—limits their

TABLE 3–4   Backgrounds of Supreme Court Justices

All U.S. Supreme Court Justices, 1789 to Present	Number of Justices (Total = 107)
Occupation before Appointment	
Private legal practice	25
State judgeship	22
Federal judgeship	25
U.S. attorney general	7
Deputy or assistant U.S. attorney general	2
U.S. solicitor general	2
U.S. senator	6
U.S. representative	2
State governor	3
Federal executive posts	10
Other	3
Religious Background	
Protestant	84
Roman Catholic	9
Jewish	6
Unitarian	7
No religious affiliation	1
Age on Appointment	
Under 40	4
41–50	30
51–60	57
61–70	15
Political Party Affiliation	
Federalist (to 1835)	13
Democrat-Republican (to 1828)	7
Whig (to 1861)	2
Democrat	43
Republican	42
Sex	
Male	105
Female	2
Race	
Caucasian	104
Other	2

SOURCES: Congressional Quarterly, *Congressional Quarterly's Guide to the U.S. Supreme Court* (Washington, D.C.: Congressional Quarterly, 1979); and *Congressional Quarterly's Guide to Government*, Spring 1983 (Washington, D.C., 1982). Updated to 1993 by author.

power. It was the Supreme Court, rather than the President or Congress, that took the lead in important issues such as eliminating segregation from public life, ensuring voter equality in representation, limiting the powers of police, and declaring abortion to be a fundamental right of women.

Social scientists have commented frequently on the class bias of Supreme Court Justices: "White; generally Protestant . . . ; fifty to fifty-five years of age at the time of his appointment; Anglo-Saxon ethnic stock . . . ;

high social status; reared in an urban environment; member of a civic-minded, politically active, economically comfortable family; legal training; some type of public office; generally well educated."[16] No blacks had served on the Supreme Court until the appointment of Associate Justice Thurgood Marshall in 1967. No women had served until the appointment of Sandra Day O'Connor in 1981. (See Table 3–4.) Of course, social background does not necessarily determine judicial philosophy. But as John R. Schmidhauser observes, "If . . . the Supreme Court is the keeper of the American conscience, it is essentially the conscience of the American upper-middle class sharpened by the imperative of individual social responsibility and political activism, and conditioned by the conservative impact of legal training and professional attitudes and associations."[17]

Clarence Thomas.   Not all Justices, however, conform to the upper-class portrait. No member of the nation's governing elite has ever had a steeper climb to the top than Justice Clarence Thomas. Born to a teenage mother who earned $10 a week as a maid, Clarence Thomas and his brother lived in a dirt-floor shack in Pin Point, Georgia, where they were raised by strict, hard-working grandparents who taught young Clarence the value of education and sacrificed to send him to a Catholic school. He excelled academically and went on to mostly white Immaculate Conception Seminary College in Missouri to study for the Catholic priesthood. But when he overheard a fellow seminarian express satisfaction at the assassination of Dr. Martin Luther King, Jr., Thomas left the seminary in anger and enrolled at Holy Cross College, where he helped found the college's Black Student Union, and went on to graduate with honors and win admission to Yale Law School.

Upon graduating from Yale, Thomas took a job as assistant attorney general working in Missouri and, after a brief stint as an attorney for the Monsanto Corporation, returned to government as a congressional aide to Republican Missouri Senator John Danforth. Despite misgivings about accepting a "black" post in government, in 1981 Thomas accepted the post as head of the Office of Civil Rights in the Department of Education, using the position to speak out on self-reliance, self-discipline, and the value of education. In 1982, he was named chairman of the Equal Employment Opportunity Commission (EEOC), where he successfully eliminated much of that agency's financial mismanagement and aggressively pursued individual cases of discrimination. At the same time, he spoke out against racial "quotas" and imposed minority hiring goals only on employers with proven records of discrimination. In 1989, President Bush nominated him to the U.S. Court of Appeals and he was easily confirmed by the Senate.

In tapping Thomas for the Supreme Court, the Bush White House rea-

---

[16] Henry Abraham, *The Judicial Process* (New York: Oxford University Press, 1962), p. 58.

[17] John R. Schmidhauser, *The Supreme Court* (New York: Holt Rinehart and Winston, 1960), p. 59.

soned that the liberal groups who had blocked the earlier nomination of conservative Robert Bork would be reluctant to launch personal attacks on an African American. But during nationally televised hearings of the Senate Judiciary Committee, University of Oklahoma law professor Anita Hill, a former legal assistant to Thomas both at the Department of Education and later at the Equal Employment Opportunity Commission, contacted the staff of the Judiciary Committee with charges that Thomas had sexually harassed her in both jobs. Initially, Hill declined to make her charges public, but when Senator Joseph Biden, the committee chairman, refused to circulate anonymous charges, she agreed to be interviewed by the F.B.I. and went on to give a nationally televised press conference, elaborating on her charges against Thomas. Her bombshell became a media extravaganza and sent the Senate into an uproar.

The Judiciary Committee reopened its hearings, with televised emotional testimony from both Anita Hill and Clarence Thomas. Indeed, the confirmation process exploded into a sleazy soap opera, with lurid stories about pubic hairs, penis sizes, and pornographic films of women with animals. The only restraint was Chairman Biden's rule that no questions would be asked about either Clarence Thomas's or Anita Hill's sex life. But the damage was done anyway, not only to Clarence Thomas and Anita Hill, but to the Senate confirmation process and the Senate as an institution.

In the end, there was no objective way to determine who was telling the truth. Too often the truth in Washington is determined by opinion polls. An astonishing 86 percent of general public said they had watched the televised hearings. A majority of blacks as well as whites, and a majority of women as well as men, sided with Clarence Thomas.[18] The final Senate confirmation vote was 52 to 48, the closest vote in the history of Supreme Court confirmations.

William H. Rehnquist. Chief Justice, U.S. Supreme Court. Raised in an upper-middle-class suburb of Milwaukee, Rehnquist attended Stanford University as an undergraduate, earned a master's degree in political science at Harvard, and then returned to Stanford for his law degree in 1952. He did his clerkship with U.S. Supreme Court Justice Robert H. Jackson and then settled in Phoenix, Arizona, to practice law. He became active in Arizona Republican politics, together with Richard Kleindienst, who later became President Richard Nixon's attorney general. Kleindienst brought Rehnquist to Washington as assistant attorney general. He was serving in that post when Nixon appointed him Associate Justice in 1971. At age forty-seven he was the youngest as well as the most conservative of the Court's Justices. In 1986 President Ronald Reagan appointed him to the post of Chief Justice upon the retirement of Warren F. Burger.

Rehnquist never really succeeded in undoing the liberal precedents set

---

[18] Gallup Opinion Reports, October 15, 1991, p. 209.

by the Supreme Court under Chief Justices Earl Warren or Warren Burger. Rehnquist wrote the *dissenting* opinion in the landmark *Roe* v. *Wade* case in 1973 declaring abortion a fundamental right of women. Rehnquist wrote so many "lone dissenting" opinions that his law clerks once presented him with a Lone Ranger doll. Rehnquist's conservative position was bolstered with President Reagan's appointment of Anton Scalia to the Court and later President Bush's appointment of Clarence Thomas. But other Reagan-Bush appointees—O'Connor, Kennedy, Souter—formed a moderate bloc that retained many liberal precedents including the right of abortion.

Ruth Bader Ginsberg. This associate justice was educated at Cornell University and Harvard Law School. Upon graduation from law school in 1958, Ginsberg reported that because she was a woman she was ignored by the prestigious firms that recruited her male classmates. She was obliged to take a job as a law secretary to a U.S. federal district court judge in New York. Soon she turned to academic work, serving as a research associate at Columbia Law School and later as a professor of law at Rutgers University. She served on the American Civil Liberties Union board of directors, and she wrote and spoke on behalf of women's issues. In 1980 President Jimmy Carter nominated her to the U.S. Court of Appeals. On the appeals court bench, she displayed a more judicial temperament in her opinions. Thus, her nomination to the Supreme Court by President Bill Clinton in 1993 won easy confirmation by the U.S. Senate.

THE MILITARY ESTABLISHMENT

In his farewell address to the nation in 1961, President Dwight D. Eisenhower warned of "an immense military establishment and a large arms industry." He observed: "In the councils of government, we must guard against the acquisition of unwarranted influence, whether sought or unsought, by the military-industrial complex."

The phrase *the military-industrial complex* caught on with many commentators over the years. It implied that a giant network of defense contractors— for example, Lockheed Aircraft, General Dynamics, Rockwell, McDonnell Douglas, Boeing, Litton, Hughes Tool, Grumman Aircraft—together with members of Congress in whose districts their plants were located, conspired with the generals in the Pentagon to create a powerful force in governmental and corporate circles. Indeed, radical social commentators held the military-industrial complex responsible for war and "imperialism."

But whatever the power of defense contractors and the military at the height of the Cold War, their influence today in governing circles is miniscule. Indeed, their goal today is to avoid complete dismantlement. Spending for national defense has declined precipitously from 10 percent of the GNP in the Eisenhower and Kennedy years to less than 4 percent today. Spending on Social Security, Medicare, and welfare, including Medicaid exceeds 52 percent of the federal budget, compared to 18 percent for national defense.[19] There are nearly three million civilian employees of the federal government, compared to only one and a half million people in the armed forces. The long-term decline of U.S. defense spending suggests that the American military-industrial complex was *not* a very powerful conspiracy.

It seems clear in retrospect that C. Wright Mills placed too much importance on the military in his work, *The Power Elite*.[20] Mills was writing in the early 1950s when military prestige was high following victory in World War II. After the war, a few high-level military men were recruited to top corporate positions to add prestige to corporate boards. But this practice ended in the 1960s. The contrast between the political prestige of the military in the post–World War II years and in the post–Vietnam years is striking: The Supreme Allied Commander in Europe in World War II, Dwight D. Eisenhower, was elected President of the United States; the U.S. Commander in Vietnam, William Westmoreland, was defeated in his bid to become governor of South Carolina! Moreover, in contrast with corporate and governmental elites, military officers do *not* come from the upper or upper-middle class of society. Military officers are more likely to be recruited from lower- and lower-middle-class backgrounds, and more likely to have rural and southern roots than are corporate or governmental elites.[21]

Colin Powell.   When General Colin Powell was named chairman of the Joint Chiefs of Staff by President George Bush in 1989, he became the first African-American and the youngest man in history to hold that post. During the Gulf War General Powell oversaw the largest military deployment of American troops since the Vietnam War. He is credited with developing and implementing a doctrine of maximum force that kept U.S. casualties to a minimum while Saddam Hussein's army was routed from Kuwait and destroyed. Powell had previously served as national security adviser to President Ronald Reagan, making him a principal military adviser to three Presidents.

Born in Harlem to Jamaican immigrant parents, Powell recounts his youth as proof that "it is possible to rise above conditions." After his graduation from Morris High School in the South Bronx, Powell's parents encouraged him to attend college, and he enrolled at City College of New York on an ROTC scholarship. He graduated with a degree in geology in 1958 at the top of his ROTC class and was commissioned a second lieutenant in the U.S. Army. Powell went to South Vietnam as a military adviser in 1962 and returned for a second tour in 1968. In Vietnam he was awarded two Purple

---

[19] *Budget of the United States Government 1994* gives this breakdown by function: Social Security: 21.2%; Medicare: 9.7%; Income Security: 14.2%; Medicaid: 7.8%.

[20] C. Wright Mills, *The Power Elite* (New York: Oxford, 1956).

[21] Morris Janowitz, *The Professional Soldier* (New York: Free Press, 1960), p. 378.

Hearts for wounds suffered in combat, and a Bronze Star and the Legion of Merit for valor under fire.

Powell returned to the classroom in 1972 and earned a master's degree in business administration from George Washington University. In 1972 he was appointed to the prestigious White House Fellows Program and was assigned to the Office of Management and Budget; there he worked under Caspar Weinberger, who later became secretary of defense in the Reagan administration. Powell's career was on a fast track after this early White House duty. He served as a battalion commander in Korea, graduated from the National War College, served as military assistant to the deputy secretary of defense, and won promotion to general and command of the Second Brigade of the 101st Airborne Division.

In 1983 Powell was recalled to Washington by Defense Secretary Weinberger to become his senior military adviser. During the invasion of Grenada in October 1983, Powell was assigned the task of running interference for the military against meddling White House and National Security Council staff. Later Powell supported Secretary Weinberger in opposing arms sales to Iran; he was overruled by President Reagan, but his memo urging that Congress be notified of the arms transfers would later stand him in good stead with the Congress after the Iran-Contra scandal became public. In 1986 Powell eagerly accepted command of the U.S. Fifth Corps in Germany, declining offers to stay on in Washington. But when President Reagan himself called and urged him to accept the post as national security adviser and reform the operations of the NSC staff, he agreed. Powell lent credibility to Reagan's promises to implement the recommendations of the Tower Commission, which had investigated the Iran-Contra affair.

President Bush chose General Powell in 1989 to be Chairman of the Joint Chiefs of Staff—the nation's highest military position. It was General Powell who helped convince the President that if military force were to be used to oust Saddam Hussein from Kuwait, it should be overwhelming and decisive force, not gradual limited escalation, as in Vietnam. Powell "ran interference" in Washington for the field commander, General Norman Schwarzkopf. Powell's televised briefings during the course of the war, together with those of General Schwarzkopf, assured the American people of the competence and effectiveness of the U.S. military. He summed up U.S. military strategy toward the Iraqi Army in Kuwait: "First we're going to cut it off. Then we're going to kill it." Under Powell's leadership, the U.S. military achieved a brilliant victory in the Gulf War with precious few casualties.

Powell retired from the Army in 1993, inspiring speculation that the popular general might enter the political arena. Throughout his military career, Powell avoided partisan affiliation. Registered as a political independent, Powell always considered himself a soldier first. Powell credits his success to those who "suffered and sacrificed to create the conditions and set the stage for me."

SUMMARY

Governmental power may be even more concentrated than corporate power in America. One indicator of its growing concentration is the increasing proportion of the gross national product produced by government. All governmental expenditures now account for over one third of the GNP, and *federal* expenditures account for nearly two thirds of all government expenditure.

Governmental elites include both elected politicians and appointed executives. The politicians' principal talent is running for office; most appointed executives, on the other hand, have had some experience in running large public or private organizations. Running for office is not the same as running a government. Presidents must depend on "serious" people to run government. Skill in campaigning does not necessarily prepare individuals for the responsibility of governing. Key government executives must be recruited from industry, finance, the law, universities, and the bureaucracy itself. These serious people do not appear to differ much in background or education from Republican to Democratic administrations.

While a significant number of top politicians have inherited wealth and power, most have climbed the ladder from relative obscurity to political success. Kennedy and Bush inherited great wealth and power, but Clinton, Reagan, Cuomo, and Kemp climbed to prominence from relatively modest backgrounds. Most politicians are lawyers but not top corporate or professional lawyers.

Congress seldom initiates programs, but rather it responds to the initiatives of the President, the executive departments, influential interest groups, and the mass media. Power *within* Congress is concentrated in the House and Senate leadership and in the chairperson and ranking minority members of the standing committees. Compared to other national elites, congressional leaders appear localistic. Their claim to national leadership must be safely hedged by attention to their local constituencies. Members of Congress are frequently recruited from very modest, middle-class backgrounds.

The Supreme Court is the most elitist branch of government. Its nine members are not elected, and they serve life terms. They have the authority to void the acts of popularly elected Presidents and Congresses. It was the Supreme Court, rather than the President or Congress, that took the lead in eliminating segregation from public life, ensuring voter equality in representation, limiting the powers of police, and declaring abortion to be a fundamental right of women. Although most Justices have been upper class in social origin, their appointment has generally been related to their political activities rather than to their experience in the law.

4 The Newsmakers

Television is the major source of information for the vast majority of Americans, and the people who control this flow of information are among the most powerful in the nation. Indeed, today the leadership of the mass media has successfully established itself as equal in power to the nation's corporate and governmental leadership.

The rise of the mass media to a position of preeminence among institutions of power is a relatively recent phenomenon. It is a direct product of the development of a national television communication network extending to nearly every home in America. Newspapers had always reported wars, riots, scandals, and disasters, just as they do today. But the masses of Americans did not read them—and fewer still read their editorials. But television reaches the masses. It is really the first form of *mass* communication devised. It also presents a *visual* image, not merely a printed word.

The mass media, particularly television, set the agenda for public discussion. They determine what we think about and talk about. Political journalist Theodore White asserts:

> The power of the press in America is a primordial one. It sets the agenda of public discussion; and this sweeping political power is unrestrained by any law. It determines what people will talk about and think about—an authority that in other nations is reserved for tyrants, priests, parties, and mandarins.[1]

As children, Americans spend more time in front of television sets than in school. As adults, Americans spend half of their leisure time watching television. In the average home, the television set is on seven hours a day. More than two thirds of Americans report that they get all or most of their "news" from television. More important, television is the "most trusted" medium of communication.[2]

The greatest asset of television is its *visual* quality—the emotional impact that is conveyed in pictures. Scenes of burning and looting in cities, dead American GIs being loaded onto helicopters, and terrorists holding

---

[1] Theodore White, *The Making of the President, 1972* (New York: Bantam, 1973), p. 327.

[2] *American Enterprise*, July–August 1991, p. 96.

frightened hostages, all convey *emotions* as well as *information*. Television tells Americans what to *feel* as well as what to think about.

The media elite—television and newspaper executives, reporters, editors, anchors, and producers—do not see themselves as neutral "observers" of American politics but rather as active "participants." They not only report events but also discover events to report, assign them political meaning, and predict their consequences. They seek to challenge government officials, debate political candidates, and define the problems of society. They see their profession as a "sacred trust" and themselves as the true voice of the people in public affairs. As the celebrated Watergate reporter Carl Bernstein put it: "The job of the press is not to follow Ronald Reagan's or George Bush's agenda, but to make its own decisions about what's important for the country."[3]

AGENDA-SETTING: CREATING THE NEWS

The power to decide what will be decided—agenda-setting—is crucial to politics. Indeed, deciding what will be the nation's "problems" is even more important than deciding what will be the solutions. Many civics textbooks imply that agenda-setting just "happens," that in a pluralist democracy any issue can be discussed and placed on the agenda of government decision-makers by anyone. It is true, of course, that we can say whatever we want to say about our society. But will anyone *listen?* Not if we do not have access to the mass media.

In reality, political issues do not just "happen." Creating an issue, dramatizing it, calling attention to it, and pressuring government to do something about it are important political tactics. These are the tactics of agenda-setting. These tactics are employed by influential individuals, organized interest groups, political candidates, government leaders, and, most of all, by the mass media.

The mass media set the agenda for conversation among people and debate among leaders. The media create some issues and obscure others. They spotlight some personalities and condemn others to anonymity. They define some conditions in society as "problems" or even "crises" and allow other conditions to go unnoticed. "TV is the Great Legitimator. TV confers reality. Nothing happens in America, practically everyone seems to agree, until it happens on television."[4]

Most Americans believe that the media have an important impact on politics and public opinion, and certainly politicians and their professional advisers behave as if they believe it. But many political scientists deny that the media are very influential. This is because voter studies show that few people *change* their voting intentions based on media endorsements of candidates. But even though the media may not change attitudes once they are formed,

---

[3] Carl Bernstein, quoted in *Vanity Fair*, March 1989, p. 106.

[4] William A. Henry, "News as Entertainment," in *What's News*, ed. Elie Abel (San Francisco: Institute for Contemporary Studies, 1981) p. 134.

the media determine what topics people will form attitudes on. "In short, the mass media may not be successful in telling us what to think, but they are stunningly successful in telling us what to think *about.*"[5]

Preplanned News. Most topics for television "news" are selected well in advance of scheduled broadcasting. It is impossible to put together a half-hour television show in twelve hours. The network "assignment desk" must decide days or weeks in advance of broadcasting what will be newsworthy, so that crews, cameras, and correspondents can be sent to the scene of the event. Videotapes must be shot and later transported, processed, and edited. "Understanding how things operate enables good assignment-desk editors to suggest stories for coverage even before they happen."[6] Many stories languish in the "bank" of already prepared news stories awaiting broadcasting time.

Television news can be categorized as either "spontaneous" or "preplanned." Spontaneous news includes fires, floods, accidents, shootings, and so on, which actually occurred the day of the news broadcast and were not planned by the media to occur on that day. In contrast, preplanned events may have occurred days or weeks before the broadcast, or may have been planned by the media and others for coverage on that day. The most common preplanned events are congressional hearings and investigations, meetings of government leaders, and press conferences. These are usually coordinated by government press agents and network producers. Ideally, they try to predict "slow" news days to schedule these media events. They are not always successful; if a hurricane, an assassination, or a violent eruption occurs (and if film of it is available), then a spontaneous event may push the preplanned event off the evening news.

Almost 70 percent of all television news stories are preplanned. One careful study of stories presented on ABC, NBC, and CBS weekday evening newscasts reported the following breakdown of stories:[7]

	Percent of Time
Preplanned events	31.8
Commentary on preplanned events	38.1
Spontaneous events	19.8
Commentary on spontaneous events	10.3
	100.0

[5] Bernard C. Cohen, *The Press and Foreign Policy* (Princeton, N.J.: Princeton University Press, 1963), p. 13. See also Maxwell E. McCoombs and Donald L. Shaw, "The Agenda Setting Function of the Press," in *Media Power in Politics*, ed. Doris Graber (Washington: Congressional Quarterly Inc., 1984), p. 66.

[6] Av Westin, "Inside the Evening News," *New York*, October 18, 1982, p. 52.

[7] Robert Rutherford Smith, "Mythic Elements in Television News," *Journal of Communication*, 29 (Winter 1979), 78–82.

CNN, however, with its twenty-four-hour news format, offers more "raw" undigested news, without preplanned packaging.

The requirement to preplan television news helps create the "media event"—an activity arranged primarily for media coverage. It is not only the press secretaries, public relations professionals, "spokespersons," and politicians who benefit from media events. It is also the network executives and producers who are searching for dramatic, sensational, or bizarre activities to videotape, and who appreciate notification well in advance of these activities so they can assign camera crews and broadcast time.

Early on the day of broadcasting the executive producer distributes the "line-up"—what "news" is scheduled, where it will originate, what priorities it will have, what graphics must be produced, what scripts need to be written, what commercials are scheduled for broadcast, and finally in what order and for how long each story is to run. Without these early decisions, the "news" would be chaos. Of course, "Change the line-up!" is a common directive during the day as "spontaneous news" arrives.

The Myth of the Mirror.   Top executives in the news media do not doubt their own power. A generation ago they credited themselves with the success of the civil rights movement. The dramatic televised images of the nonviolent civil rights demonstrators of the early 1960s being attacked by police with night-sticks, cattle prods, and vicious dogs helped to awaken the nation and its political leadership to the injustices of segregation. Later, the television networks credited themselves with "decisively changing America's opinion of the Vietnam War," and forcing Lyndon Johnson out of the presidency.

Television news, together with the Washington press corps, also lays claim, of course, to the expulsion of Richard Nixon from the presidency. *The Washington Post* conducted the "investigative reporting" that produced a continuous flow of embarrassing and incriminating information about the President and his chief advisers. But it was the television networks that maintained the continuous nightly attack on the White House for nearly two years and kept Watergate in the public eye. Richard Nixon's approval rating in public opinion polls dropped from an all-time high of 68 percent in January 1973 following the Vietnam Peace Agreement to a low of 24 percent less than one year later.

Yet publicly the leadership of the mass media claim that they do no more than "mirror" reality. Although the "mirror" argument contradicts many of their more candid claims to having righted many of America's wrongs (segregation, Vietnam, Watergate), the leadership of the television networks still claim that television "is a mirror of society."

Of course, the mirror analogy is nonsense. Newspeople decide what the news will be, how it will be presented, and how it will be interpreted. Newspeople have the power to create some national issues and ignore others, elevate obscure people to national prominence, reward politicians they favor, and punish those they disfavor. In a book significantly entitled *News from Nowhere*, Edward J. Epstein explains:

> The mirror analogy further tends to neglect the components of "will," or decisions made in advance to cover or not to cover certain types of events. A mirror makes no decisions, it simply reflects what occurs in front of it; television coverage can, however, be controlled by predecisions or "policy." . . .
>
> Policy can determine not only whether or not a subject is seen on television but also how it is depicted. . . .
>
> Intervention by the producer or assistant producers in decisions on how to play the news is the rule rather than the exception.[8]

THE CONCENTRATION OF MEDIA POWER

Media power is concentrated in the leading television networks (ABC, CBS, NBC, and CNN), the nation's leading newspapers (*New York Times, Washington Post, USA Today, The Wall Street Journal*), and the widely circulated news magazines (*Newsweek, Time,* and *U.S. News and World Report*). The reporters, anchors, editors, and producers of these "prestige" news organizations constitute a relatively small group of people in whose hands rests the power to decide what we will know about people, events, and issues.

Advertiser know the value of media influence; they spend over $42 *billion* annually on the purchase of media time and space to sell their products. Total advertising spending heavily favors television (54 percent) over newspapers (24 percent), magazines (16 percent), and radio (6 percent).[9]

Television is dominated by a few private corporations, including Capital Cities–ABC Inc.; CBS, Incorporated; the National Broadcasting Company (NBC), which is a division of General Electric Corporation; and Turner Broadcasting, Inc. Most of the 1,099 local commercial television stations are affiliated with one or another of these networks because of the high cost of producing news and entertainment programs. Local stations restrict themselves to local news coverage and then broadcast the network "feeds" of the "Evening News." In addition, each network owns five stations itself, the maximum number under the rules of the Federal Communications Commission (FCC). These network-owned stations are found in the largest "market" cities, and they cover 38 percent of all "TV households" in the nation.

However, the traditional dominance of the ABC, CBS and NBC television networks has eroded over time. Cable and satellite technology confront the corporate giants of the media with a new challenge. Indeed, in 1992 60 percent of all television homes in the United States were cable subscribers, and that number is steadily increasing. ABC, NBC, and CBS com-

---

[8] Edward Jay Epstein, *News from Nowhere* (New York: Random House, 1973), pp. 16–17.

[9] Data derived from *Advertising Age*, September 25, 1991.

bined still draw about 65 percent of total TV viewing, but this figure is down from the 95 percent enjoyed only a few years ago. The challenges of CNN (Turner's Cable News Network); Turner's TNT network; the Fox Television Network; pay television channels such as HBO; specialized channels presenting only children's programming, or sports (ESPN), or music (MTV); "superstations" such as Turner's WTBS in Atlanta broadcast via satellite; and new low-power local stations—all combined to threaten the older media giants.

Television has eroded newspaper circulation over the years. There are fewer daily newspapers today than thirty years ago, and circulation has declined from 36 to 25 percent of the population. The nation's 1,750 daily newspapers get most of their national news from the Associated Press (AP) wire service, although the larger newspapers and newspaper chains also disseminate their own national news. Radio stations also rely heavily on AP. Of course, local newspapers can "rewrite" national news stories to fit their own editorial slant, and they usually write their own headlines on the national news. But the news itself is generated from an extremely small cadre of people at the top of the media industry.

Concentration of newspaper ownership is increasing, as more and more local papers are being taken over by the major newspaper chains. Fifteen newspaper empires account for more than one half of the total newspaper circulation in the United States (see Table 4–1).

TABLE 4–1 The Newspaper Empires

	Daly Circulation (000)	Number of Dailies
Gannet Co. Inc.	5,508	90
Knight-Ridder Newspapers	3,627	27
Newhouse Newspapers	2,933	26
Tribune Co.	2,638	8
Dow Jones & Co. Inc.	2,470	23
Times Mirror Co.	2,448	8
News America Pub. Corp.	1,947	4
New York Times Co.	1,693	26
Scripps-Howard Newspapers	1,616	21
Thomson Newspapers	1,452	90
Cox Enterprises	1,210	19
Hearst Newspapers	1,125	15
Capital Cities Communications Inc.	933	8
Freedom Newspapers	892	29
Central Newspapers Inc.	809	7
Washington Post Co.	791	2

SOURCE: James L. Rowe, Jr., "Chains Seen Buying More Papers," *Washington Post*, June 1, 1986, p. F2.

Total U.S. daily circulation 62,502,000. Figures for 1986.

Media corporations are prime takeover targets in the arena of corporate mergers and acquisitions. The media are very profitable. Return on invested capital in media corporations averages above 25 percent annually, more than twice the average return for industry generally. Moreover, media ownership grants celebrity; investors are lured to the media by the promise of fame as well as fortune.

Capital Cities Communications acquired ABC in 1985 for $3.5 billion. The takeover was "friendly," that is, supported by ABC management, which was worried about a possible hostile takeover by Ted Turner. In 1986, General Electric acquired RCA Corporation, owners of NBC, in a $6 billion deal. CBS remained the only independent network, and it fought valiantly against various takeover efforts. It sought to use its political clout with the Securities and Exchange Commission to protect itself from prospective buyers. (It may seem ironic that CBS claims freedom of the press to protect itself from government regulation but seeks the protection of government to fight off corporate buyers.) The threat was a massive buyout offer by Ted Turner. In order to escape "Terrible Ted," CBS management invited billionaire hotel owner Lawrence A. Tisch to buy a controlling interest and become chairman of the board. The deal had the blessing of the aging CBS founder, William S. Paley. CBS remains independent, but Tisch has turned out to be more "bottom-line" oriented than the previously pampered network producers and reporters would prefer. The network superstars grumbled when their limousines, staff, and other perks were reduced.

MEDIA MOGULS

Who are the people who govern the flow of information to the nation? (See Table 4–2.) The top network executives—presidents, chairpersons, and corporate directors—do not make the day-to-day decisions about the news, but they choose the producers, anchors, and reporters who do. Let us examine a few brief sketches of those in the top leadership positions in the major media institutions.

Arthur Ochs Sulzberger. Publisher and president of the *New York Times.* Son of the *Times* board chairman and grandson of the newspaper's founder. Attended Loomis School and Columbia University. A corporal in World War II, but was assigned as headquarters aide to General Douglas MacArthur. He began as a reporter with the *Times* in 1953 and became president in 1963. A director of the New York Times Co., the Chattanooga Publishing Co., the Spruce Falls Power and Paper Co. of Toronto, and the Gaspesia Pulp and Paper Company of Canada. A trustee of the Boy Scouts of America, the American Association of Indian Affairs, Columbia University, and the Metropolitan Museum of Art.

Lawrence A. Tisch. Self-made billionaire, chairman of the board of CBS Inc., and "white knight" who purchased controlling interest in CBS to save the network from Ted Turner. Protégé son of a New York garment manufacturer, Tisch gradu-

TABLE 4–2   Inside the *Washington Post* Boardroom: Directors of the Washington Post Company, 1992

Inside	Outside (Corporate)

Katherine Graham, Chairman
Donald E. Graham, President
Martin Cohen, Vice-President
Allan G. Spoon, Executive Vice-President
Banjamin C. Bradlee, Vice-President at Large
	Richard D. Simmons
	   President, International Herald Tribune,
	   and a director of J.P. Morgan and
	   Union Pacific.
	George J. Gilliespie, III
	   Partner in Cravath, Swaine & Moore.
	Nicholas DeB. Katzenbach
	   Former attorney general of U.S.,
	   chairman of First American Bank
	   Shares, and a director of IBM.
	Donald R. Keough
	   President and CEO, Coca-Cola Co.
	Anthony J.F. O'Reilly
	   Chairman and CEO, H.J. Heinz
	   Company, and a director of G.E. and the
	   New York Stock Exchange.
	George W. Wilson
	   President, Newspapers of New England.
	James E. Burke
	   Former chairman, Johnson & Johnson.

Outside (Public Interest)	

Ralph E. Gomory
   President, Sloan Foundation, and director
   of Ashland Oil and Bank of New York.
Barbara Scott Preiskel
   American Womens' Economic
   Development Corporation, and director
   of G.E., Ford Foundation, and the ACLU.	

SOURCE: Based on data from *Moody's Industrial Manual, 1992.*

ated from NYU at age eighteen and obtained an M.B.A. from Wharton School at the University of Pennsylvania at nineteen. Served in the OSS (precursor to the CIA) in World War II; sampled Harvard Law School in 1946, but then left to purchase a series of resort hotels in New York and New Jersey. Expanded hotel empire to Manhattan and Florida and purchased Loews Theatre Company to obtain prime downtown locations to build more hotels. Later purchased Lorrilland, fifth largest cigarette company in the United States; CNA Financial Corporation; Bulova Watch Company; as well as oil tankers and real estate around the world. Upon taking control of CBS, Tisch shocked staffers by firing top management and cutting back the lavish perks previously enjoyed by newsroom personalities. But he does not direct news or program content. He is a director of the Bulova Watch Company, Automatic Data Processing Inc., Macy & Co., and Petrie Stores. He is a trustee of the United Jewish Appeal, the Whitney Museum, the Metropolitan Museum of Art, the New York Public Library, the Carnegie Corporation, and New York University.

Thomas S. Murphy.   Chairman of the board of Capital Cities–ABC. A Cornell University and Harvard M.B.A. graduate, who rose within Capital Cities Communications to become CEO in 1966. He presided over the acquisition of ABC—a major undertaking inasmuch as Capital Cities was only a medium-sized newspaper and magazine publisher when it swallowed the much larger network. Murphy is also a director of Texaco, Johnson & Johnson, IBM, and General Housewares.

Katherine Graham: The Most Powerful Woman in America.   Katherine Graham, the owner and publisher of the *Washington Post* and *Newsweek* magazine, was probably the most powerful woman in America even *before* Watergate. But certainly her leadership of the *Post*, which did more than any other publication to force the resignation of the President of the United States, established Graham as one of the most powerful figures in Washington. The *Washington Post* is the capital's most influential newspaper, and it vies with the *New York Times* as the world's most influential newspaper. These are the papers read by all segments of the nation's elite, and both papers feed stories to the television networks and wire services.

Graham inherited her position from her father and husband, but since 1963, when she became president of the Washington Post Company, she has demonstrated her own capacity to manage great institutional power. She is the daughter of a wealthy New York banker, Eugene Meyer. Like many elites, her education was in the fashionable private preparatory schools; she also attended Vassar College and the University of Chicago. In 1933 her father bought the *Washington Post* for less than $1 million. Katherine Meyer worked summers on her father's paper, and then took a job as a reporter with the *San Francisco News*. After one year as a reporter, she joined the editorial staff of the *Washington Post*. "Father was very strong. There was a great deal of emphasis on not behaving rich and a lot of emphasis on having to *do* something. It never occurred to me that I didn't have to work."[10]

In 1940, she married Philip L. Graham, a Harvard Law School graduate with a clerkship under Supreme Court Justice Felix Frankfurter. After service in World War II, Philip Graham was made publisher of the *Washington Post* by his father-in-law. Meyer later sold the paper to the Grahams for one dollar. The Washington Post Company proceeded to purchase other competitive papers in the nation's capital; it also bought *Newsweek* magazine from the Vincent Astor Foundation, as well as five television stations and several pulp and paper companies.

In 1963, Philip Graham committed suicide, and Katherine Graham took control of the *Washington Post–Newsweek* enterprises. By the early 1970s the *Washington Post* was challenging the *New York Times* as the nation's most powerful newspaper. Graham relied heavily on her executive editor, Benjamin Bradlee, who was directly responsible for the Watergate "investigative reporting" of Bob Woodward and Carl Bernstein that led to President Nixon's downfall. But reportedly Graham herself made the key decisions.

Indeed, the Washington Post Company's domination of the Washington scene gives it great power over federal officials and agencies. As columnist Kevin Phillips observes:

> We might note the quasi-governmental role played by the Washington Post Company. The Post Company has a five-level presence in Washington—a newspaper (the *Washington Post*), a radio station (WTOP), a television station (WTOP-TV), a news magazine (*Newsweek*), and a major news service (L.A. Times–Washington Post). Not only does the Washington Post Company play an unmatched role as a federal government information system—from the White House to Congress to the bureaucracy and back—it serves as a cue card for the

---

[10] *Current Biography* (1971), p. 170.

network news, and it plays a huge role in determining how the American government communicates to the American people.[11]

Graham is a director of Bowaters Mersey Paper Company, the John F. Kennedy School of Government of Harvard University, and a member of the Committee for Economic Development. She is a trustee of George Washington University, the American Assembly, the University of Chicago, and the Urban Institute.

In recent years Katherine Graham has turned over operating responsibility for the Washington Post Company to her son, Donald E. Graham. Donald graduated from Harvard in 1966, served in the Army for two years, and then spent over twenty years in various Washington Post management positions, before his mother named him president and chief executive officer in 1991. Katherine Graham remains as chairman of the board of directors.

Ted Turner: Maverick Media Mogul.   Media power is *less* concentrated today than a decade ago, owing to the development of satellite and cable technology that adds greater variety of communication channels. Today over 65 percent of TV households are connected to cable, diluting the power of the older established networks—ABC, CBS, and NBC—and providing diverse news and entertainment broadcasting, from C-SPAN coverage of Congress to MTV and the Cartoon Network. Perhaps no single individual is more responsible for the development of diversity in television communication than the flamboyant tycoon Ted Turner. Once ridiculed by established media elites as "the Mouth of the South," Turner changed the course of television news broadcasting with the creation of his twenty-four-hour news network, CNN.

Reportedly a mischievous child with a difficult upbringing, Turner was sent to the Georgia Military Academy before entering Brown University. He was expelled for various infractions and served a brief tour with the U.S. Coast Guard before entering the family's billboard advertising company in Atlanta. When the business floundered and his father committed suicide, young Ted took over and began building his empire. He used the restored profits from the billboard company to buy television stations and invest in the new satellite technology. With FCC deregulation of satellite broadcasting in 1975, Turner was well positioned to challenge the major networks. Turner's Atlanta-based WTBS was the first "superstation" beaming its programs via satellite throughout the nation. He purchased the Atlanta Braves and the Atlanta Hawks to help feed his programming as well as his mountainous ego. In 1988 Turner purchased the MGM film library, including the classic *Gone with the Wind*, to add to offerings shown on WTBS and his entertainment network, TNT.

But Turner's greatest achievement was the creation of CNN in 1981, despite near-unanimous predictions of financial disaster. Turner borrowed

---

[11] Kevin Phillips, "Busting the Media Trusts," *Harpers* (July 1977), p. 30.

heavily to establish CNN and nursed it financially for many years before it became profitable. The requirement to fill twenty-four hours with news, interviews, and commentary means that CNN offers more "raw" news than any other network. News on CNN is less burdened with editing, "interpretation," and context than on ABC, CBS, or NBC. And CNN recruits some conservative commentators (for example, *Crossfire*'s Pat Buchanan) in order to spark controversy. The Gulf War cemented CNN as the nation's leading source of fast-breaking news. Only CNN had live satellite coverage as bombs began to fall on Baghdad on the night of January 16, 1991. CNN would later come under criticism for broadcasts of enemy propaganda by its correspondent, Peter Arnett, but CNN established itself as a serious rival to the established news organizations. Today CNN International is shown in hotels around the world.

As Turner transformed his empire, Turner Broadcasting, Inc., into a major media corporation, he increasingly recruited professional executives and producers to manage affairs. In order to finance his purchase of MGM in 1986, he diluted some of this authority by giving some cable systems operators seats on his board of directors. Despite his success in capitalism, Turner's personal politics are decidedly left of center; his marriage to "progressive activist" Jane Fonda no doubt reinforces his often expressed cynicism toward American institutions. But Turner wisely refrains from direct interference in programming.

NETWORK CELEBRITIES

Each night nearly 40 million Americans watch one of three men—Dan Rather, Tom Brokaw, or Peter Jennings. No other individuals—Presidents, movie stars, popes—have such extensive contact with so many people. These network celebrities are recognized and heard by more people than anyone else on the planet. "The networks demand that an anchor be the network's premier journalist and principal showman, top editor and star, symbol of news excellence and the network's single most important living logo."[12]

The anchors are both celebrities and newsmen. They aspire to both journalistic power and ratings supremacy. Occasionally, they and their shows are torn between journalistic and commercial values. They must attract viewership, that is, keep their "ratings" high, and at the same time influence the course of national events.

Anchors are chosen for their mass appeal, but they must also bring journalistic expertise to their jobs. Their views on what is news shape their nightly reports. The anchors together with their producers must select from thousands of hours of videotapes and hundreds of separate stories, which stories and visuals will be squeezed into the twenty-two minutes of nightly network

---

[12] Alex S. Jones, "The Anchors," *New York Times Magazine*, July 27, 1986, p. 14.

news. (Eight minutes are reserved for commercials.) Each minute represents approximately 160 spoken words. The total number of words on the entire newscast is fewer than a single newspaper page. These restrictions of the medium itself give great power to the anchors and producers in selecting what Americans will see and hear about their world each night.

All three network anchors are middle-aged, Anglo-Saxon, male Protestants. All share liberal, reformist social values and political beliefs. Canadian-born Jennings projects an image of thoughtful, urbane sophistication. He is widely traveled (his father was a journalist), but his formal education ended in the tenth grade. ABC's *World News Tonight with Peter Jennings* devotes slightly more time to international news than its rival news shows.

Dan Rather deliberately projects an image of emotional intensity. His intensity creates both strong attachments and heated animosities among his audiences. He is despised by conservatives because of his undisguised, passionate liberal views. Rather worked his way up through the ranks of CBS news following graduation from Sam Houston State College in Huntsville, Texas. He was a reporter and news director for the CBS affiliate station in Houston, then chief of the CBS London Bureau, and later Vietnam correspondent. He came to national prominence in 1966 as CBS White House correspondent. In 1981 Rather took over the anchor position at CBS from the legendary Walter Cronkite. But he was not able to maintain the ratings lead for CBS that Cronkite had previously given the network. Over time *CBS Evening News* gradually fell behind the ABC and NBC evening news broadcasts. In 1993, Connie Chung was added as Rather's "co-anchor" in an effort to revitalize the show.

Tom Brokaw of NBC gives a calm and unemotional delivery of the news, with occasional wry humor. He is comfortable, smooth, and authoritative, yet never overbearing or hostile toward guests. Brokaw graduated from the University of South Dakota and started his career at an Omaha television station. He anchored local news in Atlanta and Los Angeles before moving up to the post of NBC White House correspondent in 1973. He hosted the NBC *Today Show* from 1978 to 1982. His show-biz and talk-show host experience have served him well as anchor of the *NBC Nightly News* since 1982. He is less ideological than Rather. He can appear relaxed and friendly, chatting with the President during a Super Bowl broadcast or emceeing a presidential debate.

BAD NEWS AND GOOD PROFITS

The economic interests of the media elite—the need to capture and hold audience attention—creates a bias toward "hype" in the selection, presentation, and interpretation of news. The media must attract and hold large audiences so that they may be sold to advertisers. On an average night, nearly 100 million people will watch television. Advertisers must pay $100,000 or more for a single thirty-second prime-time spot on any of the major networks. Advertisers pay the networks on the basis of ratings, compiled by independent services, the most popular of which is the A.C. Nielson Company. By placing electronic boxes in a national sample of television homes, Nielson calculates the proportion of all "TV households" that watch a program (the "rating"), as well as the proportion of TV households with their sets turned on that watch a specific program (the "share").

Bad news makes good profits. Bad news attracts larger audiences than good news. So television news displays a pervasive bias toward the negative in American life—in politics, government, business, the military, schools, and everywhere else. Bad news stories on television outnumber good news stories by at least three to one.[13] All presidential candidates (with the exception of Jesse Jackson in 1988) receive more bad coverage than good. Bill Clinton was no exception. Despite a liberal Democratic bias among newsmakers, stories alleging marital infidelity, pot smoking, and draft dodging followed Clinton throughout the campaign. Negative network reporting and commentary extends to the White House as well. One study of network news stories on the Reagan presidency showed that the ratio of *un*favorable to favorable stories was thirteen to one.[14] Clinton does not appear to be doing much better; the president's $200 haircut at the Los Angeles airport runway garnered more coverage than his State of the Union address.

The network's concentration on scandal, abuse, and corruption in government has not always produced the desired liberal, reformist notions in the minds of the masses of viewers. Contrary to the expectations of the media elite, their focus on political wrongdoing has produced feelings of general distrust and cynicism toward government and "the system." These feelings have been labeled "television malaise"—a combination of social distrust, political cynicism, feelings of powerlessness, and disaffection from parties and politics which seems to stem from television's emphasis on the negative aspects of American life.[15] The long-run effects of this elite behavior may be self-defeating in terms of elite interest in maintaining a stable political system.

LIBERAL BIAS IN THE NEWS

When TV newscasters insist that they are impartial, objective, and unbiased, they may sincerely believe that they are, because in the world in which they live—the New York and Washington world of newspeople, writers, intellec-

---

[13] Michael Jay Robinson, "Just How Liberal Is the News?" *Public Opinion* (February–March, 1983), pp. 55–60.

[14] Michael Robinson, Maura Clancey, and Lisa Grand, "With Friends Like These . . . ," *Public Opinion* (June–July 1983), pp. 2–3.

[15] Michael Robinson, "Public Affairs Television and the Growth of Political Malaise," *American Political Science Review*, 70 (June 1976), 409–32; and "Television and American Politics," *The Public Interest* (Summer 1977), pp. 3–39.

tuals, artists—the established liberal point of view is so uniformly voiced. TV news executives can be genuinely shocked and affronted when they are charged with slanting their coverage toward liberal concerns. But the media elite—the executives, producers, reporters, editors, and anchors—are decidedly "liberal" and "left-leaning" in their political views. Political scientist Doris A. Graber writes about the politics of the media: "economic and social liberalism prevails, as does a preference for an internationalist foreign policy, caution about military intervention, and suspicion about the ethics of established large institutions, particularly government."[16] One study of news executives reported that 63 percent described themselves as "left-leaning," only 27 percent as "middle-of-the-road," and 10 percent as "right-leaning." Newsmakers describe themselves as either "independent" (45 percent) or Democratic (44 percent); very few (9 percent) admit to being Republican.[17]

There is very little diversity in television news. ABC, CBS, and NBC present nearly identical "packages" each evening. They are "rivals in conformity."[18] Liberal and conservative views can be found in newspapers and magazines—for example, the *New York Times* versus *The Wall Street Journal, Harpers* versus the *National Review*. But a standard liberal position is presented on all three television networks in both news and entertainment programming.

The owners and directors of the major media corporations usually share the moderate conservatism of the big business community; but the executives, producers, reporters, and other media professionals are clearly liberal and left-leaning in their political views. Generally, newsmakers in the larger, or prestigious organizations—CBS, ABC, NBC, *New York Times, Washington Post–Newsweek*—are more liberal in their social, cultural, and political values than those in smaller, regional organizations, including individual television stations.

The responses of the media elite to various economic, social, and foreign policy questions reflects upper-class liberalism. Most of the media elite enjoyed socially privileged upbringings. Fewer than one in five came from working-class families. Few of them are outright socialists; they overwhelmingly reject the idea that major corporations should be taken over by the government. Most reject rigid egalitarianism and support the idea that people with more ability should be paid more money. Most believe that free enterprise is fair (see Table 4–3). However, the media elite is strongly committed to the welfare state. They believe the government should reduce income differences between the rich and the poor, and nearly half believe that the gov-

---

[16] Doris A. Graber, *Mass Media and American Politics* (Washington, D.C.: Congressional Quarterly Press, 1980), p. 49.

[17] S. Robert Lichter, Stanley Rothman, and Linda S. Lichter, *The Media Elite* (New York: Hastings House, 1990), p. 47.

[18] Graber, *Mass Media and American Politics*, p. 68.

Table 4–3   Liberal Values among News and Entertainment Leaders

	Percent of Leaders in Agreement		
	Business	News	Entertainment
Economic liberalism			
Government should redistribute income.	23	68	69
Government should guarantee jobs.	29	48	45
Big corporations should be publicly owned.	6	13	19
Private enterprise is fair.	89	70	69
People with more ability should earn more.	90	86	94
Reformism			
Structure of society causes alienation.	30	49	62
Institutions need overhaul.	28	32	48
Social liberalism			
Strong affirmative action for blacks is needed.	71	80	83
Women have the right to abortions.	80	90	97
Homosexuals should not teach in schools.	51	15	15
Homosexuality is wrong.	60	25	20
Adultery is wrong.	76	47	49

SOURCES: Robert Lichter and Stanley Rothman, "Media and Business Elites," *Public Opinion* (October–November 1981), pp. 42–46; Linda S. Lichter, S. Robert Lichter, and Stanley Rothman, "Hollywood and America: The Odd Couple," *Public Opinion* (December–January 1983), pp. 54–58.

ernment should guarantee jobs. They favor affirmative action and believe environmental problems are serious. They are liberals on social issues such as abortion and homosexuality.

Of course, the argument by many newsmakers is that they do not allow their personal values to affect the news. But newsmakers, like all of us, must rely on our personal values in making decisions, including decisions about what is "newsworthy." Newsmakers must choose from an almost infinite number of stories in the real world which stories will be presented as "news." Even as broadcast time approaches, hundreds of hours of film and videotape are available for selection as "news." Most of these stories must be rejected; there is simply not enough time to report all of the news. It would be impossible for the newsmakers' own values *not* to influence the selection of news.

PRIME-TIME: SOCIALIZING THE MASSES

Prime-time entertainment programming suggests to Americans how they ought to live and what values they ought to hold. Socialization—the learning, accepting, and approving of customs, values, and life styles—is an important function of the mass media. Network television entertainment is the most widely shared experience in the country. America's favorite TV shows are shown to over 50 million individual viewers in 20 million households (see Table 4–4). This is two-and-one-half times the average audience for network news. The network executives who decide what will be shown as entertainment have a tremendous impact on the values, aspirations, and life styles of Americans.

Throughout the 1970s no one had a more direct effect on the themes of television entertainment than Fred Silverman. Silverman was vice-president for programming at CBS-TV from 1970 to 1975, president of entertainment for ABC-TV from 1975 to 1978, and president of NBC-TV from 1978 to 1981. It was Silverman who championed liberal programming with *M.A.S.H.* (antiwar), *All in the Family* (antiracist), and later *Roots* (black experience). He favored the producer Norman Lear, whose work—*All in the Family, Maude, The Jeffersons, One Day at a Time*, and *Mary Hartman, Mary Hartman*—emphasized different and often controversial life styles. When Silverman moved to ABC, he boldly predicted that he would raise a lackluster network to number one in viewing audience; he did just that. It was Silverman, more than anyone else, who introduced sex-oriented shows to prime-time television with *Charlie's Angels* and *Three's Company*. He also went after young audiences—*Happy Days* and *Laverne and Shirley*—with the notion that children in the family really control the TV dial. Silverman was never accused of overestimating the intelligence of TV audiences.

When he moved to NBC, Silverman faced the problem of beating his own program line-ups on CBS and ABC. By 1978, NBC had dropped to third in the audience ratings. Silverman made numerous changes in program line-ups to try to restore NBC audience ratings, but he failed. He spent millions on poor shows, and in 1981 NBC was still in the network cellar. Its only long-run, top-ten show, *Little House on the Prairie*, predated Silverman's tenure and emphasized traditional family values. When a new

Table 4–4   America's Favorite Television Programs in 1991

Program	Average Number of Households Viewing (Millions)
1. *60 Minutes*	23.4
2. *Roseanne*	20.6
3. *CBS Sunday Movie*	18.9
4. *Home Improvement*	18.3
5. *Coach*	17.6
6. *Murder, She Wrote*	17.5
7. *Cheers*	17.2
8. *Designing Women*	17.1
9. *Major Dad*	17.0
10. *Murphy Brown*	16.4

SOURCE: A.C. Nielsen, as reported in *The World Almanac 1993* (New York: Newspaper Enterprises Association, 1988), p. 304.

chairman, Thornton Bradshaw, took over the reins of NBC's parent company, RCA, Silverman was encouraged to resign. His replacement was Grant Tinker.

Tinker had founded MTM Enterprises with his former wife, Mary Tyler Moore. He had produced shows generally considered superior to those of Silverman: *The Mary Tyler Moore Show, Phyllis, Rhoda,* and *Lou Grant.* These shows emphasized feminism, liberalism, and crusading journalism.

When Tinker took over the chairmanship of NBC in 1981, the network's prime-time ratings were the lowest in its history. Five years later Tinker had propelled the network to the top of the ratings again and sent corporate profits soaring. He mastered late night TV by giving Johnny Carson a shorter show and adding the popular David Letterman show. The NBC *Today Show* already captured most of the early morning viewers. He brought the award-winning *Hill Street Blues* to NBC, and its upscale viewership grew. He fed a younger audience's thirst for violence with the hip *Miami Vice.* And he hooked the entire country on *The Cosby Show,* which quickly became the nation's number one prime-time television show. He added *Cheers, Family Ties, The Golden Girls,* and *Night Court.* No one exercised greater influence over prime-time television broadcasting for more than two decades than Grant Tinker.[19]

Silverman, Tinker, and other top network executives and producers are generally "coast oriented" in their values and life styles; that is, they reflect popular culture in New York and California. Almost all are from the big cities of the East and West coasts. Almost all are white males. A majority are Jewish. They are well-educated, extraordinarily well-paid, and independent or Democratic in their politics. They are *not* radicals or socialists. Almost all believe that "people with ability should earn more," and most support free enterprise and oppose government ownership of the economy. However, these television programmers are very critical of government and business; they believe strongly that society is unfair to women, blacks, and minorities; and they are socially very liberal in terms of their views on abortion, homosexuality, and adultery.

More important, perhaps, the programmers believe that they have a responsibility to change America's views to fit their own. They believe that television should "promote social reform." (Fully two thirds of the programmers interviewed agreed with this definition of their role in society). "This is perhaps the single most striking finding in our study. According to television's creators, they are not in it just for the money. They also seek to move their audience toward their own vision of the good society."[20]

Much of our learning is subconscious. If these televised images are inaccurate, we end up with wrong impressions of American life. If television shows

---

[19] Diane K. Smith, "Starting Over: TV's Grant Tinker," *New York Times Magazine,* October 23, 1987.

[20] Linda S. Lichter, S. Robert Lichter, and Stanley Rothman, "Hollywood and America: The Odd Couple," *Public Opinion* (December–January 1983), p. 58.

emphasize sex and violence, we come to believe that there is more sex and violence in America than is actually the case. For millions of Americans, television is a way of keeping in touch with their environment. Both entertainment and advertising provide model ways of life. People are shown products, services, and life styles that they are expected to desire and imitate. By creating these desires and expectations, the media help to define how Americans should live.

SUMMARY

The people who control the flow of information in America are among the most powerful in the nation. Television network broadcasting is the first form of truly *mass* communication; it carries a visual image with emotional content as well as information. Television news reaches virtually everyone, and for most Americans it is the major source of information about the world.

The power of mass media is primarily in agenda-setting—deciding what will be decided. The media determine what the masses talk about and what the elite must decide about. Political issues do not just "happen." The media decide what are issues, problems, even crises, which must be acted upon.

Control of the television media is highly concentrated. A few private corporations (CBS, NBC, ABC, and Turner Broadcasting, Inc.) largely determine what the people will see and hear about their world; they feed 1,099 local TV stations that account for 80 percent of the news and entertainment broadcasts. Most of the nation's 1,750 daily newspapers receive their news from the AP wire service. The fifteen largest newspaper empires account for more than one half of the total newspaper circulation in the country.

Those at the top of the mass media include both inheritors and individuals who worked their way up the management ladder. Among the media elite are the heads of CBS, NBC, and ABC; the *New York Times; Washington Post–Newsweek;* Time, Inc.; and the fifteen largest newspaper empires.

The mass media must attract large audiences to sell to advertisers. The principal source of bias in the news originates from the need to capture large audiences with drama, action, and confrontation. The result is an emphasis on "hard" news—unfavorable stories about prominent people and business and government. However, media attention to scandal, abuse, violence, and corruption has not always produced liberal reformist values. Many scholars believe it has produced "television malaise"—distrust, cynicism, and disaffection from public affairs caused by negative reporting on American life. This reporting may also be contributing to the public's decline in confidence in the media.

The media elite is the most liberal segment of the nation's elite. While this elite supports the free enterprise system and reward based on merit, it favors government intervention to reduce income differences and to aid women, blacks, and minorities. News executives claim only to "mirror" reality, yet at the same time they take credit for civil rights laws, ending the Vietnam War, and expelling Richard Nixon from the White House. Prime-time programming executives are even more liberal in their views, and they acknowledge that their role is to "reform" society.

5 The Civic Establishment

In an advanced, complex society, there are many specialized institutions and organizations that exercise power. In addition to economic organizations (corporations, banks, insurance companies, and investment houses), governmental bureaucracies, television networks, and news organizations, there are other, less visible institutions that also provide bases of power in American society. An operational definition of a national elite must include individuals who occupy positions of power in influential law firms, major philanthropic foundations, recognized national cultural and civic organizations, and prestigious private universities. We shall refer to these institutions collectively as the "civic establishment."

The identification of a civic establishment involves many subjective judgments. We shall try to defend these judgments, but we recognize that equally valid defenses of alternative judgments might be made in many cases.

THE "SUPERLAWYERS"

As modern societies grow in size and complexity, the need for rules and regulations increases geometrically, and so does the power of people whose profession is to interpret those rules and regulations. As early as 1832, deTocqueville felt that the legal profession in this country would become the "new aristocracy" of the Republic. C. Wright Mills asserts that lawyers are indeed a key segment of the nation's aristocracy of power:

> The inner core of the power elite also includes men of the higher legal and financial type from the great law factories and investment firms who are professional go-betweens of economic, political, and military affairs, and who thus act to unify the power elite.[1]

The predominance of lawyers among political elites has already been noted. Within the corporate elite—presidents and directors of the nation's largest industries, banks, utilities, and insurance companies—over 15 percent

[1] C. Wright Mills, *The Power Elite* (New York: Oxford, 1956), p. 289.

are lawyers. But neither the politician-lawyer nor the businessperson-lawyer really stands at the top of the legal profession. The "superlawyers" are the senior partners of the nation's most highly esteemed New York and Washington law firms. These are the firms that represent clients such as General Motors, AT&T, Du Pont, CBS, and American Airlines,[2] not only in the courts but, perhaps more importantly, before Congress and the federal regulatory agencies. Of course, the nation's largest corporate and financial institutions have their own legal departments; but attorneys in these departments, known as "house counsels," usually handle routine matters. When the stakes are high, the great corporations turn to the superlawyers.

Identification of the "top" New York and Washington law firms is necessarily a subjective task. Prestigious firms do not provide lists of clients, claiming that to do so would violate "lawyer-client confidentiality." So we cannot be

TABLE 5–1   The Top Law Firms

Wall Street	Washington
Shearman & Sterling	Arnold & Porter
Cravath, Swaine & Moore	Covington & Burling
White & Case	Arrent, Fox, Kintner, Plotkin & Kahn
Dewey, Ballantine, Bushby, Palmer & Wood	Wilmer, Cutler & Pickering
Simpson, Thacher & Bartlett	Clifford, Warnke, Glass, McIlwain & Finney
Davis, Polk & Wardwell	Fried, Frank, Harris, Shriver & Kampelman
Milbank, Tweed, Hadley & McCloy	Rodgers & Wells
Cahill, Gordon & Reindel	
Sullivan & Cromwell	
Chadbourne, Parke, Whiteside & Wolff	
Breed, Abbott & Morgan	
Winthrop, Simpson, Putnam & Roberts	
Cadwalader, Wickersham, & Taft	
Wilkie, Farr & Gallagher	
Donovan, Leisure, Newton & Irvine	
Lord, Day & Lord	
Dwight, Royall, Harris, Koegel & Caskey	
Mudge, Rose, Guthrie & Alexander	
Kelley, Drye & Warren	
Cleary, Gottlieb, Steen & Hamilton	

These firms were selected on the basis of reputed power and prestige. If gross revenues were considered, the following firms would be at the top of the list: Skadden, Arps, Slate, Meagler & Flom (New York); Finley, Kumble, Wagner, Heine, Underberg, Manley, Meyerson & Casey (New York); Baker and McKenzie (Chicago); Gibson, Dunn & Crutcher (Los Angeles); O'Melveny & Myers (Los Angeles).

[2] Quoted as clients of Covington & Burling by Joseph C. Goulden, *The Superlawyers* (New York: Dell, 1971), p. 27.

certain what firms actually represent the nation's largest corporations. The listing in Table 5–1 was compiled from a variety of sources and represents our best estimate of the nation's legal elite. The senior partners of these firms are our superlawyers.

These selected firms represent the nation's largest banks and corporations. A partial listing of their clients include:[3]

Cravath, Swaine & Moore	IBM, CBS, Chemical Bank
Davis, Polk & Wardwell	ITT, LTV, Morgan Guaranty
Donovan, Leisure, Newton & Irvine	Mobil, Westinghouse
Milbank, Tweed, Hadley & McCloy	Chase Manhattan, Rockefellers
Shearman & Sterling	United Technologies, Citibank
Simpson, Thacher & Bartlett	Paramount Communications, Manufacturers Hanover
Sullivan & Cromwell	Exxon, General Foods, GE

The names of the firms themselves, of course, do not always identify the senior partners. Firms often retain the names of deceased founders, and most large firms have so many senior partners (twenty or thirty is not uncommon) that it would be impossible to put all their names in the title of the firm. Then, too, some firms change names upon the resignation of partners.[4]

The senior partners of the nation's top law firms generally feel an obligation to public service. According to superlawyer Arthur Dean, the experience of serving in such a firm provides "an exceptional opportunity to acquire a liberal education in modern government and society. Such partnerships are likely in the future, as they have in the past, to prepare and offer for public service men exceptionally qualified to serve."[5] The arrogance of such an assertion has too much basis in fact to be dismissed as mere self-congratulation.

Superlawyers among the serious men who have been called upon over the years for governmental leadership include:

[3] James B. Stewart, *The Partners: Inside America's Most Powerful Law Firms* (New York: Simon & Schuster, 1983).

[4] For example, Mudge, Stern, Baldwin & Todd placed the name of Richard M. Nixon at the head of the firm during his Wall Street years, and later added John Mitchell's name to the firm. The result was "Nixon, Mudge, Rose, Guthrie, Alexander & Mitchell." When Nixon became President and Mitchell became attorney general, the firm went back to Mudge, Rose, Guthrie & Alexander. Despite the legal difficulties of its former partners, the firm remains one of the most powerful on Wall Street. Likewise, when one of Arnold, Fortas & Porter's clients, Lyndon Johnson, became President of the United States, and named his personal attorney Abraham Fortas to the Supreme Court (and then later tried unsuccessfully to make him Chief Justice), the Fortas name was removed from the firm. The firm is now Arnold & Porter, but it is still one of the most powerful in Washington.

[5] Quoted in Goulden, *The Superlawyers*, p. 36.

Dean Acheson. Secretary of state under President Harry Truman (Covington & Burling)

John Foster Dulles. Secretary of state under President Dwight Eisenhower (Sullivan & Cromwell)

Clark Clifford. Secretary of defense under President Lyndon Johnson (Clifford, Warnke, Glass, McIlwain & Finney)

William P. Rogers. Secretary of state under President Richard Nixon (Rodgers & Wells)

Cyrus Vance. Secretary of state under President Jimmy Carter (Simpson, Thacher & Bartlett)

In an even earlier era, the New York Wall Street law firms supplied presidential candidates:

John W. Davis. Democratic party nominee for President of the United States, 1924 (Davis, Polk, Wardwell, Sunderland & Kiendl)[6]

Wendell Willkie. Republican party nominee for President of the United States, 1940 (Willkie, Farr, Gallagher, Walton & Fitzgibbon)

Thomas E. Dewey. Republican party nominee for President of the United States, 1944 and 1948 (Dewey, Ballantine, Bushby, Palmer & Wood)

Equally important are the top lawyers who were called upon to represent the United States itself in periods of crisis where matters were considered too serious to be left to State Department bureaucrats:

Paul Warnke. U.S. negotiator in the Strategic Arms Limitation Talks (SALT). (Clifford, Warnke, Glass, McIlwain & Finney).

John J. McCloy. Chairman of the Coordinating Committee on the Cuban Crisis, 1962. Member of the President's commission on the assassination of President Kennedy. (Milbank, Tweed, Hadley & McCloy).

Arthur H. Dean. Chairman of the U.S. delegation on Nuclear Test Ban Treaty. Chief U.S. negotiator of the Korean Armistice Agreement. (Sullivan & Cromwell).

Lawrence Walsh. U.S. delegate to the Paris Peace Conference ending the Vietnam War; special prosecutor in the "Iran Contra" affair (Davis, Polk & Wardwell).

The typical path to the top of the legal profession starts with a Harvard, Yale, or Stanford law school degree, clerkship with a Supreme Court Justice, and then several years as an attorney with the Justice

---

[6] Davis unsuccessfully argued the case for racial segregation on behalf of the Board of Education of Topeka, Kansas, in the famous case of *Brown v. Board of Education* (1954); opposing counsel for Brown, of course, was Thurgood Marshall, later to become Supreme Court Justice.

Department or a federal regulatory commission. Young government lawyers who are *successful* at defeating a top firm in a case are *more* likely to be offered lucrative junior partnerships than those who lose to big firms. Talented younger government lawyers are systematically recruited by the top firms.

CLARK CLIFFORD: THE RISE AND FALL OF A WASHINGTON SUPERLAWYER

For over forty years Washington's premier superlawyer was the shrewd, courtly, and dapper Clark Clifford. Clifford was an inside fixer; he seldom appeared in an open courtroom. But his firm—Clifford, Warnke, Glass, McIlwain & Finney—produced results for their legion of wealthy clients.

Consider the clever style of the restrained Clifford as he solemnly disclaimed having any "influence":

> There is one point I wish to make clear. This firm has no influence of any kind in Washington. If you want to employ someone who has influence, you will have to go somewhere else. . . . What we do have is a record of working with the various departments agencies of the government, and we have their respect and confidence, and that we consider to be a valuable asset.[7]

Clifford's "valuable assets" brought him clients such as Exxon, ABC–Capital Cities, Hughes Tool Co. (Howard Hughes), Time Inc., General Electric, Du Pont Corporation, Phillips Petroleum, W.R. Grace Shipping, TWA, and so on. His former personal clients included John F. Kennedy and Lyndon Johnson.

Clifford is the son of an auditor for the Missouri-Pacific Railroad. He attended Washington University St. Louis Law School, graduating in 1928. He promptly established a successful law practice in St. Louis and included in his contacts Missouri Senators Harry S. Truman and Stuart Symington. Clifford enlisted in the U.S. Navy in World War II, but when Truman became President, he was called to the White House as counsel to the President. Clifford's title never changed, but he soon became a dominant figure on Truman's staff. He supervised foreign and domestic policy in the White House, as well as Truman's successful come-from-behind 1948 presidential campaign. In 1950, he left the White House, after five years of service, to open his own Washington firm.

Bureaucrats had become accustomed to answering Clifford's phone calls when he called from the White House, so they answered them when he called from his firm. His first big clients were Phillips Petroleum, Pennsylvania Railroad, Standard Oil of California, and Howard Hughes.

[7] Quoted in Goulden, *The Superlawyers*, p. 78.

Even during Republican years Clifford prospered. After Du Pont had lost its complex ten-year antitrust case and was ordered to sell its ownership of General Motors, it called upon Clifford in desperation. If Du Pont were forced to sell its huge holdings of GM stock immediately, the price would plummet, and income from the sale would be heavily taxed. Clifford obtained passage of a special congressional act allowing distribution of the GM stock to Du Pont stockholders as a capital gain—and a tax savings to Du Pont of $500 million (which of course was a tax loss to the U.S. Treasury of an equal amount).

When President Kennedy prepared to take over the reins of government from his predecessor, Dwight Eisenhower, he sent his personal attorney, Clark Clifford, to arrange the transition. He also sent Clifford to investigate the Bay of Pigs disaster and reorganize the CIA and the Defense Department's intelligence operations. Later he sent Clifford to the headquarters of U.S. Steel to force a rollback of steel prices by threatening tax audits, contract cancellations, and FBI investigations. But Clifford did not accept any formal government appointment under Kennedy.

When the Vietnam War controversy shattered the Johnson administration, and Robert McNamara was forced to resign as secretary of defense, President Johnson persuaded his attorney and friend Clark Clifford to assume the leadership of the Defense Department. Clifford reluctantly accepted the position of secretary of defense and began America's slow and painful withdrawal from Vietnam. Clifford later returned to his Washington law firm; he subsequently accepted the directorships of Phillips Petroleum and the Knight-Ridder newspapers. His partner, Paul Warnke, was arms control and disarmament adviser to President Carter, with special responsibilities for the SALT negotiations with the Soviet Union.

Clifford carefully nurtured a reputation for honesty and integrity over the years, and by so doing added to his tremendous influence in Washington circles. But sometime in the early 1980s, he became enmeshed in a worldwide banking scandal that led to his downfall. Clifford undertook to represent First American Bank in its dealings with the Federal Reserve Board. Federal regulators were concerned that First American was really a front for the sleazy Bank of Credit and Commerce International (BCCI), which regularly laundered international drug money. But Clifford won approval for the bank by personally persuading the regulators that BCCI had no control over it. Clifford was rewarded for his efforts by being named chairman of First American. In 1990 an investigation into drug laundering through First American revealed that BCCI in fact owned a controlling interest in Clifford's bank. Clifford publicly claimed that he had been duped. But later it was revealed that Clifford had received a $12 million loan from BCCI which he used to gain personal profits on First American stock totaling over $20 million. Clifford was indicted by a federal grand jury in 1992, but the charges were dropped in 1993 because of his age and ill health.

THE "FIXERS": PEDDLING POWER FOR PROFIT

Washington is a city of "representatives"—agents, advocates, lawyers, lobbyists, and "fixers" who offer to influence government policy for a price. Washington representatives number in the thousands; their clients include individual corporations; professional and trade associations; communications, transportation, and utility companies; consumer and environmental groups; and foreign governments and corporations. As government *regulation* has grown, so also has the profitable business of defending clients from regulatory activity. As government *spending* has grown, so also has the lucrative profession of seeking out government grants and contracts. As government *power* has grown, so also have the profits of lawyers, lobbyists, consultants, and spokespersons, whose job it is to advance their clients' interests in Washington.

The fixers include the nation's prestigious law firms as well as professional public relations firms and individual lobbyists. Their work includes legal counseling—representation before regulatory commissions or in civil or criminal proceedings—as well as legal advice on proposed laws and regulations and assistance in petitioning for special treatment under them. Their work also includes information and intelligence gathering—monitoring, analyzing, and informing their clients of current and future government activity. They may also provide public relations services—promoting a favorable climate of opinion for their clients. Their services usually include the various forms of direct lobbying—testifying before congressional committees and regulatory commissions; buttonholing Congress members, Cabinet officials, or White House staff; and trying to directly influence legislation or executive decisions. But perhaps most important of all, the Washington fixers provide their clients with *access* to the corridors and cocktail parties of power.

"Opening doors" is big business in Washington. To influence decision-makers, people must first acquire access to them. The Washington law firms, public relations agencies, and "consultants" all offer their insider connections along with their advice to their clients. Indeed, most of the top fixers are former government officials—former Congress members, Cabinet secretaries, White House aides, and the like—who "know their way around." The personal prestige and background of the fixer helps to open doors, to "just get a chance to talk" with top officials.

These are the services offered by notable Washington fixers such as Joseph A. Califano, of the Washington office of Dewey, Ballantine, Bushby, Palmer & Wood. Califano's clients reportedly include Bethlehem Steel, Bristol Myers, Chrysler, Walt Disney, Presidential Insurance, Seagrams, and Xerox. Califano also serves as a director of Chrysler, Primerica, Automatic Data Processing, and as a trustee of Urban Institute, New York University, Georgetown University, and the 20th Century Fund. He was secretary of Health Education and Welfare under President Jimmy Carter and special assistant to the President under Lyndon Johnson.

In recent years Wall Street investment firms have also seen the wisdom of bringing Washington insiders into their fold. It helps in putting together big deals to have "big names to help you get through the door." Paul Volcker, former chairman of Federal Reserve Board, returned to Wall Street as a consultant after his successful years at "the Fed." William Simon did so after serving as secretary of the treasury.

Consider the new partners in the Carlyle Group, a Washington-based investment firm. In 1993 it added James Baker as a partner. Baker had been the most powerful appointed official in the Reagan and Bush administrations, serving first as secretary of the treasury, then chief of staff in the Reagan White House, and finally as secretary of state in the Bush administration. Baker's Washington and worldwide connections are unsurpassed. Baker was recruited to the Carlyle Group by its chairman, Frank Carlucci, former deputy CIA director who served briefly as secretary of defense in the Reagan administration. The Carlyle Group also includes Richard Darman, former budget director under President Bush. Carlucci acknowledges the value of good connections and powerful names in opening doors: "I'd be a fool to deny that having a number of high profile officeholders does provide Carlyle with certain advantages."[8]

THE FOUNDATIONS

The power of the nation's largest foundations derives from their support of significant research projects in social problems, arts, and humanities. Actually, the foundations spend far less for research and development than does the federal bureaucracy. But the principal research components of the federal bureaucracy—the National Science Foundation, the U.S. Public Health Service—channel most of their funds into the physical, biological, and medical sciences. Thus, it has been the role of the nation's largest foundations to support and direct innovations in the social, intellectual, and cultural life of the nation.

The major foundations are in the forefront of national policy-making. They channel corporate and personal wealth into the policy-making process, providing both financial support and direction for university research and the activities of various policy-planning groups (see Chapter 9). Foundations are tax-exempt; contributions to foundations may be deducted from federal corporate and individual income taxes, *and* the foundations themselves are not subject to federal income taxation.

Foundations can be created by corporations or by individuals. These corporations or individuals can name themselves and their friends as directors or trustees of the foundations they create. Large blocs of corporate stock or large amounts of personal wealth can be donated as tax-exempt contributions to the

---

[8] Quoted in *Time*, March 22, 1993, p. 39.

foundations. The foundations can receive interest, dividends, profit shares, and capital gains from these assets without paying any taxes on them. The directors or trustees, of course, are not allowed to use foundation income or assets for their personal expenses, as they would their own taxable income. Otherwise, however, they have great latitude in directing the use of foundation monies—to underwrite research, investigate social problems, create or assist universities, establish "think tanks," endow museums, theaters, operas, symphonies, and so on.

According to *The Foundation Directory*, there were 6,334 foundations large enough to deserve recognition and listing in 1993; these are the foundations with at least $1 million in assets or $100,000 in yearly distributions. (There are tens of thousands of other smaller foundations and trusts, some established as tax dodges by affluent citizens and therefore not having any appreciable effect on public policy except to reduce tax collections.) These foundations controlled $151 billion in assets.[9] But as in other sectors of society, these foundation assets are concentrated in a small number of large foundations. The fifty largest foundations control over 40 percent of all foundation assets in the nation (see Table 5–2).

Historically, the largest and most powerful foundations have been those established by the nation's leading families—Ford, Rockefeller, Carnegie, Mellon, Pew, Duke, Lilly, Danforth. Over the years, some foundations—for example, the Ford Foundation and the Carnegie Corporation—have become independent of their original family ties. Independence occurs when the foundation's own investments prosper and new infusions of family money are not required; however, some Rockefellers, Mellons, Lillys, Danforths, and other wealthy individuals still sit on the boards of directors of their family foundations. A number of foundations limit their contributions to specific fields: The Johnson Foundation, for example, sponsors research in health care, and the Lilly Endowment supports advances in education and religion. In contrast, the Ford and Rockefeller foundations deliberately focus on a wide range of key national policy areas.

The Rockefeller Foundation.   A glance at some of the people who serve on the Rockefeller Foundation board of trustees confirms its ties in other top institutions.

Richard H. Jenrette.   Chairman of the board of Equitable Life.

Arthur Levitt.   Chairman of the American Stock Exchange.

Thomas S. Johnson.   Former president of Manufacturers Hanover Trust Bank.

Robert C. Maynard.   Owner and publisher of the Oakland (Calif.) Tribune.

Frank G. Wells.   Former president and CEO of Walt Disney Co.

Harold Brown.   Former secretary of defense. Former president of Cal Tech. A director of AMAX, CBS, and IBM.

---

[9] *The Foundation Directory*, 1993 ed. (New York: Russell Sage Foundation, 1993).

TABLE 5–2   The Leading Foundations

Rank (by Assets)	Foundation	Assets ($ millions)
1	The Ford Foundation	$6,253
2	W.K. Kellogg Foundation	5,396
3	J. Paul Getty Trust	5,251
4	The Robert Wood Johnson Foundation	4,085
5	Lilly Endowment Inc.	3,592
6	John D. and Catherine T. MacArthur Foundation	3,393
7	The Pew Charitable Trusts	3,330
8	The Rockefeller Foundation	2,171
9	The Andrew W. Mellon Foundation	1,701
10	Robert W. Woodruff Foundation, Inc.	1,495
11	The Annenberg Foundation	1,477
12	The Kresge Foundation	1,422
13	The Duke Endowment	1,211
14	Charles Stewart Mott Foundation	1,095
15	DeWitt Wallace–Reader's Digest Fund, Inc.	1,088
16	The McKnight Foundation	1,067
17	The New York Community Trust	1,030
18	Carnegie Corporation of New York	981
19	Richard King Mellon Foundation	964
20	Lila Wallace–Reader's Digest Fund, Inc.	821
21	W.M. Keck Foundation	821
22	The Starr Foundation	780
23	Houston Endowment, Inc.	776
24	The Harry and Jeanette Weinberg Foundation, Inc.	762
25	The William and Flora Hewlett Foundation	752
26	Alfred P. Sloan Foundation	727
27	The David and Lucille Packard Foundation	718
28	The Cleveland Foundation	693
29	The Freedom Forum	687
30	The Annie E. Casey Foundation	666
31	Howard Heinz Endowment	629
32	The James Irvine Foundation	608
33	Knight Foundation	605
34	Meadows Foundation, Inc.	558
35	Robert R. McCormick Tribune Foundation	550
36	The William Penn Foundation	550
37	Marin Community Foundation	548
38	The J.E. and L.E. Mabee Foundation, Inc.	544
39	Joseph B. Whitehead Foundation	520
40	The George Gund Foundation	498
41	The Brown Foundation, Inc.	496
42	Weingart Foundation	458
43	Conrad N. Hilton Foundation	457
44	The Ahmanson Foundation	445
45	Hall Family Foundations	444
46	The Edna McConnell Clark Foundation	430
47	The Bush Foundation	428
48	Horace W. Goldsmith Foundation	420
49	The Henry Luce Foundation, Inc.	415
50	The Henry J. Kaiser Family Foundation	406

Total Number of Foundations = 6,334

Total Foundation Assets = $151,181 million

SOURCE: *The Foundation Directory*, 1993 ed. (New York: Russell Sage Foundation, 1993).

The Ford Foundation. The president of the Ford Foundation is Franklin A. Thomas, an African American New York attorney (Columbia Law School), who made his mark as president of the Bedford Stuyvesant Restoration Corporation (urban renewal). He is a director of Citicorp, CBS, Aluminum Company of America, Allied Stores, and Cummins Engine; he is also a trustee of Columbia University. Recent trustees of the Ford Foundation have included:

> **Henry B. Schacht.** Chairman of the board of Cummins Engine; and a director of AT&T, CBS, and Chase Manhattan. He is also a trustee of the Brookings Institution and Yale University.
>
> **Robert D. Haas.** Chairman of Levi Strauss Co.; and a trustee of the Brookings Institution; a member of the Council on Foreign Relations and the Trilateral Commission.
>
> **Barbara Scott Preiskel.** A director of General Electric, Massachusetts Mutual Life Insurance, Textron, American Stores, and the *Washington Post.*
>
> **Donald F. McHenry.** Former U.S. ambassador to the United Nations; and a director of AT&T, International Paper, Coca-Cola, Bank of Boston, Smith Kline Beecham, American Stock Exchange; a trustee of the Brookings Institution.
>
> **Vernon E. Jordan, Jr.** Former president of the National Urban League; and a director of American Express, Bankers Trust, Union Carbide, J.C. Penney, Xerox, Corning Glass, Dow Jones & Co., Ryder System, Sara Lee; a trustee of the Brookings Institution.
>
> **Yvonne Barthwaite Burke.** Attorney and former member of Congress and chair of the Congressional Black Caucus. A regent of the University of California and a trustee of the Brookings Institution.

THE CULTURAL ORGANIZATIONS

The identification of the nation's leading cultural and civic institutions requires qualitative judgments about the prestige and influence of a variety of organizations. Five cultural organizations were selected:

Metropolitan Museum of Art

Museum of Modern Art

Lincoln Center for the Performing Arts

Smithsonian Institution

John F. Kennedy Center for the Performing Arts

It is difficult to measure the power of particular institutions in the world of art, music, and theater. Certainly there are a number of viable alternatives that might be added to or substituted for our choices.

The Metropolitan Museum of Art. This organization in New York City is the largest art museum in the United States, with a collection of nearly one-half million *objects d'art.* Decisions of the Metropolitan Museum regarding exhibitions, collections, showings, and art objects have tremendous impact on what is or is not to be considered valued art in America. These decisions are the formal responsibility of the governing board. This board includes names such as:

Arthur Ochs Sulzberger. Chairman of the board of trustees of the Metropolitan Museum of Art. Former chairman of the board of the New York Times Co.

James R. Houghton. Chairman of the board of Corning Glass and a director of Metropolitan Life Insurance and J.P. Morgan.

Leonore Annenberg. Spouse of Walter H. Annenberg, retired chairman and owner of *T.V. Guide.*

Lawrence A. Tisch. Chairman of the Board of CBS.

Henry A. Kissinger. Former secretary of state.

Mrs. Henry J. Heinz II. Spouse of the chairman of the H.J. Heinz Company.

Richard S. Perkins. Former chairman of the board of Citicorp; and a director of Allied Chemical, New York Life Insurance, Southern Pacific, ITT, and Hospital Corporation of America.

The Museum of Modern Art. This museum in New York City is the leading institution in the nation devoted to collecting and exhibiting contemporary art. It houses not only paintings and sculpture but also films, prints, and photography. Its loan exhibitions circulate artworks throughout the world. The determination of what is to be considered "art" in the world of modern art is extremely subjective. The directors of the Museum of Modern Art, then, have great authority in determining what is or is not to be viewed as art. Its directors include illustrious names such as:

William S. Paley. Chairman emeritus. Former chairman of the board of CBS.

Mrs. John D. Rockefeller III. Widow of the oldest of four sons of John D. Rockefeller, Jr.

David Rockefeller. Former chairman of the board of Chase Manhattan.

David Rockefeller, Jr. Son of David Rockefeller.

Thomas S. Carroll. Former president of Lever Brothers.

Peter G. Peterson. Former chairman of the board of Lehman Brothers, Kuhn Loeb (investments); and a director of RCA, General Foods, Minnesota Mining & Manufacturing, Black and Decker, and Cities Service.

The Lincoln Center for the Performing Arts. The Lincoln Center in New York City is a major influence in the nation's serious theater, ballet, and music. The Lincoln Center houses the Metropolitan Opera, the New York

Philharmonic, and the Julliard School of Music. It also supports the Lincoln Repertory Company (theater), the New York State Theater (ballet), and the Library-Museum for Performing Arts.

The Metropolitan Opera, which opened in 1883, is the nation's most influential institution in the field of serious operatic music. Decisions about what operas to produce influence greatly what is, or is not, to be considered serious opera in America, and indeed, in the world. Such decisions are the formal responsibility of a board that includes such luminaries as:

William Rockefeller. Chairman of the Metropolitan Opera. A cousin of the Rockefeller brothers. Senior partner in Shearman & Sterling, a top Wall Street law firm.

Richard R. Shinn. Former chairman of the board of Metropolitan Life.

John T. Conner. Former chairman of the board of Allied Chemical; and a director of General Motors, Chase Manhattan, ABC, and Warner Lambert.

The Smithsonian Institution. The Smithsonian Institution in Washington supports a wide variety of scientific publications, collections, and exhibitions. It also exercises nominal control over the National Gallery of Art, the John F. Kennedy Center for the Performing Arts, and the Museum of Natural History, although these component organizations have their own boards of directors. The Smithsonian itself is directed by a board consisting of the Vice-President of the United States, the Chief Justice of the Supreme Court, three U.S. senators, three U.S. representatives, and nine private citizens.

Its "private citizens" turn out to be people such as:

Anne Armstrong. Former U.S. ambassador to Great Britain; and a director of General Motors, Halliburton, General Foods, Boise Cascade, and First City Bancorp. of Texas.

Hanna Gray. President of the University of Chicago; and a director of Cummins Engine, J.P. Morgan, and Atlantic Richfield.

William G. Bowen. President of Princeton University; and a director of NCR Corp., Merck & Co., and Reader's Digest, Inc.

Samuel C. Johnson. Chairman of the board of Johnson Wax Co.; and a director of Deere & Co. and Mobil Oil.

The John F. Kennedy Center for the Performing Arts. The Kennedy Center in Washington, which was begun in 1964, also has considerable influence on the arts in America. It describes itself as a "national showcase for the performing arts" (music, opera, drama, dance). It is officially part of the Smithsonian Institution, but it is administered separately by a forty-five-member board, most of whom are appointed by the President. The board is largely "political" in origin and includes:

Roger L. Stevens. Chairman of the board of the John F. Kennedy Center for the Performing Arts. Producer of *West Side Story, Cat on a Hot Tin Roof, Bus Stop, Tea and Sympathy, A Man for All Seasons*. Former chairman of the National Endowment for the Arts. A director of the Metropolitan Opera.

Mrs. Bob Hope. Spouse of the prominent entertainer and heavy financial contributor to political campaigns.

Joan Mondale. Spouse of the former vice-president.

Cary Grant. Actor.

Mrs. J.W. Marriott. Spouse of the president of Marriott Motor Hotels, a heavy financial contributor to political candidates.

Patricia Roberts Harris. Former secretary of Health, Education and Welfare; and senior partner in a top Washington law firm.

Mrs. Jean Kennedy Smith. Sister of John F., Robert F., and Edward M. Kennedy.

THE CIVIC ASSOCIATIONS

Our judgments about the power and influence of civic associations are necessarily qualitative, as they were for cultural organizations. We shall focus particular attention on the political power of the nation's leading policy-planning organizations—the Council on Foreign Relations, the Business Roundtable, and the Brookings Institution—both in this chapter and later in Chapter 9. These organizations are central coordinating mechanisms in national policy-making. They bring together people in top positions from the corporate world, the universities, the law firms, and the government to develop explicit policies and programs for submission to Congress, the President, and the nation.

The Council on Foreign Relations. The most influential policy-planning group in foreign affairs is the Council on Foreign Relations. The origins of the CFR go back to the Versailles Treaty in 1919 ending World War I. Some Americans, including Woodrow Wilson's key adviser, Edward M. House, believed that top leadership in the United States was not sufficiently informed about world affairs. The Council on Foreign Relations was founded in 1921 and supported by grants from the Rockefeller and Carnegie foundations and later the Ford Foundation. Its early directors were internationally minded Wall Street corporation lawyers such as Elihu Root (who was secretary of state), John W. Davis (1924 Democratic presidential nominee), and Paul Cravath (founder of the famous law firm of Cravath, Swaine & Moore), as well as Herbert Hoover (later to become President), Yale University president Charles Seymour, Harvard professor Archibald Cary Coolidge, and Columbia professor James T. Shotwell.

The CFR is designed to build consensus among elites on foreign policy questions. It initiates new policy directions by first commissioning scholars to undertake investigations of foreign policy questions. Its studies are usually made with the financial support of foundations. Upon their completion, the CFR holds seminars and discussions among its members and between its members and top government officials.

CFR publishes the journal *Foreign Affairs*, considered throughout the world to be the unofficial mouthpiece of U.S. foreign policy. Few important initiatives in U.S. policy have not been first outlined in articles in this publication. It was in *Foreign Affairs* in 1947 that George F. Kennan, chief of the policy-planning staff of the State Department, writing under the pseudonym of "X," first announced U.S. intentions of "containing" Communist expansion in the world. Current CFR concerns, as reflected in the pages of *Foreign Affairs*, the *Annual Report*, and other public sources, are discussed in Chapter 9.

The CFR limits its membership to 2,200 individuals who are proposed by existing members and who meet "high admissions standards." There is a long waiting list of individuals seeking membership in this prestigious organization. Broadly categorized, the membership profile look like this:[10]

Business and banking executives	25%
Academic scholars and administrators	21
U.S. government officials	14
Foundation, nonprofit administrators	19
Journalists, media executives	11
Lawyers	9
Other	1

The CFR's list of former members includes every person of influence in foreign affairs from Elihu Root, Henry Stimson, John Foster Dulles, Dean Acheson, Robert Lovett, George F. Kennan, Averill Harriman, and Dean Rusk, to Henry Kissinger, Cyrus Vance, Alexander Haig, George Schultz, and George Bush. The CFR describes itself as "a unique forum for bringing together leaders from the academic, public, and private worlds."

For almost two decades the CFR chairman was David Rockefeller, then chairman of the board of Chase Manhattan Bank (see Chapter 6). The international investment activity of Chase and the foreign policy influence and expertise of CFR dovetailed neatly in the person of the chairman. Rockefeller became honorary chairman in 1985 and turned over the reins of power to Peter G. Peterson. The CFR board of directors has always been a compendium of power and prestige:

Peter G. Peterson. Chairman of the board of the CFR. Former chairman and chief executive officer of Lehman Brothers, Wall Street investment firm. Former chairman of Bell and Howell Co., and former secretary of commerce. A director of

[10] Council on Foreign Relations, *Annual Report*, 1993, p. 105.

Minnesota Mining & Mfg., General Foods, and the Rockefeller Center; and a trustee of the Committee on Economic Development and the Museum of Modern Art.

Cyrus R. Vance. Director emeritus of CFR. Former secretary of state. Former chairman of the Rockefeller Foundation; senior partner in the prestigious Wall Street law firm of Simpson, Thacher & Bartlett.

Clifton R. Wharton, Jr. Chairman of TIAA-CREF insurance. Former chancellor of the State University of New York; and a director of Ford Motor Co. and the New York Stock Exchange.

B.R. Inman. Chairman of the board of Westmark. Former deputy director of the CIA and former director of the National Security Agency. Admiral, U.S. Navy. Named secretary of defense to replace Les Aspin in January 1994, but withdrew.

Paul A. Volcker. Former chairman of the Federal Reserve Board.

James E. Burke. Former chairman and chief executive officer of Johnson & Johnson; and a director of IBM and Prudential Insurance; a member of the Trilateral Commission.

John L. Clendenin. Chairman and chief executive officer of Bell South Corp.; and a director of Equifax, Wachovia, Coca-Cola, and the New York Stock Exchange.

Robert F. Erburu. Chairman and chief executive officer of Times-Mirror Co., Los Angeles; and a trustee of Brookings Institution, Hewlett Foundation, and J. Paul Getty Trust.

James R. Houghton. Chairman and chief executive officer Corning Glass Co., and a director or Metropolitan Life, J.P. Morgan, Dow-Corning; a trustee of the Metropolitan Museum of Art; and a member of the Trilateral Commission.

The Business Roundtable. The Business Roundtable provides direct representation of the chief executive officers of the nation's 200 largest corporations in the policy process. Unlike other policy-planning groups, which emphasize policy formation and consensus-building, the Roundtable engages in direct lobbying on behalf of specific bills it wants passed by the Congress and supported by the President.

The Roundtable has formed task forces on a wide variety of policy issues—antitrust, energy, environment, inflation, government regulation, health, social security, taxation, welfare, and so on. These task forces submit their policy recommendations to a powerful policy committee. The strength of the organization is derived from the willingness of its member chiefs to appear *in person* in Washington. In 1993 its leadership consisted of the following individuals, together with fifty other chairmen and CEOs of the largest corporations, banks, utilities, and investment firms that serve on its policy committee:

John D. Ong. Chairman of the Business Roundtable and chairman and chief executive officer of B.F. Goodrich.

Robert E. Allen. Chairman of the board of AT&T.

Charles A. Corry.   Chairman of the board of USX.

Richard C. Mahoney.   Chairman of the board of Monsanto.

Robert C. Winters.   Chairman of the board of Prudential Insurance.

The Brookings Institution.   Over the years, the foremost policy-planning group in domestic affairs has been the Brookings Institution. Since the 1960s, it has overshadowed the CED (Council on Economic Development), the American Enterprise Institution, the American Assembly, the Twentieth Century Fund, the Urban Institute, and all other policy-planning groups. Brookings has been extremely influential in planning the war on poverty, welfare reform, national health care, defense programs, and taxation programs. The Brookings Institution is generally regarded as moderate-to-liberal in its policy orientation. The American Enterprise Institute (AEI) was reorganized in the 1970s to try to offset Brookings' influence by providing moderate-to-conservative advice on public policy. While the AEI enjoyed a resurgence in Washington in the Reagan administration, its long-term influence was no match for the well-established Brookings Institution.

The Brookings Institution's trustees today are as impressive a group of top elites as assembled anywhere:

Louis W. Cabot.   Honorary trustee and former chairman of the Brookings Institution. Chairman of the board of the Cabot Corporation. Served as director of Owens-Corning Fiberglas and New England Telephone, as chairman of the Federal Reserve Bank of Boston, and as a trustee of the Carnegie Corporation, M.I.T., and Northeastern University; a member of the Council on Foreign Relations. Ancestors discovered America.

Robert V. Roosa.   Honorary trustee and former chairman of the Brookings Institution. Senior partner, Brown Brothers, Harriman & Co. (New York investment firm). Served as a director of American Express, Anaconda Copper, Owens-Corning Fiberglas, and Texaco. He was a former undersecretary of the treasury and a director of the Council on Foreign Relations.

Alden W. Clausen.   Former chairman and chief executive officer of BankAmerica; former president of the World Bank.

Vernon E. Jordan, Jr.   Former president of the National Urban League; and a director of American Express, Bankers Trust, Union Carbide, J.C. Penney, Xerox, and Corning Glass.

Thomas G. Labrecque.   Chairman and chief executive officer, Chase Manhattan.

Donald F. McHenry.   Former UN Ambassador; and a director of AT&T, International Paper, Coca-Cola, Bank of Boston, and Smith Kline Beecham.

David Rockefeller, Jr.   Son of David Rockefeller.

If some names are growing repetitious by now, it is for good reason. Those who occupy top posts in the leading corporate, governmental, and mass media institutions are frequently the same individuals who direct the leading foundations, cultural organizations, and civic associations. Our purpose in "naming names," even when they become repetitive, is to suggest the frequent interlocking of top elites in different institutional sectors. In Chapter 6, we will examine interlocking in greater detail.

THE UNIVERSITIES

The growth of public higher education since World War II—the creation of vast state university, state college, and community college systems in every state in the nation—has diminished the influence of the prestigious private universities. There are now nearly 3,000 separate institutions of higher education in America, enrolling over 12 million students—more than one half of all high school graduates. Only about one quarter of these students are enrolled in *private* colleges and universities. Moreover, some leading public universities—for example, the University of California at Berkeley and the

TABLE 5–3   Private Universities with Largest Endowments

Rank (by Assets)	Foundation	Assets ($ millions)
1	Harvard University	$5,118
2	Princeton University	3,003
3	Yale University	2,833
4	Stanford University	2,428
5	Columbia University	1,683
6	Emory University	1,658
7	Massachusetts Institute of Technology	1,589
8	Washington University	1,533
9	Rice University	1,254
10	Northwestern University	1,198
11	University of Chicago	1,151
12	Cornell University	1,078
13	University of Pennsylvania	974
14	University of Notre Dame	726
15	Vanderbilt University	668
16	Dartmouth College	661
17	Johns Hopkins University	639
18	University of Rochester	619
19	New York University	615
20	University of Southern California	588
21	California Institute of Technology	583
22	Duke University	555
23	Rockefeller University	551
24	Case Western Reserve University	499
25	Brown University	484

SOURCE: *Chronicles of Higher Education*, February 10, 1993, p. A30.

University of Michigan—are consistently ranked with the prestigious private universities in terms of the quality of higher education offered. Thus, the leading private universities in the nation no longer exercise the dominant influence over higher education that they did before World War II.

Nonetheless, among private colleges and universities it is possible to identify those few top institutions which control most of the resources available to private higher education. The twenty-five universities listed in Table 5–3 control two thirds of all private endowment funds in higher education; this was the formal basis for their selection. (Only three *public* universities rank with the top twenty-five private universities in endowments. These are the University of Texas, the University of California, and the University of Virginia.) Moreover, they are consistently ranked among the "best" educational institutions in the nation. Finally, as we will see, a disproportionate number of the nation's top leaders attended one or another of these institutions.

The trustees of private universities are generally charged with the responsibilities of selecting the president, setting broad policy goals and direction for their institutions, and securing financing for growth and development. The prestigious universities, of course, recruit top elites to their governing boards, including:

YALE UNIVERSITY

Sid R. Bass. Independent oil operations (see Chapter 8).

David L. Boren. U.S. Senate, chairman of the Senate Intelligence Committee.

Vernon R. Loucks, Jr. Chairman of Baxter International (drug co.); and a director of Dun & Bradstreet, Nestlé, Quaker Oats, Emerson Electric, Anheuser-Busch, and the Business Roundtable.

Henry B. Schacht. Chairman of Cummins Engine; and a director of AT&T, CBS, and Chase Manhattan; and a trustee of the Brookings Institution.

Richard T. Franke. Chairman of John Nuveen & Co. (investments).

HARVARD UNIVERSITY

Elizabeth H. Dole. President of the American Red Cross and former secretary of transportation.

Hanna H. Gray. President of the University of Chicago; and a director of Cummins Engine, J.P. Morgan, and Atlantic Richfield.

Arthur A. Hartman. Former U.S. ambassador to the Soviet Union; and a director of Hartford Insurance, Dreyfus Funds, American Telephone and Electronics, and First American Bank of New York.

Theodore M. Hesburgh. Former president of Notre Dame and a director of Chase Manhattan.

John Lithgow. Actor.

Thomas S. Murphy. Chairman of the board of Capital Cities–ABC Inc.

We have already acknowledged the growing importance in higher education of the nation's leading *state* universities. Their rise to prominence since World War II has distributed power in education more widely and opened positions of authority to persons whose elite credentials are not necessarily as impressive as the ones we have seen again and again in our lists of top leaders. State boards of regents for state universities are generally composed of individuals who would probably *not* be among the top institutional elites according to our definition in Chapter 1. Many of these regents hold directorships in smaller corporations, smaller banks, and smaller utility companies; they frequently have held state rather than national political office; their legal, civic, cultural, and foundation affiliations are with *state* institutions rather than with prestigious and powerful *national* institutions.[11]

University presidents, particularly the presidents of the nation's top institutions, are frequently called upon to serve as trustees or directors of other institutions and to serve in high government posts. Most university presidents today have come up through the ranks of academic administration, suggesting that universities themselves may offer a channel for upward mobility into the nation's elite. We must keep in mind, however, that presidents are hired and fired by the trustees, not by students or faculty.

THE AMERICAN ESTABLISHMENT

Is there a unifying "Establishment" in this nation, separate from business and government, which seeks to use its power, prestige, and wealth to further its own vision of America? The notion of an Establishment—with its old school ties, inherited wealth, upper-class life style, position, and privilege—flourishes even in a democratic society. Harvard historian Mark Silk and his brother, *New York Times* columnist Leonard Silk, write:

> Although the origins of the Establishment are ecclesiastical and aristocratic, in America it is firmly joined to both democratic and capitalist institutions. But its ambitions go beyond: it seeks to protect and advance social, moral, and aesthetic values that transcend the interests of any single person, economic group, or political constituency or organization; it affects to be a harmonizer, an arbiter, a wise instructor of the nation—and particularly of its political and business leaders.[12]

This Establishment traces its roots, and even its name, to the established church in early Massachusetts. The nation's earliest democrats sought to ensure that there would be "no establishment of religion" by writing those words into the First Amendment of the Constitution. But in the early years

[11] David N. Smith, *Who Rules the Universities?* (New York: Monthly Review Press, 1974), pp. 30–33.

[12] Leonard Silk and Mark Silk, *The American Establishment* (New York: Basic Books, 1980), p. 325.

the First Amendment applied only to the national government and not to the states; Massachusetts supported the established Congregationalist church well into the nineteenth century. Harvard College was the center of established religion, even after the more rigid Calvinists abandoned it in favor of more orthodox instruction at newer Yale College. This early schism in the established church was partly due to the greater openness, humanism, and tolerance of dissent at Harvard, traits which are supposed to characterize the Establishment even today.[13]

The Establishment today is said to "inhabit" the nation's most influential institutions. The Establishment is not an institution itself but rather a "collective entity" or "third force" (the other two being business and government) which links together various institutions in separate segments of society. The Establishment is concerned with maintaining a public ethos—a civic morality emphasizing toleration, individual liberty, and goodness. The institutions which it "inhabits" are said to be:

Harvard University

New York Times

Ford Foundation

Brookings Institution

Council on Foreign Relations

Committee for Economic Development

Not every person associated with these institutions is a member of the Establishment. And there are other institutions which also possess Establishment connections:

Yale University

Princeton University

Columbia University

University of Chicago

Stanford University

Carnegie Endowment for International Peace

RAND Corporation

Twentieth Century Fund

Russell Sage Foundation

Century Club

[13] According to the Silks, Harvard represented a middle religious ground between the Calvinists at Yale and the Enlightenment Deists of the Virginia planters, notably Thomas Jefferson. Only six of the fourteen faculty members at Harvard in 1831 were Unitarians; the faculty even included three Roman Catholics and a Quaker. See Silk and Silk, ibid., p. 13.

> Metropolitan Museum of Art
>
> Museum of Modern Art
>
> Metropolitan Opera[14]

But these institutions do not define the Establishment. Instead, the Establishment is defined as "a national force, outside government, dedicated to truth, liberty, and however defined, the broad public interest."[15]

SUMMARY

Using the term *civic establishment,* we refer collectively to the nation's top law firms, its major foundations, its national cultural institutions, influential civic organizations, and prestigious private universities. At the top of the legal profession, the senior partners of the nation's best-known New York and Washington law firms exercise great power as legal representatives of the nation's largest corporations. These superlawyers are frequently called upon for governmental leadership, particularly when high-level, delicate negotiations are required. Most superlawyers have been educated at Ivy League law schools and served apprenticeships in governmental agencies before entering law firms.

The power of the nation's large foundations rests in their ability to channel corporate and personal wealth into the policy-making process. They do this by providing financial support and direction over university research and the activities of policy-oriented, civic associations. There is great concentration of foundation assets. There is also a great deal of overlapping among the directorates of the leading foundations and corporate and financial institutions, the mass media, universities, policy-planning groups, and government.

A small number of cultural organizations exercise great power over the nation's art, music, theater, and ballet. A brief glance at the directors of these institutions confirms that they are the same group of people identified earlier as influential in business, finance, government, and the mass media.

The civic associations, particularly the leading policy-planning groups—the Council on Foreign Relations, the Business Roundtable, and the Brookings Institution—play key roles in national policy-making. They bring together leaders at the top of various institutional sectors of society to formulate recommendations on major policy innovations. More will be said about the important role of policy-planning groups in Chapter 9. But we have noted here that the directors of these groups are top leaders in industry, finance, government, the mass media, law, and the universities.

There may not be as much concentration of power in higher education

---

[14] Ibid., p. 18.

[15] Ibid., p. 20.

as in other sectors of American life. The development of state universities since World War II has diminished the influence of the private, Ivy League–type universities. However, among *private* universities, only twenty-five institutions control over two thirds of all private endowment funds.

Commentators have speculated about an American "Establishment," separate from business and government, which inhabits influential civic organizations, universities, and foundations.

6 Interlocking and Specialization at the Top

CONVERGENCE OR SPECIALIZATION AT THE TOP?

Is there a convergence of power at the top of an institutional structure in America, with a single group of individuals—recruited primarily from industry and finance—who occupy top positions in corporations, education, government, foundations, civic and cultural affairs, and the military? Or are there separate institutional structures, with elites in each sector of society having little or no overlap in authority and many separate channels of recruitment? In short, is the structure of power in America a hierarchy or a polyarchy?

Social scientists have differed over this important question, and at least two varieties of leadership models can be identified in the literature on power.[1] A *hierarchical model* implies that a relatively small group of individuals exercises authority in a wide variety of institutions—forming what has been called a "power elite." In contrast, a *polyarchical model* implies that different groups of individuals exercise power in various sectors of society and acquire power in separate ways.

The hierarchical model derives from the familiar "elitist" literature on power. Sociologist C. Wright Mills argues that "the leading men in each of the three domains of power—the warlords, the corporation chieftains, and the political directorate—tend to come together to form the power elite of America."[2] According to Mills, leadership in America constitutes "an intricate set of overlapping cliques." And Floyd Hunter, in his study *Top Leadership, U.S.A.*, concludes: "Out of several hundred persons named from all sources, between one hundred and two hundred were consistently chosen as top leaders and considered by all informants to be of national policy-making stature."[3] The

[1] This literature is voluminous, and any characterization of positions results in some oversimplification. For good summary statements of positions, see the works of Mills, Hunter, Kolko, and Dahl, cited elsewhere in chapter notes. See also Nelson Polsby, *Community Power and Political Theory*, 2nd ed. (New Haven: Yale University Press, 1980); David Ricci, *Community Power and Democratic Theory*, (New York: Random House, 1971); and Robert J. Waste, ed., *Community Power: Directions for Future Research* (Beverly Hills, Calif.: Sage, 1986).

[2] C. Wright Mills, *The Power Elite* (New York: Oxford University Press, 1956), p. 9.

[3] Floyd Hunter, *Top Leadership, U.S.A.* (Chapel Hill: University of North Carolina Press, 1959), p. 176.

notion of interlocking directorates has widespread currency in the power elite literature. Gabriel Kolko writes that "interlocking directorates, whereby a director of one corporation also sits on the board of one or more other corporations, are a key device for concentrating corporate power. . . ."[4] The hierarchical model also implies that top leaders in all sectors of society—including government, education, civic and cultural affairs, and politics—are recruited primarily from business and finance.

In contrast, pluralist writers have implied a polyarchical leadership structure, with different sets of leaders in different sectors of society and little or no overlap, except perhaps by elected officials responsible to the general public. According to this view, leadership is exercised in large measure by "specialists" who limit their participation to a narrow range of societal decisions. These specialists are believed to be recruited through separate channels—not drawn exclusively from business and finance. Generally, pluralists have praised the dispersion of authority in American society. Robert A. Dahl writes: "The theory and practice of American pluralism tends to assume, as I see it, that the existence of multiple centers of power, none of which is wholly sovereign, will help (may indeed be necessary) to tame power, to secure the consent of all, and to settle conflicts peacefully."[5]

SOURCES OF ELITE COHESION

It is the responsibility of elitist scholars to demonstrate the cohesiveness of the nation's leadership, and to counter the pluralist argument that elites are plural, specialized, relatively independent, frequently competitive, and occasionally conflictual. Elite theorists postulate several different mechanisms which provide the necessary cohesion among the leaders of different institutions in American society.

Interlocking Directorates.   Institutions are linked by a network of interlocking memberships, whereby the directors of various industrial corporations, banks, foundations, newspapers and television networks, civic and cultural corporations sit on the governing boards of more than one institution. Banks and other financial institutions are often considered central to this network. Banks may function to mediate in intercorporate conflict since they usually have investments in many different segments of the economy.[6]

[4] Gabriel Kolko, *Wealth and Power in America* (New York: Praeger, 1962), p. 57.

[5] Robert A. Dahl, *Pluralist Democracy in the United States* (Chicago: Rand McNally, 1967), p. 24.

[6] See, for example, Beth Mintz and Michael Swartz, "Interlocking Directorates and Interest Group Formations," *American Sociological Review*, 46 (1981), 851–69; Ronald F. Burt, "A Structural Theory of Interlocking Corporate Directorates," *Social Networks*, 1 (1979), 415–35; Ronald S. Burt, et al., "Testing a Structural Theory of Corporate Cooptation: Intraorganizational Directorate Ties," *American Sociological Review*, 45 (1980), 821–41; Thomas Koenig, "Interlocking Corporate Directorates as a Social Network," *American Journal of Economics and Sociology*, 40 (1981), 37–50.

An Inner Group.   An "inner group" thesis suggests that even though most corporate leaders have a direct interest in only a single corporation, a relatively small group of business leaders have broader interests which transcend the boundaries of industrial corporations to encompass the long-term interests of business as a whole.[7]

Institutional Experiences.   In addition to *concurrent* interlocking where individuals hold more than one top institutional post at the same time, members of the elite may enjoy *sequential* interlocking, where individuals hold a number of leadership positions over their lifetime. This is especially important in securing cohesion between governmental and corporate elites. Government officials are usually expected to resign their corporate directorships when they assume a government post, but many top government leaders bring their corporate experience to government and return to corporate life after their government work.

Class Backgrounds, Education, Clubs, Kinship.   Still another source of cohesion may be the shared social class backgrounds which transmit relatively uniform upper- and upper-middle-class values and aspirations to future elite members. These class values are transmitted through uniform educational experiences for a large proportion of elite members, including attendance at prestigious private prep schools and Ivy League universities. These social class and educational ties are frequently reinforced through marriage and family relations. Finally, elite cohesion is abetted through a network of private prestigious social clubs, which purposefully encourage interaction and solidarity within the elite.[8]

Shared Attitudes and Beliefs.   The result of shared social class backgrounds, similar educational experiences, and numerous social, family, and business ties, is broad agreement on societal values. Elites agree on the goals and purposes of public policies; disagreement is limited to specific means for achieving these goals and purposes. Elite consensus includes support for the free enterprise system, limited government, and rewards based on individual merit; a devotion to personal liberty, due process of law, and equality of opportunity; opposition to discrimination; a desire to mitigate the worst effects of poverty and ill-health; an impulse to do good and instill middle-class values in all citizens; a desire to exercise influence in international affairs and spread Western cultural values throughout the world. The range of disagree-

---

[7] See, for example, Maurice Zeitlin, "Corporate Ownership and Control," *American Journal of Sociology*, 79 (1974), 1073–119; Michael Useem, "The Inner Group of the American Capitalist Class," *Social Problems*, 25 (1978), 225–40.

[8] See, for example, G. William Domhoff, *The Bohemian Grove and Other Retreats* (New York: Harper and Row, 1974); Gwen Moore and Richard D. Alba, "Class and Prestige Origins in the American Elite," in *Social Structure and Network Analysis*, eds. Peter V. Marsden and Nan Lin (Beverly Hills, Calif.: Sage, 1982).

ment among elites is relatively narrow compared to this broad consensus on fundamental values.[9]

Private Policy-Planning Organizations. Planning, coordination, and consensus-building in national policy is achieved through a complex process which ensures that major policy directions are determined *before* the "proximate policy-makers"—Congress, the White House, administrative agencies, and so on—become directly involved. Central to this process are a small number of private policy-planning organizations. These organizations bring together leaders from corporate and financial institutions, universities, foundations, the mass media, the top law firms, and government, in order to set the agenda of national decision-making, direct research into policy questions, and most important, try to reach a consensus on the major policy directions for the nation.[10]

These potential sources of elite cohesion are discussed in the remainder of this volume. In Chapter 6 we examine interlocking directorates, the "inner group," and the institutional experiences of our national elite. In Chapter 7 we examine the social class origins of the top elites, their educational experiences, and their social activities. In Chapter 8, we assess the extent of consensus and factionalism among the nation's elite. In Chapter 9 we describe the policy-planning process and the role of the private policy-planning organizations.

"INTERLOCKERS" AND "SPECIALISTS"

Earlier we identified 7,314 top institutional positions in 12 different sectors of society which we defined as the nation's elite (see Chapter 1). Individuals in these positions control more than one half of the nation's industrial and financial assets, nearly half of all the assets of private foundations, and two thirds of the assets of private universities; they control the television networks, the news services, and leading newspapers; they control the most prestigious civic and cultural organizations; and they direct the activities of the executive, legislative, and judicial branches of the national government.

These 7,314 top positions were occupied by 5,778 individuals. In other words, there were fewer top individuals than top positions—indicating multiple holding of top positions by some individuals. Table 6–1 presents specific data on this phenomenon, which we shall call *interlocking*.

Approximately 15 percent of those we identified as the nation's elite

---

[9] See Richard Hofstadter, *The American Political Tradition* (New York: Knopf, 1948).

[10] See, for example, Thomas R. Dye, "Oligarchic Tendencies in National Policy-Making," *Journal of Politics*, 40 (May 1978), 309–31; G. William Domhoff, *The Powers That Be* (New York: Vintage, 1979); Michael Useem, "The Social Organization of the American Business Elite and Participation of Corporate Directors in the Governance of American Institutions," *American Sociological Review*, 44 (August 1979), 553–72.

TABLE 6–1   Interlocking and Specialization in Top Institutional Positions

	Number of Top Institutional Positions	Percent of Total Positions	Number of Individuals in Top Positions	Percent of Total Individuals
Total	7,314	100.0	5,778	100.0
Specializd	4,981	68.1	4,911	85.0
Interlocked	2,333	31.9	867	15.0
Number of Interlocks:				
Two	1,046	14.3	520	9.0
Three	614	8.4	202	3.5
Four	278	3.8	69	1.2
Five	197	2.7	40	0.7
Six	110	1.5	17	0.3
Seven or more	88	1.2	11	0.2

held more than one top position at a time. These are our "interlockers." Most of them held only two top positions, but some held five, six, seven, or more! Eighty-five percent of the people at the top are "specialists"—individuals who hold only one top position. Many of these specialists hold other corporate directorships, governmental posts, or civic, cultural, or university positions, but not *top* positions as we have defined them. Thus, our specialists may assume a wide variety of lesser positions: directorships in corporations below the top 100; positions on governmental boards and commissions; trusteeships of less well-known colleges and foundations; and directorships of less influential civic and cultural organizations. We will also observe that over a lifetime, many specialists tend to hold a number of top positions serially, rather than concurrently.

About 32 percent of all top positions are interlocked with other top positions. The reason that 32 percent of the top positions are interlocked, but only 15 percent of the top individuals hold more than one position, is that some individuals are "multiple interlockers"—they hold three or more positions.

The multiple interlockers turned out to be individuals of considerable stature, as the list that follows indicates. This list was compiled from extensive data collected and analyzed in 1980–81. These individuals comprised our top group of multiple interlockers—individuals occupying *six or more* top positions concurrently. By any criteria whatsoever, these individuals must be judged important figures in America. The fact that our investigation of positional overlap revealed such impressive names lends some face validity to the assertion that interlocking is a source of authority and power in society. However, despite the impressive concentration of interlocking authority in this top group, it should be remembered that most of the remaining 85 percent of top position holders were specialists.

A. Robert Abboud. President, Occidental Petroleum. Former chairman of the board of First National Bank of Chicago; a director of Hart Schaffner & Marx, Inland Steel, Standard Oil of Indiana. A director of the Committee for Economic Development, a trustee of the University of Chicago, and member of the Council on Foreign Relations.

J. Paul Austin. Chairman of the board of Coca-Cola Co. A director of Federated Department Stores, Morgan Guaranty Trust, General Electric, Trust Company of Georgia, Dow Jones & Co.

Thornton Bradshaw. Chairman of the board of RCA. Former president of Atlantic Richfield. A director of Security Pacific Corp., NBC, Los Angeles Philharmonic, Aspen Institute, American Petroleum Institute; and a trustee of Howard University.

Andrew F. Brimmer. President of Brimmer & Co. A director of BankAmerica, American Security Bank, International Harvester, United Airlines, Du Pont Corp., the Trilateral Commission, the Committee for Economic Development, the Ford Foundation, the Urban League, and the Council on Foreign Relations.

Ralph Manning Brown, Jr. Chairman of the board of New York Life Insurance Co. A director of Union Carbide, Morgan Guaranty Trust, A&P, and Avon Products. A trustee of the Sloan Foundation, and Princeton University; and a director of the Metropolitan Museum of Art.

Edward W. Carter. Chairman of the board of Carter Hawley Hale Stores (including Nieman Marcus, Bergdorf, and so on). A director of AT&T, Del Monte, Lockheed Corp., Pacific Mutual Life Insurance, Southern California Edison, Western Bancorp. A trustee of the Brookings Institution, the Committee for Economic Development, Rockefeller University, Howard University.

Frank T. Cary. Chairman of the board of IBM. A director of J.P. Morgan & Co. and the American Broadcasting Company. A director of the Brookings Institution, the Business Roundtable, and the Committee for Economic Development.

Catherine B. Cleary. Former chairman of the board of First Wisconsin Corp. A director of Northwestern Mutual Life Insurance, General Motors, Kohle Corp., Kraft.

William T. Coleman. Former secretary of transportation. Washington attorney. A director of IBM, Chase Manhattan, Pepsi Co., American Can, Pan American World Airways, Philadelphia Electric. A trustee of the Brookings Institution and Harvard University, and a member of the Trilateral Commission and the Council on Foreign Relations.

John D. Debutts. Former chairman of the board of AT&T. A director of Citicorp, U.S. Steel, Kraft, General Motors, Hospital Corporation of America. A trustee of the Brookings Institution, the Business Roundtable, the Duke Endowment, and Duke University.

Clifton C. Garvin. Chairman of the board of Exxon. A director of Citicorp, Pepsi Co., Sperry Rand. Chairman of the Business Roundtable. A trustee of the Committee for Economic Development, Memorial Sloan-Kettering Cancer Center, and Vanderbilt University.

J. Richardson Dilworth. Chairman of the board of the Rockefeller Center. A director of R.H. Macy & Co., Chase Manhattan, Chrysler. A trustee of colonial Williamsburg and Yale University.

Harry Jack Gray. Chairman of the board of United Technologies. A director of Exxon, Citicorp, Aetna Life & Casualty, Carrier Corp., Otis Elevator, Pratt & Whitney.

Fred L. Hartley. Chairman of the board of Union Oil Co. A director of Rockwell International, Union Bank, Daytona International Speedway. A trustee of Cal Tech Pepperdine University, the Council on Foreign Relations, and the Committee for Economic Development.

Gabriel Hauge. Former chairman of the board of Manufacturers Hanover Trust. A director of New York Life Insurance, Amax, N.Y. Telephone, Chrysler, Royal Dutch Petroleum. A trustee of the Committee for Economic Development and the Julliard School of Music.

Robert S. Hatfield. Chairman of the board of Continental Can. A director of Citicorp, Johnson & Johnson, the New York Stock Exchange, Kennecott Copper, General Motors, Eastman Kodak. A director of the Business Roundtable; and a trustee of the Committee for Economic Development and Cornell University.

Carla A. Hills. Former secretary of Housing and Urban Development. Washington attorney. A director of IBM, American Airlines, Signal Companies, Standard Oil of California. A trustee of the Brookings Institution and the University of Southern California.

George P. Jenkins. Chairman of the board of Metropolitan Life. A director of Citicorp, ABC, St. Regis Paper, Bethlehem Steel, W.R. Grace & Co.; and a trustee of the University of Southern California.

Howard W. Johnson. Former president of M.I.T. A director of Federated Department Stores, John Hancock Mutual Life Insurance, Du Pont Corp., Morgan Guaranty Trust, Champion International. A trustee of the Committee for Economic Development and Radcliffe College.

J. Paul Lyet. Chairman of the board of Sperry Rand Corp. A director of Armstrong Cork, Continental Can, Manufacturers Hanover Trust, Hershey Trust, Eastman Kodak; and a trustee of the University of Pennsylvania.

Lee L. Morgan. Chairman of the board of Caterpillar Tractor. A director of 3M, Commercial National Bank, Mobil Oil.

Ellmore C. Patterson. Former chairman of the board of Morgan Guaranty Trust. A director of General Motors, Bethlehem Steel, Acheson Topeka and Santa Fe Railroad, J.P. Morgan & Co., Standard Brands, and Comsat. A trustee of the Alfred P. Sloan Foundation, Memorial Sloan-Kettering Cancer Center, the University of Chicago, and M.I.T.

Donald S. Perkins. Chairman of the board of Jewel Companies. A director of Time Inc., AT&T, Inland Steel, Corning Glass, Cummins Engine. A trustee of the Ford Foundation, the Business Roundtable, and the Brookings Institution.

Richard S. Perkins. Former chairman of the board of Citicorp. A director of Allied Chemical, New York Life, Southern Pacific, ITT, the Hospital Corporation of America. A trustee of Chapin School, Miss Porter's School, and the Metropolitan Museum of Art.

Peter G. Peterson. Chairman of the board of Lehman Brothers, Kuhn Loeb Inc. Former secretary of commerce. A director of RCA, Black & Decker, Cities Service, 3M Co., General Foods, Federated Department Stores. A trustee of the

Museum of Modern Art, the Council on Foreign Relations, and the University of Chicago.

Edmund T. Pratt. Chairman of the board of IBM. A director of Chase Manhattan, International Paper Co., General Motors. A trustee of the Committee for Economic Development and Duke University.

David Rockefeller. Chairman of the board of Chase Manhattan Bank. Chairman of the Council on Foreign Relations. A trustee of the Rockefeller Foundation, the Museum of Modern Art, Rockefeller Center, Downtown Lower Manhattan Association, the University of Chicago, and Howard University.

Robert V. Roosa. Senior partner, Brown Brothers, Harriman & Co. A director of American Express, Owens-Corning Fiberglas, Texaco. Chairman of the Brookings Institution. A trustee of the Rockefeller Foundation, Memorial Sloan-Kettering Cancer Center, and the National Bureau of Economic Research.

Irving Saul Shapiro. Chairman of the board of E.I. du Pont de Nemours & Co. A director of Citicorp, Bank of Delaware, IBM, Continental American Insurance. A director of the Business Roundtable; and a trustee of the Conference Board, the University of Delaware, and the Ford Foundation.

Richard R. Shinn. Chairman of the board of Metropolitan Life Insurance. A director of Allied Chemical, Sperry Rand, Norton Simon. A director of the Business Roundtable and the Committee for Economic Development. A trustee of the Metropolitan Opera and the University of Pennsylvania.

Rawleigh Warner. Chairman of the board of Mobil Oil. A director of Caterpillar Tractor, AT&T, Chemical Bank of New York, American Express, Wheelabrator. A trustee of Princeton University.

THE INNER GROUP: AN ELITE WITHIN THE ELITE

Let us label these multiple interlockers as the *inner group* of the nation's institutional leadership.[11] These individuals are only a small percentage of the total number of leaders we identified, but they are in a unique position to communicate and coordinate the activities of a variety of institutions. The members of the inner group have significant "connections" with corporations, banks, media, cultural organizations, universities, foundations, and civic associations. The inner group is really a metaphor, and the boundary between it and other top leaders is not sharp. The individuals listed here have *six* or more *top* institutional positions; they certainly can be thought of as the central core of the inner group. But we might also picture concentric rings surrounding the inner group—those persons with five, four, three, or two interlocking positions.

The existence of a "core elite," or an "elite within the elite," has been suggested by several social scientists.[12] However, there is no clear-cut defini-

---

[11] Maurice Zeitlin, "Corporate Ownership and Control," *American Journal of Sociology*, 79 (September 1974), 1073–119; Michael Patrick Allen, "Continuity and Change within the Core Corporate Elite," *Sociological Quarterly*, 19 (Autumn 1978), 510–21.

[12] W. Lloyd Warner and James D. Abegglen, *Big Business Leaders in America* (New York: Harper, 1955); Allen, "Continuity and Change within the Core Corporate Elite."

tion of these terms. Our notion of an *inner group* involves not only multiple directorships of large corporate and financial institutions but also the governance of large, influential foundations, universities, cultural organizations, and civic associations.

Members of the inner group are differentiated from other leaders in that their multiple position-holding encourages them to take a broader view of business problems. "They move from the industrial point of interest and outlook to the interest and outlook of the class of all big corporate property as a whole."[13] Indeed, members of the inner group cannot take narrow positions based upon the interests of a single firm, but instead they must consider the well-being of a wide range of American institutions.

Members of the inner group know each other socially. They come together not only in multiple corporate boardrooms but also at cultural and civic events, charitable endeavors, foundation meetings, and university trustee and alumni get-togethers. They are also members of the same exclusive *social clubs*—the Links, Century, Knickerbocker, Burning Tree, Metropolitan, Pacific Union.

Most importantly, the inner group plays a major role in linking the corporate world with government, foundations, universities, cultural organizations, and civic associations. Members of the inner group are highly valued and generally preferred as members, advisers, and trustees of government and nonprofit organizations. "The multiple corporate connections place inner group members in an exceptionally good position to help mobilize the resources of many firms on behalf of policies they favor—and institutions whose governance they assist—making inner group members preferable to other businessmen when appointments to positions of governance are decided."[14] Indeed, it turns out that multiple corporate directors have a participation rate in government and nonprofit organizations which is more than twice the participation rate of single directors (specialists).

However, interlocking of directorates appears to be declining modestly over time. In 1970, we estimated from our own data that about 20 percent of all top leaders were interlockers. In 1980, our estimate was only 15 percent. The 1990s have brought added responsibilities to the boardroom (see Chapter 2) and a resulting decline in the number of directorships an individual can comfortably handle. Leading business sources report a new reluctance on the part of corporate leaders to assume more than two corporate directorships at a time.[15] Thus, increasing proportions of top leaders are specialists.

[13] Mills, *The Power Elite*, p. 121.

[14] Useem, "The Social Organization of the American Business Elite," p. 557.

[15] See "Board Games," *Time*, February 8, 1993, pp. 54–55; "The King Is Dead," *Fortune*, January 11, 1993, pp. 34–40; however, for evidence that interlocking among all corporations remained fairly constant from 1935 to 1970, see Michael Patrick Allen, "The Structure of Interorganizational Elite Corporation: Interlocking Corporate Directorates," *American Sociological Review*, 39 (June 1974), 393–406.

TABLE 6–2 Institutional Experience of Top Leaders

	Corporate					Public Interest					Government		All
	Industry	Banking	Utilities	Insurance	Investment	Media	Law	Foundation	Education	Civic	Government	Military	
Average number of positions ever held:													
Total	10.5	6.6	10.9	9.1	4.6	7.1	7.9	10.2	7.9	11.4	8.0	1.0	9.3
Corporate	5.9	4.1	6.0	5.1	3.1	2.1	2.0	5.2	3.2	6.0	1.0	.0	5.2
Public interest	3.8	2.0	3.9	3.1	1.2	3.8	4.2	4.0	3.8	4.2	3.8	0.8	3.1
Governmental	.8	.5	1.0	.9	.3	1.2	1.7	1.0	.9	1.2	3.2	0.2	1.0
Percent having ever held positions in:													
Corporate	99.8	88.8	99.6	86.5	72.4	48.1	46.8	96.2	76.2	98.6	25.2	.0	80.2
Public interest	76.9	59.0	72.5	69.1	59.6	76.5	80.2	88.0	70.8	82.2	72.2	38.6	78.4
Governmental	39.2	24.8	40.6	38.0	19.2	40.2	56.5	45.1	42.5	58.6	76.6	14.5	42.3

PREVIOUS INSTITUTIONAL EXPERIENCE OF TOP LEADERS

How many positions of authority in all types of institutions have top leaders *ever held* in a lifetime? We carefully reviewed the biographies of our top position holders to see how many authoritative positions—president, director, trustee, and so on—were ever held by these people. Their record of leadership turned out to be truly impressive. Table 6–2 shows the average number of authoritative positions ever held by top leaders in each sector of society. The average corporate leader held 10.5 positions in a lifetime; the average foundation trustee, 10.2; the average civic group leader, 11.4; the average governmental leader, 8.0. (The only exception is military leaders, whose experience is generally limited to the military itself.) Of course, these positions are not all in *top-ranked* institutions. But it is clear that top leaders occupy a number of institutional positions in their lifetime.

Leaders in government have held somewhat fewer top positions in their lifetime than leaders in the corporate world, but nonetheless their record of leadership experience is impressive. However, governmental leaders tended to gain their experience in *governmental or public interest* positions—over 70 percent of governmental leaders had held previous governmental posts and had held posts in the public interest sector. Only about one quarter of top governmental elites had previously held any top positions in the corporate world.

The tradition of public service is very much alive among top institutional leaders in every sector. Both corporate and governmental elites reported one or more public appointments during their lifetime. Nearly 40 percent of corporate elites held at least one government post at some time during their careers.

As we might expect, corporate directorships are common among top leaders in industry, communications, utilities, and banking. It is common for these individuals to have held four or more directorships in a lifetime. In contrast, top government officials have *not* held many corporate directorships. Their experience in institutional positions is derived mainly from public service and government.

AT&T: EVIDENCE OF CONVERGENCE

Our aggregate data indicate that a majority of the people at the top are specialists, that corporate and governmental elites are not closely interlocked, and that there appear to be multiple, differentiated structures of power in America. Earlier we suggested that many corporate, governmental, and public interest leaders were self-made managerial elites rather than inheritors who started at the top. All of these findings tend to undermine confidence in the hierarchical model, at least as it is represented in the traditional power elite literature.

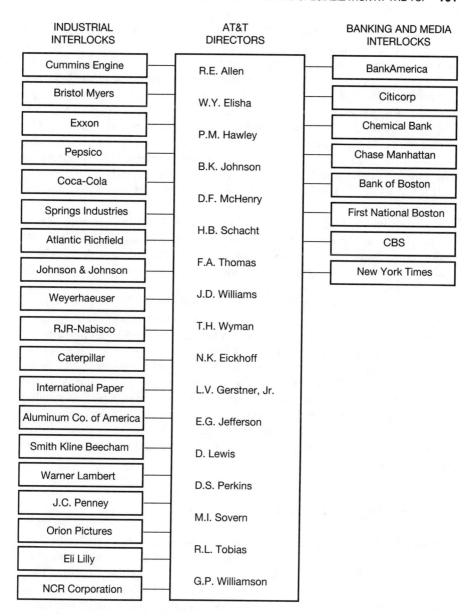

FIGURE 6–1   AT&T and Its Friends

Nonetheless, there are important concentrations of corporate power in America as evidenced in interlocking directorates of major corporations. Figure 6–1 is our own diagram of the interlocking of AT&T directors with industrial corporations, banks, and media companies in 1992.

It might be possible to greatly expand Figure 6–1 and observe all the corporate interlocks of corporations that interlock with AT&T. We might observe "indirect" interlocking of AT&T with any corporation that has an interlocking board member with any of the corporations in Figure 6–1. An indirect interlock does not mean that a director serves on two boards (this is a direct interlock); it means instead that a director of one corporation and a director of another both belong to the board of a third corporation. For example, AT&T and IBM are competitors in satellite communications. The AT&T and IBM boards are *not* interlocked. However, an AT&T director and an IBM director may meet on the board of an oil company. Is this evidence of collusion? Probably not. It requires "a touch of paranoia" to believe that indirect interlocks can create a concentration of power that would threaten the corporate structure.

The pattern of interlocking directorates with AT&T is illustrative of relationships and interests in the boardrooms of major corporations. AT&T, like many other giant corporations, has direct contacts with a wide variety of industrial corporations—oil, drugs, paper, foods, publishing, and so on—as well as banks.

The forcible break-up of AT&T, previously the world's largest corporation, significantly reduced concentration of resources in corporate America. In order to end a seven-year antitrust suit brought by the U.S. Department of Justice, AT&T agreed in 1984 to divest itself of twenty-two telephone-operating companies, comprising over two thirds of its total corporate assets. While it is true that AT&T itself remains the nation's largest utility company, and the seven new telephone holding companies created out of AT&T themselves are utility giants,[16] nonetheless, this government-imposed action reduced the power of AT&T directors and created new multiple centers of power in the regional companies. In brief, the AT&T break-up contributed to polyarchy in corporate America.

THE ROCKEFELLERS: END OF A DYNASTY?

Historically the greatest concentration of power in America centered on the Rockefeller empire—a network of industrial, financial, political, civic, and cultural institutions under the control of the Rockefeller family. Until recently this empire was actively directed by David Rockefeller. But David Rockefeller retired as chairman of the board of the core financial institution of the Rockefeller empire, Chase Manhattan Bank, in 1981. He gradually relinquished direct control over New York's Rockefeller Center and various Rockefeller investment holding companies, including Rockefeller Group Inc. and the Rockefeller Brothers Fund. Earlier he had set the Rockefeller Foundation on an independent course. Finally, in 1985 he gave up his chair-

[16] Ameritech, Bell Atlantic, BellSouth, NYNEX, Pacific Telesis, Southwestern Bell, US WEST. See Table 2–2.

manship of the Council on Foreign Relations. No other member of the Rockefeller family, numbering nearly 100 today, has stepped forward to hold the empire together. Nonetheless, the Rockefeller empire, as it evolved over the last century, remains our best illustration of convergence of power in America.

The Rockefeller family fortune was founded by John D. Rockefeller, originator of the Standard Oil Company. With his partners, H.M. Flagler and S.V. Harkness, Rockefeller created the company that controlled 90 percent of the nation's oil production by the 1880s. A series of antitrust cases, culminating in the Supreme Court in *U.S.* v. *Standard Oil* (1911), resulted in the forced dissolution of the company into several separate corporations: Exxon, formerly Standard Oil of New Jersey (the nation's number-five-ranked industrial corporation); Mobil (ranked number 8); Chevron (ranked number 11); Atlantic Richfield (ranked number 17); and other large oil companies.[17] The Rockefeller family continues to hold large blocs of stock in each of these companies. But gradually the center of Rockefeller power shifted to banking and finance.

The core financial institution of the Rockefeller family was Chase Manhattan Bank, which David Rockefeller supervised for nearly thirty years. However, the family was also interested in Citicorp, which was headed for many years by James Stillman Rockefeller, a cousin of David's.

The Rockefeller financial influence in corporate decision-making was felt in several ways: by giving or withholding loans to corporations, by placing representatives on corporate boards of directors, and by owning or controlling blocs of common stock of corporations. Chase Manhattan directors (there are 25 of them) were interlocked with more than 100 major industrial corporations, banks, utilities, and insurance companies. These included giants such as Exxon, AT&T, ITT, Metropolitan Life, Equitable Life, and United States Steel. In addition, Chase Manhattan owned or held in trust over 5 percent of the corporate stock of many other large companies, including Eastern Airlines, Pan American World Airways, Boeing, TWA, Mobil Oil, and CBS. The rules of the Securities and Exchange Commission presume that 5 percent of a corporation's stock can give the holder dominant influence in the corporation.

The Rockefeller interest in foreign affairs was particularly strong. The oil companies, which were the industrial core of Rockefeller holdings, required constant attention to foreign sources of supply. In addition, Chase Manhattan was deeply involved in overseas banking and investment activities. The Rockefellers supplied many of the top foreign affairs personnel for the nation, including Secretaries of State John Foster Dulles, Dean Rusk, and Henry Kissinger. Dulles, secretary of state under President Eisenhower, was a senior partner in the Wall Street law firm of Sullivan & Cromwell, whose principal client for many years was the Standard Oil Company (Exxon). Dulles

---

[17] See Table 2–1 for rankings.

was also chairman of the trustees of the Rockefeller Foundation. Dean Rusk, secretary of state under Presidents Kennedy and Johnson, served seven years as president of the Rockefeller Foundation. John J. McCloy, a Chase Manhattan director, served as U.S. high commissioner for Germany during the postwar occupation; in 1962, he was chairman of the Coordinating Committee on the Cuban Missile Crisis. Henry Kissinger was personal adviser on foreign policy to Nelson Rockefeller before becoming national security adviser and later secretary of state under President Richard Nixon. Cyrus Vance, secretary of state under President Carter, was a Wall Street lawyer and a director of the Rockefeller Foundation, as well as of Pan American World Airlines, Aetna Life Insurance, and IBM. Zbigniew Brzezinski, President Carter's national security adviser, was director of the Trilateral Commission— David Rockefeller's influential group of top leaders from industrialized nations of the world. David Rockefeller himself served as chairman of the influential Council on Foreign Relations, which has been responsible for many of the nation's most important foreign policy initiatives (see the section "The Council on Foreign Relations and the Trilateral Commission" in Chapter 9).

For many decades, the single most powerful private citizen in America was David Rockefeller—"the only man for whom the presidency of the United States would be a step down." David Rockefeller is the youngest of five sons of John D. Rockefeller, Jr., himself the only son of the founder of the Rockefeller empire, John D. Rockefeller. Despite the seniority of his brothers,[18] it was recognized that David was the serious and scholarly one. It was to David that the family wisely entrusted its wealth.

David was raised with his brothers at the Rockefeller's 3,500-acre Pocantico Hills estate, east of Tarrytown, New York. He attended nearby Lincoln School. As a child, he traveled about to Rockefeller holdings—the Seal Harbor, Maine retreat, the Virgin Islands estate, the Venezuela ranch, the Grand Teton Mountains ranch—and collected beetles as a hobby. It soon became clear to David's father and grandfather that Nelson, Lawrence, and Winthrop were more interested in politics and pleasure than hard work, and that John D. III was content to pursue cultural interests. The elder Rockefellers wanted a businessman to care for the family fortune, and they were successful in motivating David in this direction.

David's undergraduate career at Harvard was undistinguished. But later he spent a year at the Harvard Graduate School of Business and a year at the London School of Economics. He married Margaret "Peggy" McGrath, whose father was a senior partner in the esteemed Wall Street law firm of Cadwalader, Wickersham & Taft. He enrolled at the Rockefeller-

---

[18] John D. III (deceased), former chairman of the Rockefeller Foundation and the Lincoln Center for the Performing Arts; Nelson A. (deceased), former Vice-President of the United States and four-term governor of New York; Lawrence S., family dilettante in "venture capitalism" and "conservationist"; and Winthrop (deceased), former governor of Arkansas and cattle rancher.

funded University of Chicago and *earned* a Ph.D. in economics in 1940. He returned to New York for a short stint in public service as an unpaid assistant to Mayor Fiorello La Guardia. In 1942 he enlisted in the Army as a private, went through Officers Training School, and served in North Africa and Europe as an intelligence officer. He was fluent in French, Spanish, and German.

After the war he began his banking career in his uncle Winthrop W. Aldrich's bank, the Chase Manhattan. His first post was assistant manager of the foreign department; three years later he became vice-president and director of the bank's business in Latin America. When his uncle became ambassador to England in 1952, David became successively executive vice-president, vice-chairman of the board, and finally, president and chairman of the board.

Of course, David Rockefeller was active in civic and cultural affairs. He was chairman of the Museum of Modern Art, president of the Board of Overseas Study of Harvard University, a trustee of the Carnegie Endowment for International Peace, a trustee of the University of Chicago, a trustee of the John F. Kennedy Library, and so forth.

Above all, David Rockefeller was an internationalist. His active intervention in American foreign policy produced remarkable results. He was personally involved in Nixon's arrangement of détente with the USSR, the Strategic Arms Limitations Talks (SALT), and the "normalization" of U.S. relations with the mainland People's Republic of China. He was chairman of the board of the Council on Foreign Relations, and he formed the Trilateral Commission in 1972. Through the CFR, Rockefeller was instrumental in most of the nation's important foreign policy initiatives of recent years: from the Paris Peace Agreement ending the Vietnam War, through détente with the Soviet Union and the international human rights campaign, to new concerns over U.S.–Soviet relations in the 1980s. David Rockefeller was personally involved in the decision to permit the Shah of Iran to come to the United States for medical treatment, the decision not to hand over the dying Shah to ransom the U.S. hostages, and the financial agreement that finally secured the release of the hostages.

Under David Rockefeller's direction, Chase Manhattan developed a reputation in the business world for "social responsibility," which included the active recruitment and promotion of blacks, women, and other minorities; the granting of a large number of loans to minority-owned business enterprises; and active involvement in a variety of social projects. Indeed, this may be one reason why Chase Manhattan fell as the nation's leading bank. Another reason for Chase's performance may be that David Rockefeller was so deeply involved in national and international affairs that he did not devote full attention to banking matters.

David Rockefeller exercised great power but always with *modesty*, of course, as one would expect of a man who has no reason to try to impress anyone. Indeed, he consistently understated his own power:

> I feel uncomfortable when you ask how I exert power. We accomplish things through cooperative action, which is quite different than exerting power in some mysterious and presumably evil way. I have no power in the sense that I can call anybody in the government and tell them what to do. Because of my position, I'm more apt to get through on the telephone than somebody else, but what happens to what I suggest depends on whether they feel this makes sense in terms of what they are already doing.[19]

Of course, what Rockefeller was really saying is that when David Rockefeller called, people answered their phone; when he asked them to serve on a committee, they were flattered to be asked; when he suggested that they do something, they did it.

Yet it may be that all great family dynasties eventually splinter and disperse. Despite the best efforts of the founders, the passage of time and the multiplication of family inheritors, together with an erosion of the entrepreneurial spirit in generations born to great wealth, gradually dissolve family concentrations of wealth and power.[20]

SUMMARY

The question of hierarchy versus polyarchy in America's elite structure is a familiar one in the literature on power. The elitist literature describes a convergence of power at the top, with a single group of leaders recruited primarily from industry and finance, exercising power in many different sectors of society. The pluralist literature describes many separate structures of power in different sectors of society, with little or no overlap in authority and many separate channels of recruitment.

Our findings do not all fit neatly into either the elitist or the pluralist leadership model. The fact that roughly 7,000 persons in 6,000 positions exercise formal authority over institutions that control over half of the nation's resources is itself an indication of a great concentration of power. But despite institutional concentration of authority, there is considerable specialization among these leaders. Eighty-five percent of them hold only one "top" position. Only 15 percent are interlockers—holders of two or more top positions. However, because of these interlockers, about 30 percent of all top positions were found interlocked with another top position. Moreover, the top multiple interlockers (those people with six or more top positions) turned out to be impressive figures in America, lending support to the notion of an inner group of national leaders.

There is very little concurrent interlocking among people at the top of the governmental and military sectors of society. To the extent that high government officials are interlocked at all, it is with civic and cultural and educa-

---

[19] "Beyond Wealth, What?" *Forbes*, May 15, 1972, pp. 250–52.

[20] For argument to the contrary, see Michael Patrick Allen, *The Founding Fortunes* (New York: Dutton, 1988).

tional institutions. It is *within* the corporate sector that interlocking is most prevalent. If there is a "coming together" of corporate, governmental, and military elites, as C. Wright Mills contends, it does not appear to be by means of interlocking directorates.

The notion of hierarchy is strengthened, however, if we examine the record of leadership experience of top institutional elites *over a lifetime*. Most top leaders have held more than one top position in their career. Governmental leaders, however, have generally gained their leadership experience in governmental positions or in the law; only one quarter of top governmental leaders have ever held high positions in the corporate world.

These aggregate figures suggest specialization rather than convergence at the top of the nation's institutional structure. However, we agree that there are special cases of concentrated corporate, governmental, and social power. AT&T, for example, is linked through its board of directors to a wide variety of manufacturing companies, as well as to banks and media companies. A few years ago, the Rockefeller family, through its dominance of Chase Manhattan Bank and its family holdings in many large corporations, utilities, and insurance companies, together with its activities in cultural organizations, universities, foundations, and civic associations, represented a very important concentration of power.

7 Elite Recruitment: Getting to the Top

A RULING CLASS OR AN OPEN LEADERSHIP SYSTEM?

Are there opportunities to rise to the top of the institutional structure of America for individuals from all classes, races, religions, and ethnic groups, through multiple career paths in different sectors of society? Or are opportunities for entry into top circles limited to white, Anglo-Saxon Protestant, upper- and upper-middle-class individuals whose careers are based primarily in industry and finance?

Social scientists have studied data on the social backgrounds of corporate and governmental leaders for many years. But there is still disagreement on the interpretation of the data. A "ruling class" school of thought stresses the fact that elites in America are drawn disproportionately from among wealthy, educated, prestigiously employed, socially prominent, "WASP" groups in society. These ruling-class social scientists are impressed with the fact that leadership in industry, finance, government, education, the law, the mass media, and other institutional sectors is recruited primarily from society's upper social classes. Many of the elite have been educated at a few esteemed private prep schools and gone to Ivy League colleges and universities. They have joined the same private clubs, and their families have intermarried. Moreover, a disproportionate share of the top leadership in all sectors of society has made its career mark in industry and finance. Ruling-class social scientists infer that these similarities contribute to cohesion and consensus among the institutional leaders in America.

By contrast, pluralists describe an open leadership system that enables a significant number of individuals from the middle and lower classes to rise to the top. High social background, or wealth, or WASPishness *itself* does not provide access to top leadership positions. Instead, top institutional posts go to individuals who possess outstanding skills of leadership, information, and knowledge, and the ability to organize and communicate. Admittedly, opportunities to acquire such qualities for top leadership are unequally distributed among classes. But lower-class origin, the pluralists believe, is not an insurmountable barrier to high position.

Classical elitist writers such as Mosca acknowledge that some "circulation of elites" is essential for the stability of a political system. The opportunity for the brightest among the lower classes to rise to the top siphons off potentially revolutionary leadership, and the elite system is actually strengthened when talented and ambitious individuals enter top positions. The fact that only a minority of top leaders are drawn from the lower classes is not really important. It is the availability of a modicum of opportunity that encourages talented people to believe they can rise to the top and strengthens support for the system throughout all social classes.

Defenders of the pluralist theory also argue that social background, educational experience, and social group membership are poor predictors of decision-making behavior. Members of the social elite often hold very different views about policy questions, differences that can be attributed to a variety of factors, all of which are more influential than social background. Among these are the nature of the top position occupied, the individual's perception of his or her own role, the institutional constraints placed upon the individual, systems of public accountability, interest-group pressures, public opinion, and so forth. Thus, pluralists argue that the class homogeneity among top leaders that is reported in many social background studies is meaningless, since the class background/decision-making behavior linkage is weak.

The recruitment of some non-upper-class individuals to elite positions may be essential to society, because these individuals bring new and different perspectives to societal problems. Sociologist Suzanne Keller speaks of "two irreconcilable tendencies in social life—the need for order and the need for change":

> If the social leadership becomes so conservative as to be immune to new ideas and social developments, the pressure for unfulfilled needs mounts until that leadership declines, resigns, or is violently displaced. If it is so receptive to the new as to neglect established traditions, social continuity is endangered.[1]

Thus, we would expect to find some recruitment of non-upper-class individuals to elite positions even in an essentially hierarchical society. The question remains, *how much* opportunity exists in America for middle- and lower-class individuals to climb to the top?

GETTING AHEAD IN THE SYSTEM

The American ideal is not a classless society, but rather a society in which individuals are free to get ahead on the basis of merit, talent, hard work, and good luck. Upward mobility is valued very highly in American culture. The nation is portrayed in its own literature as a "land of opportunity" where individuals can better themselves if they work at it.

And, indeed, there is a great deal of social mobility in America. The results of a typical study of social mobility are shown in Table 7–1. A majority

---

[1] Suzanne Keller, *Beyond the Ruling Class: Strategic Elites in Modern Society* (New York: Random House, 1968), p. 172.

TABLE 7–1   Social Mobility in America

Father's Occupation	Son's Current Occupation						Father's Percentage Totals
	Upper White Collar	Lower White Collar	Upper Manual	Lower Manual	Farm	Total	
Upper white collar	52.0	16.0	13.8	17.1	1.1	100.0	18.2
Lower white collar	42.3	19.7	15.3	21.9	0.8	100.0	9.0
Upper manual	29.4	13.0	27.4	29.0	1.1	100.0	20.5
Lower manual	22.5	12.0	23.7	40.8	1.0	100.0	29.7
Farm	17.5	7.8	22.7	37.2	14.8	100.0	22.6
Son's percentage totals	29.9	12.7	21.7	31.5	4.1	100.0	100.0

SOURCE: David Featherman and Robert Hauser, *Opportunity and Change* (New York: Academic Press, 1978). Data are from March 1973 current population surveys and occupational changes in a generation survey. Occupation groups are upper white collar: professional and kindred workers and managers, officials and proprietors, except farm; lower white collar: sales, clerical and kindred workers; upper manual: craftspeople, forepersons and kindred workers; lower manual: operatives and kindred workers, service workers, and laborers, except farm; farm: farmers and farm managers, farm laborers, and forepersons.

Mobility from father's (or other family head's) occupation to current occupation: U.S. men in the experienced civilian labor force aged 20 to 64 in 1973. Figures in percentages.

of the sons of upper-white-collar fathers (52 percent) are themselves in upper-white-collar occupations. This means that slightly less than half of these sons have descended to less prestigious occupations than their fathers. At the other end of the scale, only about 40 percent of the sons of lower-manual workers end up in the same manual occupations as their fathers. This means that nearly 60 percent of these sons have risen to more prestigious occupations than their fathers (22.5 percent rose to upper-white-collar occupations). In the past, there has been more upward mobility than downward mobility in the American system, a pattern that results from economic growth. But as the rate of growth slows, the balance in favor of upward mobility diminishes. Nonetheless, there continues to be a great deal of both upward and downward mobility.

SOCIAL CHARACTERISTICS OF INSTITUTIONAL LEADERS

What do we know about the people who occupy top institutional positions in American society? Over the years studies have consistently shown that top institutional leaders are *atypical* of the American public.[2] They are recruited

[2] Among the early studies, see Donald R. Matthews, *The Social Background of Political Decision-Makers* (New York: Doubleday, 1954); David T. Stanley, Dean E. Mann, and Jameson W. Doig, *Men Who Govern* (Washington: Brookings Institution, 1967); Morris Janowitz, *The Professional Soldier* (New York: Free Press, 1960); and Lloyd Warner and James C. Abegglen, *Big Business Leaders in America* (New York: Harper & Row, 1955).

TABLE 7–2 Social Characteristics of Top Leaders

	Corporate					Public Interest					Government		
	Industry	Banking	Utilities	Insurance	Investment	Media	Law	Foundation	Education	Civic	Government	Military	All
Average age	61	61	61	62	58	61	64	62	62	60	56	56	60
Female %	2.4	2.3	4.3	1.1	0.9	6.8	1.8	14.7	10.6	9.0	7.7	0	4.3
Education %													
Non-College	3.0	5.8	7.6	5.0	0.9	18.4	0	5.1	4.3	3.6	8.8	4.7	5.7
College	42.7	43.0	40.6	42.7	51.3	39.2	100.0	24.9	32.8	37.0	10.7	30.2	37.4
Law	22.6	22.2	25.1	22.6	8.8	20.9	100.0	26.9	28.1	24.8	41.0	9.3	25.8
Advanced	29.8	29.0	26.7	29.8	39.0	21.6	5.3	43.1	34.7	34.7	33.5	55.8	31.1
Schools %													
Public	25.3	28.5	28.3	25.3	21.2	28.5	8.4	13.7	15.5	21.4	37.9	23.3	24.9
Private	18.2	20.7	18.8	18.2	17.7	13.9	8.4	19.8	10.2	17.9	17.2	7.0	16.9
Prestigious*	54.9	49.5	51.0	54.9	61.1	51.9	83.2	66.5	73.7	59.7	41.9	20.9†	56.1

*Harvard, Yale, Chicago, Stanford, Columbia, M.I.T., Cornell, Northwestern, Princeton, Johns Hopkins, Pennsylvania, and Dartmouth.

†U.S. Military Academy (West Point) and U.S. Naval Academy (Annapolis) account for an additional 48.8 percent.

from the well-educated, prestigiously employed, older, affluent, urban, white, Anglo-Saxon, upper- and upper-middle-class male populations of the nation. We had expected our top institutional elites to conform to the pattern, and we were not at all disappointed (see Table 7–2).

Age: The average age of all the corporate leaders identified in our study is sixty. Leaders in foundations, law, education, and civic and cultural organizations are slightly older—average age sixty-two. Top positions in the governmental sector are filled by slightly younger people—average age fifty-six.

Sex: The feminine sector of the population is seriously underrepresented at the top of America's institutional structure. Male dominance in top positions is nearly complete in the corporate world. But even in government, women hold less than 10 percent of the key posts. Only in cultural affairs, education, and foundations are women found in significant numbers among the top position-holders.

Ethnicity: WASPs are preeminent in America's institutional structure. Our own data do not include ethnic identification, but the work of sociologists Richard D. Alba and Gwen Moore confirm the disproportionate representation of WASPs in high positions in business and government. Their studies revealed that WASPs (who made up only 22.9 percent of all persons born before 1932) made up 57.3 percent of top business leaders and 53.4 percent of Congress. ("Other Protestants" increase these figures to 79.4 percent for business and 72.4 percent for Congress.) However, ethnics have made some inroads: 37 percent of union leaders are Irish Catholics, and 25.8 percent of mass media leaders are Jews. A WASP background, they conclude, is an "incremental advantage" in achieving elite status.[3]

Education: Nearly all our top leaders are college-educated, and more than half hold advanced degrees. Some 25.8 percent hold law degrees, and 31.1 percent hold advanced academic or professional degrees. (These are earned degrees only; there are a host of honorary degrees that were not counted.) Governmental leaders are somewhat more likely to hold advanced degrees than corporate leaders. What is even more impressive is the fact that 54 percent of the corporate leaders and 42 percent of the governmental leaders are graduates of twelve heavily endowed, prestigious "name" private universities—Harvard, Yale, Chicago, Stanford, Columbia, M.I.T., Cornell, Northwestern, Princeton, Johns Hopkins, Pennsylvania, and Dartmouth. Elites in America are notably Ivy League.[4]

---

[3] Richard D. Alba and Gwen Moore, "Ethnicity in the American Elite," *American Sociological Review,* 47 (June 1982).

[4] Our figures are confirmed in a separate study of over 55,000 top executives by Standard & Poor's Corporation, showing that half received degrees from these twelve universities. See *Chronicle of Higher Education,* September 29, 1980, p. 1.

Urban: Most of our top leaders were urban dwellers. Governmental leaders (notably members of Congress) are somewhat more likely to be drawn from rural areas than are leaders in business, finance, and law, but less than one third of the key government posts in our study were found to be filled by individuals from rural areas.

Preppy: Elites are notably "preppy." At least 10 percent of the corporate leaders and 6 percent of the governmental leaders attended one of only thirty-three prestigious private prep schools before entering college.[5] (Actually, the proportion of "preppies" among top leaders may be double these figures—up to 20 percent for corporate leaders and 10 percent for government leaders. The reason for suggesting these higher figures is that less than half of known preppies reported their prep school affiliation to *Who's Who in America.*[6] Thus, their prep school backgrounds would be overlooked in our biographical search.) It is astonishing to realize that these proportions of top leaders went to only thirty-three prep schools, since these schools educate an infinitesimal proportion of the nation's population. As *The Official Preppy Handbook* explains: "There are preparatory schools and then there are Prep Schools, those institutions that bless you with a certain luster along with your diploma."[7] Among the Eastern Establishment, the phrase "old school ties" refers to prep schools, not to colleges or universities. It is considered more prestigious to have attended Groton, Hotchkiss, Phillips Exeter, Loomis, Phillips at Andover, or Choate, than to have attended Harvard, Yale, Princeton, or Columbia.

These social background characteristics suggest a slight tendency for corporate elites to be more "upper class" in origin than government elites. Among governmental leaders there are slightly fewer Ivy Leaguers. Moreover, there is a slight tendency for governmental leaders to have had more advanced professional education.

CLASS: A TOUCHY SUBJECT

All known societies have some system of ranking individuals along a superiority-inferiority scale. Yet in America, the ideological assertion "All men are created equal" is so pervasive that people are reluctant to even acknowledge the

---

[5] Andover, Buckley, Cate, Catlin, Choate, Cranbrook, Country Day, Deerfield, Episcopal, Exeter, Gilman, Groton, Hill, Hotchkiss, Kingswood, Kent, Lakeside, Lawrenceville, Lincoln, Loomis, Middlesex, Milton, St. Andrew's, St. Christopher's, St. George's, St. Mark's, St. Paul's, Shattuck, Taft, Thatcher, Webb, Westminster, Woodberry Forest. Listing courtesy of G. William Domhoff.

[6] Unpublished reports by Michael Useem and G. William Domhoff, November 1980.

[7] Lisa Birnbach, ed., *The Official Preppy Handbook* (New York: Workman, 1980), p. 50.

existence of social classes. Most Americans describe themselves as "middle class"; nearly nine out of ten will choose "middle class" when they are asked in surveys to choose between this term and either upper class or lower class.[8] Sociologists use measures of occupation, income, and education to assess class position and to study social classes. But members of America's upper classes avoid using the term *class* altogether. In her *Women of the Upper Class*, sociologist Susan A. Ostrander reports that her interviewees preferred describing themselves as "being from an old family," "established," or "respected in the community."

> I hate [the term] upper class. Its so non-upper class to use it. I just call it "all of us," those of us who are well-born.
>
> I hate to use the word "class." We're responsible, fortunate people, old families, the people who have something.[9]

According to writer Paul Fussell, a tendency to get very anxious about discussions of social class—"It's the dirtiest thing I ever heard of"—reveals a middle-class outlook toward social classes.[10] Upper-class members will discuss class in subtle terms; lower-class members will discuss class in terms of humor and derision ("snobs," "fat cats," "fancy pants"). The middle class prefers to avoid the topic altogether. Fussell also contends that people reveal their own class by the way they define class. The lower classes believe class is defined by the amount of money a person has; the middle class grants that money has something to do with it but thinks that education and occupation are more important; the upper class thinks that taste, values, style, and behavior define class, regardless of money or education or occupation.

The ambiguities about class in America make it difficult to assess the role of class in elite composition. We must avoid the circularity of saying "the power elite is the upper class" and then defining the upper class as "the power elite." We have already defined our elite as individuals who occupy the top positions in the institutional structure of society. Certainly these people are granted high status and accorded great deference by virtue of the institutional positions they occupy. But their institutional status cannot itself be synonymous with upper social class; upper social class must have some independent meaning if it is to have any meaning at all.

One of the few class analysts to recognize this distinction between class and power is sociologist G. William Domhoff:

---

[8] See *The American Enterprise* (May–June, 1993), pp. 82–83, reporting National Opinion Research Center data on class identifications.

[9] Susan A. Ostrander, "Upper-Class Women," in *Power Structure Research*, ed. G. William Domhoff (Beverly Hills, Calif.: Sage, 1980), pp. 78–79; see also Ostrander, *Women of the Upper Class* (Philadelphia: Temple University Press, 1984).

[10] Paul Fussell, *Class: A Guide Through the American Status System* (New York: Summit Books, 1983).

> The upper class as a whole does not rule. Instead class rule is manifested through the activities of a wide variety of organizations and institutions. . . . Leaders within the upper class join with high-level employees in the organizations they control to make up what will be called the *power elite*. This power elite is the leadership group of the upper class as a whole, but it is not the same thing as the upper class. It is the members of the power elite who take part in the processes that maintain the class structure.[11]

To demonstrate upper-class "dominance" of the elite, Domhoff employs several upper-class "indicators": (1) listing in the *Social Register*; (2) attendance at a private prestigious preparatory school; or (3) membership in a private prestigious club. But Domhoff fails to acknowledge that listing in the *Social Register* and membership in a prestigious club usually come to an individual *after* he or she has attained high institutional position. In other words, one may attain these indicators of upper social class as a result of climbing the institutional ladder from a middle-class background. We certainly cannot contend that the upper class "dominates" the elite, if it turns out that elite membership is what determined upper-class status.

The only way to avoid circularity in studying the class composition of an elite group is to focus on social *origins*. Are top institutional positions largely limited to the sons and daughters of upper-class families? Our own estimate is that approximately *30 percent* of our total institutional elite are upper class in social origin. This estimate derives from a sample of our elite for whom we endeavored to learn their parents' class circumstances. We attributed *upper-class social origin* on the basis of the following: (1) attendance at a private prestigious preparatory school; (2) parent is an officer or a director of a major corporation, bank, insurance company, or utility; (3) parent is a high government official or general in the military; (4) parent is an attorney in a top law firm, a newspaper owner or director, or a university president or trustee of a university, foundation, or major civic or cultural association.

Certainly individuals with upper-class family origins are disproportionately represented in institutional leadership positions. (Far less than 1 percent of the general population would meet our definition of upper-class origin.) But we cannot conclude that the upper class "dominates" on the basis of our estimate of 30 percent upper-class origins. On the contrary, 70 percent of our institutional elite appeared to be middle class in family origin; their parents were able to send them to college, but there is no indication that their parents ever achieved high institutional position.

BLACKS AT THE TOP

There are very few blacks in positions of power in America. African-Americans remain noticeably absent from top positions in the corporate world. In 1979 only 3 of 1,700 senior executives of Fortune "1000" companies

---

[11] G. William Domhoff, *Who Rules America Now?* (Englewood Cliffs, N.J.: Prentice Hall, 1983), p. 2.

were black. A 1985 follow-up study found only 4 blacks, 6 Asians, and 3 Hispanics among 1362 senior executives.[12]

Corporations say that the main reason that blacks are not found in top management positions is that they did not enter the corporate ranks until the late 1960s, and it takes anyone, white or black, over twenty years to rise to the top. However, many blacks feel that discrimination continues to play a major role in obstructing black progress up the corporate ladder. White corporate executives feel more comfortable in dealing with other whites, and they do not aggressively recruit blacks into management. The Equal Employment Opportunity Commission and other federal agencies assigned to investigate job discrimination focus their attention on entry-level cases rather than on very subtle discrimination in the ranks of top corporate management. Instead of assigning promising black executives to key operating posts, many corporations tend to move them to positions overseeing personnel or affirmative action programs. This removes blacks from the "fast track" in corporate promotions.

Edward W. Jones Jr., a black business consultant and former AT&T executive, argues that "colorism"—"a predisposition to act in a certain manner because of a person's skin color"—is the major obstacle to black advancement to top corporate positions. He distinguishes "colorism" from "racism," which he defines as overt bigotry and hatred. "All people possess stereotypes, which act like shorthand to avoid mental overload. . . . a decision about a promotion is a subjective thing. For blacks, colorism adds an extra layer of subjectivity."[13]

Illustrative of African-Americans who have gained positions at the top of the corporate structure are:

William T. Coleman. Former secretary of transportation under President Gerald Ford. Senior partner, O'Melveny & Myers, Washington. Attended the University of Pennsylvania and Harvard Law School. Chairman of the board of the NAACP Legal Defense and Education Fund. Served as a director of IBM, Chase Manhattan, Pepsico, American Can, Pan American World Airways, Philadelphia Electric. A trustee of the Brookings Institution; a member of the Council on Foreign Relations and the Trilateral Commission; and a trustee of Harvard University.

Andrew F. Brimmer. Independent financial consultant. Served as a director of BankAmerica, International Harvester, United Airlines, Du Pont, BellSouth, Gannett Newspapers, Mercedes Benz, and Navistar International. A graduate of the University of Washington with a Ph.D. (economics) from Harvard. He taught at the Wharton School of the University of Pennsylvania and moved on to be assistant secretary of commerce and later a member of the Federal Reserve Board. He now heads Brimmer and Company, an independent financial and managerial consulting firm. He is a member of the Council on Foreign Relations and the Trilateral Commission, and he is a trustee of Atlanta University, Tuskegee Institute, the Urban League, and the Ford Foundation.

---

[12] See Edward W. Jones Jr., "Black Managers: The Dream Deferred," *Harvard Business Review* (May–June, 1986), 84–93.

[13] Ibid., p. 88.

Vernon E. Jordon, Jr. Former president of the National Urban League. A graduate of DePauw University and Howard University Law School. He began his career in civil rights affairs as the Georgia field secretary of the NAACP in the early 1960s, and later became director of the Vote Education Project of the Southern Regional Council, leading black voter registration drives in the south. He served briefly as executive director of the United Negro College Fund before becoming head of the National Urban League in 1972. In recent years he has accepted directorships of Bankers Trust of New York, American Express, Celanese Corporation, J.C. Penney Co., Union Carbide, Corning Glass, Dow Jones & Co., Revlon, RJR-Nabisco, Ryder Systems, Sara Lee, and the Xerox Corporation. He is also a trustee of the Rockefeller Foundation and the Brookings Institution.

Franklin A. Thomas. President of the Ford Foundation. Former president of the Bedford Stuyvesant Restoration Corporation in New York. He received his B.A. and law degree from Columbia University, and served as deputy police commissioner under New York's Mayor John Lindsay. Served as a director of Citicorp, AT&T, Aluminum Co. of America, CBS, Cummins Engine, and New York Life Insurance. He is also a trustee of the Lincoln Center for the Performing Arts, the Urban Institute, and Columbia University.

Clifton R. Wharton, Jr. Chairman and CEO of TIAA-CREF (insurance) and former chancellor of the State University of New York. Educated at the private prestigious Boston Latin School and later Harvard and Johns Hopkins; he received his Ph.D. (economics) from the University of Chicago. Former president of Michigan State University. Served as a director of Ford Motors, Burroughs Corp., Equitable Life, and the New York Stock Exchange. A trustee and later chairman of the board of the Rockefeller Foundation. A director of the Carnegie Corporation and the Council on Foreign Relations.

No African-Americans have ever been chairman or chief executive officer of a major industrial corporation, bank, utility, insurance company, investment firm, or communication network. Black leadership has been confined to a small number of board members. In contrast, African-Americans have served in high *government* posts in all recent presidential administrations.

President Carter's Cabinet included:

Patricia Roberts Harris. Secretary of Health, Education, and Welfare. The daughter of a railroad dining-car waiter and a graduate of Howard University (B.A., 1945). Received a law degree from George Washington University in 1960. She began her career as a YWCA director in Chicago and later as executive director of Delta Sigma Theta, a national black sorority. She was a delegate to the Democratic National Convention in 1964, and seconded the nomination of Lyndon Johnson; President Johnson appointed her ambassador to Luxembourg (1965–67). She became a law partner of Sargent Shriver (Kennedy brother-in-law) and a prominent Washington attorney. She served as a director of IBM, Chase Manhattan, and Scott Paper Co. She was a member of the Council on Foreign Relations.

President Reagan's Cabinet included:

Samuel R. Pierce. Secretary of Housing and Urban Development. Pierce was a senior partner in the New York law firm of Fowler, Jaffin, Pierce & Kneel and a governor of the American Stock Exchange. Pierce received his law degree from Cornell in 1949 and began his long career as an assistant district attorney in New York. He was named an assistant U.S. attorney under President Eisenhower and later assistant to the undersecretary of labor. He was a Ford Foundation fellow at Yale for a year, and a New York City judge. Under Nixon, he was general counsel for the U.S. Department of the Treasury (1970–73). He served as a director of General Electric, Prudential Insurance, First National Boston Corp., International Paper, and U.S. Industries.

President Bush's Cabinet included:

Dr. Louis W. Sullivan.   Secretary of Health and Human Services. A graduate of Morehouse College and Boston University Medical School, Sullivan took his residency at Cornell Medical Center in New York, and then Massachusetts General Hospital. He served in a number of teaching and research positions at Harvard's Thorndike Labs, and Harvard and Boston University Medical Schools. In 1978 he was named the first dean and founding director of the Morehouse School of Medicine.

And President Clinton's Cabinet includes:

Mike Espy.   Secretary of Agriculture. A native of Mississippi who received his B.A. from Howard University in Washington, D.C., and law degree from Santa Clara Law School in California in 1978. He served as an attorney in the Mississippi Legal Services Corporation (1978–80), the office of secretary of state (1980–84), and the state attorney general's office (1984–85), before running successfully for Congress in 1986. In Congress (1987–93), he served on the Agricultural and Budget committees.

Jesse Brown.   Secretary of Veterans Affairs. An honor graduate of Chicago City College, Brown enlisted in the Marine Corps in 1963. He was wounded in combat in Vietnam and his right arm was partially paralyzed. He joined the Chicago area staff of the Disabled American Veterans (DAV) in 1967 and moved to the DAV National Office in Washington in 1973, eventually becoming national director.

Ron Brown.   Secretary of Commerce (see below).

Ron Brown: Political Insider.   The first African-American to become chairman of a major political party, Ron Brown, would rather be known as the man who regained the White House for the Democrats. A long-time Washington lobbyist and insider, Brown has worked to unite the Democratic party. "We'll all work together—brown, black, yellow, and white." Democratic leaders described Brown as a team player who avoided racial and ethnic politics and concerned himself with the process of electing Democrats to national office.

Brown grew up in Harlem. Both of his parents were college graduates and his father managed the Theresa Hotel next to the Apollo Theater. As a youth, Brown was exposed to the upper strata of black society in New York, including many of the famous entertainers that played the Apollo. He attended an exclusive New York preparatory school and went on to graduate from Middlebury College in Vermont. At Middlebury, Brown was the only black student in his freshman class. He was popular among his classmates and was invited to join a then all-white fraternity. When the national organization prohibited Brown's membership, his Middlebury fraternity brothers renounced their national affiliation. The college also stood by Ron Brown and barred all exclusionary fraternities from campus. Today Brown is a trustee of Middlebury College.

After a stint in the Army, Brown earned a law degree at St. John's University and became a Washington lobbyist for the National Urban League. He worked as a deputy campaign manager for Senator Edward Kennedy in 1979–80, becoming Kennedy's general counsel and staff director. From 1981–85, he was a deputy director of the Democratic National Committee; in 1988, he managed Jesse Jackson's presidential campaign. Brown joined the powerful Washington lawyer-lobbying firm of Patton, Boggs, and Blow.

It was Brown's role in bringing Jackson and his supporters into the Dukakis camp that propelled him to the party's chair. Brown's negotiating skills resolved the platform differences between the candidates. Both candidates were able to save face, and a serious racial split within the Democratic party was averted. As national chairman, Brown proved to be an impressive fund-raiser, and under his leadership the Democrats gained four congressional seats in 1989 off-year elections, including Dan Quayle's former seat in Indiana. That the Democrats and Ron Brown achieved this while President Bush was still riding high in the post–Gulf War approval ratings made the victories even more impressive.

As comfortable on the tennis courts as in national politics, Brown proved to be an extremely likable and popular national chairman. As Michael Dukakis said, "If Ron were a pop singer, he would have crossover appeal." Brown vowed to take the Clinton campaign into the White House: "I promise you my chairmanship will not be about race; it will be about the races we win," and win he did. Brown's reward was appointment to the Clinton Cabinet as secretary of commerce, the first African-American ever to hold that post.

WOMEN AT THE TOP

The nation's institutional elite are predominately male. Overall, about 10 percent of top institutional leaders—presidents, directors, and trustees of the nation's largest industrial corporations, banks, utilities, insurance companies, television networks and newspaper chains, foundations, universities, civic and cultural organizations; full partners in the nation's leading law firms and investment houses; and top elected and appointed federal government officials—are women.

However, women have made impressive gains in securing top institutional positions over the past twenty years. Our figures show an overall increase in women in top positions from a meager 1.9 percent in 1970, to 4.3 percent in 1980, to 10.1 percent in 1992 (see Table 7–3).

TABLE 7–3   Percentage of Women in Top Institutional Positions

	1992	*1980*	*1970*
Industry	9.2%	2.4%	0.2%
Banking	8.1	2.3	0.2
Media	13.3	6.8	4.1
Foundations	26.2	14.7	6.2
Universities	25.0	10.0	2.0
Government (1993)			
Cabinet members	16.6	5.5	0
House members	10.8	3.7	2.3
Senate members	7.0	2.0	1.0
Supreme Court	22.2	11.1	0
All	10.1	4.3	1.9

SOURCES: Figures for 1970 and 1980 from all top institutional positions in industry, banking, media, foundations, universities, and government as described in Chapter 1. Figures for 1992 based on ten largest industrial corporations, ten largest banks, six most influential media corporations, ten largest foundations, and the ten most heavily endowed private universities. Government figures under each column are those elected that year and taking office the following January, including the Clinton Cabinet and the 103rd Congress serving 1993–95.

Most corporate boardrooms continue to resemble male clubs. Few of the nation's largest corporations have more than one or two women on their boards of directors. The General Motors board, for example, includes two women on its fifteen-member board: Ann Armstrong (see below) and Ann D. McLaughlin, former secretary of labor in the Reagan administration and a director of Unocal, Travelers Insurance, Union Camp, Kellogg, Vulcan Materials, AMR Corporation, and Potomac Electric Power. Most of the women serving on corporate boards are *outside* directors; few are inside manager-directors. No woman serves as chairman or chief executive officer of any of the nation's one hundred largest industrial corporations.

Women have made only modest improvements in their leadership positions in *banking*. Today most of the nation's largest banks have at least one female director, including Citicorp and BankAmerica, the nation's two largest financial institutions. Yet women have only about 8 percent of the total number of big bank directorships.

Women have been more successful in the *mass media* than in industry or banking. Today women hold about 13 percent of the officer and director posts in the leading media corporations. For nearly twenty years, Katherine Graham, owner of the *Washington Post* and *Newsweek* magazine empire, served as chairman of the board of the Washington Post Company. Three women serve on the board of directors of the New York Times Company; all of them are "outside" directors. Each of the three television broadcasting networks has at least one woman on its board.

The nation's leading private *universities* have begun to appoint more women to their governing boards of trustees. Today about 25 percent of the governing trustees of the nation's leading private universities are women, an increase over the 10 percent found in 1980, and the scant 2 percent in 1970. Eight of Harvard's thirty trustees are women. All of the leading universities have at least one woman trustee.

Women are frequently encountered on the governing boards of trustees of leading *foundations*. The Ford and Rockefeller foundations each have five women trustees, and the Carnegie Corporation has six women trustees on its sixteen-member board. Some women, of course, have long served as foundation trustees because of their family associations: Mary Ethel Pew, Pew Memorial Trust; Doris Duke, Duke Endowment; Harriet Bush Melin, Bush Foundation; Mary Moody Northern, Moody Foundation; Josephine Hartford Bryce, Hartford Foundation; Mary Ann Mott Meynet, Mott Foundation; Ida Calloway, Calloway Foundation; Drue M. Heinz, Heinz Endowment.

Women are frequently encountered as trustees of *cultural organizations*. The influential *civic associations* have only a few women trustees; for example, the Brookings Institution has three women trustees on its thirty-two-member board. But the nation's leading cultural institutions appoint significant numbers of women to their governing boards. The John F. Kennedy Center for the Performing Arts has ten women on its twenty-five-member board of trustees. Unlike most of the women in the corporate world who list themselves by their own name, many women in cultural organizations list themselves by their husband's name (for example, Mrs. Howard H. Baker, Jr.; Mrs. Edward Finch Cox; Mrs. Jean Kennedy Smith; Mrs. Bob Hope; Mrs. Vincent Astor; Mrs. Henry J. Heinz II). Overall, about 9 percent of the trustees of the leading cultural and civic associations are women.

Women have made greater inroads in *government* than in the corporate world. Women's major gains in government have occurred in both Republican and Democratic administrations. Three women served in Cabinet-level positions under President Reagan:

Margaret Heckler. Secretary of Health and Human Services. Catholic College, Boston College law degree; fourteen years a Republican congresswoman from Massachusetts.

Elizabeth Hanford Dole. Secretary of Transportation. Duke University and Harvard Law School; Commissioner, Federal Trade Commission; later assistant to President Reagan.

Jeanne Kirkpatrick. UN ambassador. Barnard College, Columbia University, Ph.D. Political science; Georgetown University professor.

The Bush Cabinet included two women, both of whom were Washington "insiders" who had served in previous Cabinet posts:

Elizabeth Dole. Reappointed Secretary of Transportation.

Carla Anderson Hills. Cabinet-level post as U.S. trade representative. She had formerly served as secretary of Housing and Urban Development in the Ford administration. She was a prominent Washington lawyer and a director of IBM, Corning Glass, American Airlines, Chevron, and the Signal Corporation. She was a member of the Council on Foreign Relations and the Trilateral Commission; she was once a trustee of the Brookings Institution but later became an adviser to the American Enterprise Institute. She was also chairman of the board of trustees of the Urban Institute. She earned her bachelors at Stanford and her law degree at Yale.

The Clinton cabinet includes three women: Attorney General Janet Reno, Secretary of Health and Human Services Secretary Donna E. Shalala, and Energy Secretary Hazel R. O'Leary.

Janet Reno. She received a B.A. in chemistry from Cornell and her law degree from Harvard Law School. She worked in private law practice and served briefly as staff director for the judiciary committee of the Florida House of Representatives, before becoming assistant state attorney in Miami in 1973. She was initially appointed state attorney in 1978 and subsequently elected and reelected to that post.

Donna E. Shalala. She earned a Ph.D. in political science at Syracuse University, served in the Peace Corps in Iran, and taught at City University of New York and Columbia University, before going to Washington in the Carter administration as assistant secretary of Housing and Urban Development. Following Reagan's victory she was a successful candidate for president of Hunter College, part of the City University of New York; she was appointed chancellor of the University of Wisconsin in 1988. She was a governor of the American Stock Exchange; a member of the Council on Foreign Relations and the Trilateral Commission; and a trustee of the Brookings Institution.

Hazel R. O'Leary. She received degrees from Fisk University and Rutgers School of Law and served briefly in state and county government legal posts in New Jersey. She went to Washington, first to serve in the Federal Energy Administration in the Ford administration, and later the department of energy in the Carter administration. From 1981 to 1989 her Washington-based O'Leary Associates lobbied state and federal agencies on energy issues. She was recruited to a high management post in Northern States Power Company, became executive vice-president in 1990, and won promotion to president just prior to her appointment as secretary of energy by President Clinton.

A few women at the top deserve closer observation. Our list of top women leaders includes:

Katherine Graham. Chairman of the board of the Washington Post Company. (See "Katherine Graham: The Most Powerful Woman in America" in Chapter 4.)

Ruth Bader Ginsberg. Associate Justice, U.S. Supreme Court. (See "The Judges" in Chapter 3).

Sandra Day O'Connor. Associate Justice, U.S. Supreme Court. (See "Sandra Day O'Connor: In the Center of the Court" in this chapter.)

Barbara Scott Preiskel. Wellesley College, Yale Law School. Formerly an associate with the prestigious Wall Street firm of Dwight, Royal, Harris, Hoege, and Caskey, and attorney for the Motion Picture Association of America. Now an independent attorney with corporate directorships at American Stores, General Electric, Massachusetts Mutual Life Insurance, Textron, and the Washington Post Company. She is also a trustee of the Ford Foundation, Wellesley College, and Yale University.

Judith Richards Hope. Wellesley College and Harvard Law School. Senior partner in the Washington firm of Hastings, Janofsky, and Walker. A director of the Budd Company, Union Pacific, General Mils, and IBM; a trustee of Harvard University; and a member of the Council on Foreign Relations.

Helene L. Kaplan. Barnard College and New York University Law School. A partner in the New York firm of Webster and Shelfield; a director of May Department Stores, Metropolitan Life Insurance, Mobil Corporation, NYNEX, and Verde Explorations; and a trustee of Mt. Sinai Hospital, Guggenheim Foundation, Carnegie Corporation, and the American Museum of Natural History.

Marina VonNeumann Whitman. Chief economist for General Motors Corporation and former member of the Council of Economic Advisers. A director of Manufacturers Hanover Trust, Westinghouse Electric, and Procter & Gamble. Earned a bachelors degree from Radcliffe and a Ph.D. from Columbia. A director of the Council on Foreign Relations, and a member of the Trilateral Commission.

Anne L. Armstrong. Served as a director of General Motors, Braniff International, First City Bankcorp. of Texas, General Foods, American Express, Halliburton Company, and Boise Cascade. Has a bachelor's degree from Vassar College. Former cochairperson of the Republican National Committee and former U.S. ambassador to Great Britain. A member of the Council on Foreign Relations. A trustee of the Smithsonian Institution and Southern Methodist University.

Jane Cahill Pfeiffer. Former chairman of the board of the National Broadcasting Company. A director of International Paper, Ashland Oil, J.C. Penney, Chesebrough-Ponds Inc., and the Bach investments group. A member of the Council on Foreign Relations. Earned a bachelors degree from the University of Maryland. Former vice-president of IBM. A trustee of the University of Notre Dame, Catholic University, and the Rockefeller Foundation.

Sandra Day O'Connor: In the Center of the Court. For nearly 200 years the U.S. Supreme Court was America's most exclusive male club. After 101 male justices, Sandra Day O'Connor was named to the Supreme Court by President Reagan in 1981. At the time of her appointment, O'Connor was a fifty-one-year-old state appellate court judge in Arizona. Justice O'Connor had no previous experience as a federal court judge, but she had the active support of Arizona's senior U.S. senator and Republican warhorse, Barry Goldwater. More important, she was a "she." Reagan was anxious to deflect attacks on his opposition to the Equal Rights Amendment and his failure to appoint many women in his own administration. As one Reagan aide put it: "This is worth twenty-five assistant secretaries, maybe more!" Feminist groups were forced to support the appointment, even though O'Connor's record in Arizona was moderately conservative.

Sandra Day grew up on her family's large Arizona ranch, graduated from Stanford with honors, and then went on to Stanford Law School. She finished near the top of her class, along with Chief Justice of the Supreme

Court William Rehnquist (who was first in the class). She married John Jay O'Connor, a Phoenix attorney, and raised three sons. She entered Arizona politics about the time her youngest son entered school. She was appointed to the Arizona State Senate in 1969 and was later elected twice to that body. She rose to majority leader in 1973. She left the Arizona legislature in 1975 to become a Phoenix trial judge. In 1979, she was appointed by a Democratic governor to the Arizona Court of Appeals. Work on this state intermediate court, however, does not involve major constitutional questions.

O'Connor had some business experience; she was formerly a director of the First National Bank of Arizona and Blue Cross/Blue Shield of Arizona. But until her appointment to the U.S. Supreme Court, she was an obscure state court judge. Her service as a Republican leader in the Arizona State Senate qualified her as a moderately conservative party loyalist. However, it appears that her professional and political friendships had more to do with bringing her to President Reagan's attention than her record as a jurist. She had known Justice William Rehnquist since her law school days. She had known former Chief Justice Warren Burger for a long time. And Barry Goldwater had been her mentor in Arizona Republican politics. When Reagan's political advisers told him during the presidential campaign that he was not doing well among women voters, the candidate responded by pledging to appoint a woman to the Supreme Court. Reagan's fulfillment of his campaign pledge was a politically popular decision.

In recent years Sandra Day O'Connor has emerged as the leader of a middle bloc of votes on the High Court, mediating between the liberal and conservative blocs. O'Connor has taken the lead in shaping Supreme Court policy on women's issues—including abortion. O'Connor strongly reaffirmed a woman's fundamental right to abortion, yet recognized a state's interest in protecting a "viable" fetus (a late-term fetus capable of surviving outside of the womb).[14] She has also taken the lead in deciding Supreme Court policy in the controversial area of affirmative action, arguing that laws that distinguish between individuals based on their race must be narrowly tailored to remedy specific injustices. "Racial classifications of any sort pose the risk of lasting harm to our society. They reinforce the belief, held by too many for too much of our history, that individuals should be judged by the color of their skin."[15]

SOCIAL CHARACTERISTICS OF WOMEN LEADERS

Women leaders, like their male counterparts, are disproportionately upper class in social origin. More than half of the nation's women leaders attended prestigious private colleges. About one quarter of them attended one of the "Seven Sisters": Vassar, Radcliffe, Smith, Wellesley, Barnard, Bryn Mawr, or

[14] *Planned Parenthood* v. *Casey* (1992).

[15] *Shaw* v. *Reno* (1993).

Mt. Holyoke. Another one quarter attended one of the traditional prestigious private universities: Harvard, Yale, Chicago, Stanford, Columbia, Cornell, Northwestern, Princeton, Johns Hopkins, or Pennsylvania.

The educational level of top women leaders is very high; nearly half possess earned masters or doctorate degrees, and an additional quarter possess law degrees. (Honorary degrees were not counted.) Thus, a total of 71 percent of the women leaders earned advanced degrees; the comparable figure for male leaders is 55.8 percent. This strongly suggests that women need more education than men to compete effectively for top posts. (Only one woman in our entire group failed to indicate that she held a bachelors degree. Marian Sulzberger Heiskell, daughter of the owner of the *New York Times* and a director of the New York Times Co., Consolidated Edison, Ford Motors, and Merck & Co., does not list an earned degree in her biography.)

The average age of top women leaders was fifty-four in 1980. This is younger than the average age of men in comparable positions, which was sixty-one. We suspect that this difference is largely a product of the recent appointment of many of the women leaders to their positions. Newer members of an elite can be expected to be younger than established members.

An examination of the career backgrounds of women leaders reveals a number of separate recruitment paths. Table 7–4 includes the principal lifetime occupational activity of women at the top of each sector of society.

TABLE 7–4   Social Characteristics of Women in Top Institutional Positions

	Total	Corpo- rate	Govern- ment	Law, News	Civic, Cultural, Education
Average age	54	55	49	55	54
Career					
Corporate	15.9%	19.0%	17.6%	0%	4.3%
Government	19.6	8.5	58.8	9.1	17.4
Law	13.1	11.9	5.9	18.2	21.7
News	15.0	14.2	5.9	54.5	13.0
Education	29.9	40.5	11.8	18.2	34.8
Other	6.5	4.8	0	0	8.7
Education					
Advanced degree	46.7	47.6	47.0	18.2	52.2
Law degree	24.3	23.8	23.5	18.2	34.8
Bachelors degree	28.0	28.6	29.4	54.5	13.0
No degree	0.8	0	0	9.1	0
Schools					
Women's prestigious	34.0	26.2	17.6	60.0	47.8
Prestigious	26.4	28.6	17.6	20.0	39.1
Private	9.4	7.1	29.4	0	4.3
Public	30.2	38.1	35.3	30.0	8.7
Married	76.2	69.2	70.6	100.0	87.0
Has Children	61.0	57.7	52.9	90.9	61.0

In the corporate world—industrials, banks, utilities, insurance companies, and investment firms—a surprising percentage of women are recruited to boards of directors from *universities.* Only 19 percent of female corporate directors were recruited from the corporate world itself; over 40 percent were recruited from universities. This is *not* the pattern of recruitment of male corporate directors, most of whom (89 percent) are recruited from corporations, and few of whom (0.6 percent) come from universities. This leads to the suspicion that many corporations deliberately reached out to universities in the 1970s to find talented women to join their boards. The corporations, in brief, raided the universities.

In contrast, women leaders in government tend to be recruited through government itself (58.8 percent). Only 17.6 percent of female governmental leaders are recruited from the corporate world. Likewise, top female lawyers are recruited through law firms, and top female leaders in the mass media are recruited from news organizations. The career backgrounds of civic, cultural, foundation, and educational leaders are balanced between various sectors of society. The largest single source of female leadership in these institutions is the academic world, supplying approximately one third of the trustees of the largest and most influential institutions.

Finally, it is interesting to observe that three quarters of the nation's top women leaders are married, and over 60 percent of them are mothers. Most of the women at the top today have combined marriage and family with careers that have taken them to the nation's highest institutional positions. Of course, these are extraordinary women. They comprise less than 5 percent of the nation's top leadership. Most were born in the 1920s and 1930s and reached adulthood in a period of history when marriage and family were seemingly more central to American culture.

WHY WOMEN AREN'T GETTING TO THE TOP

Despite the impressive progress of women in leadership positions in the last two decades, women still have not achieved the top rung—chairperson or chief executive officer. Only one woman, Katherine Graham of the Washington Post Company, chairs a major corporate institution in America. (Liz Claiborne, founder of the clothing company that bears her name, was the only other woman CEO in the top 1,000 corporations in 1987; Catherine B. Cleary of First Wisconsin Bank was the only female president of a large bank in 1980.) A *Fortune* survey asking executive recruiters to identify women who *might* become chief executive officers drew a complete blank; even the few companies with women in senior management positions conceded that these women were not going to win the top job.[16]

Serious explanations are not easy to develop. Blatant sexism—dirty

---

[16] Susan Fraker, "Why Women Aren't Getting to the Top," *Fortune,* April 16, 1984, pp. 40–45.

jokes, references to "girls," or overt hostility toward women—is seldom encountered in high corporate and banking circles. The barriers women confront are very subtle and often not recognized by men. Women frequently fail to get "fast-track" assignments or especially sensitive posts. Yet these are the jobs that lead to the top. The reasons are difficult to pinpoint. One observer remarked, "At senior management levels competence is assumed. What you're looking for is someone who fits, someone who gets along, someone you trust. Now that's subtle stuff. How does a group of men feel that a woman is going to fit? I think it's very hard."[17] A woman bank executive says, "The men just don't feel comfortable."

There are many other explanations, and all of them are controversial. Men are reluctant to openly criticize a woman, and therefore women executives do not receive constructive feedback. Government affirmative-action efforts are directed primarily at entry-level positions rather than senior management posts. Women choose staff assignments rather than fast-track, operating-head assignments; they are cautious and unaggressive in corporate politics. Women have lower expectations about peak earnings and positions, and these expectations become self-fulfilling. Women bear children, and even during relatively short maternity absences they fall behind their male counterparts. Women are less likely to want to change locations than men, and immobile executives are worth less to a corporation than mobile ones. Women executives in sensitive positions come under even more pressure than men in similar posts; women executives believe that they get much more scrutiny than men and must work harder to succeed.

Cross-national elite studies confirm these patterns of women in elite positions. Results of a systematic study of institutional elites in the United States, West Germany, and Australia by sociologist Gwen Moore indicate that (1) few women have achieved elite positions in major national institutions; (2) women elites are concentrated in the political and the voluntary association sectors; (3) women elites have fewer inter-sectoral ties; (4) marriage and parenthood is less common among women elites than their male counterparts; (5) most women elites are recruited from very high-status social backgrounds; and (6) women elite participation, while still very low, has increased significantly over the last two decades.[18]

MULTIPLE PATHS TO THE TOP

How do people at the top get there? Certainly, we cannot provide a complete picture of the recruitment process. But we can learn whether the top leadership in government is recruited from the corporate world, or whether there are separate and distinct channels of recruitment.

---

[17] Ibid., p. 40.

[18] Gwen Moore, "Women in Elite Positions," *Sociological Forum*, Vol. 3 (December, 1988), 566–85.

TABLE 7–5 Recruitment to Top Institutional Positions

Sector from which Top Elites Recruited*	Corporate					Public Interest					Government		
	Indus-try	Bank-ing	Utilities	Insur-ance	Invest-ment	Media	Law	Founda-tions	Educa-tion	Civic	Govern-ment	Military	All
Corporate %													
Industry	67.5	52.6	28.1	32.7	4.4	24.4	0	27.9	42.9	56.7	4.0	2.3	43.4
Banking	6.7	22.3	12.5	8.4	12.4	3.1	0	10.2	10.0	7.1	1.3	0	9.9
Utilities	3.8	7.6	36.2	6.7	0	1.2	0	3.0	6.1	4.8	0	0	7.3
Insurance	1.7	2.2	4.1	32.3	0	1.2	1.1	3.0	2.6	2.7	0	0	5.2
Investments	2.6	2.1	3.0	1.6	77.0	3.1	0	3.6	4.9	2.9	.4	0	4.6
Total	82.3	86.8	83.9	81.7	93.8	33.0	1.1	47.7	66.5	74.2	5.7	2.3	70.4
Public Interest %													
Media	.7	0.9	1.9	.9	.9	55.6	0	6.6	5.5	3.6	3.1	2.3	4.2
Law	7.7	6.3	6.3	5.3	1.8	5.6	96.8	9.6	11.6	5.5	61.5	7.0	9.4
Foundations	.6	0.3	.5	.9	0	0	0	6.6	1.8	1.1	.4	0	1.0
Education	7.7	4.0	6.5	9.5	1.8	4.4	2.1	23.4	12.0	8.2	10.1	7.0	8.2
Civic	.1	0.1	0	.2	0	0	0	2.0	.4	2.1	.4	0	0.5
Total	16.8	11.6	15.2	16.8	4.5	65.6	98.9	48.2	31.3	20.5	25.5	16.3	23.4
Governmental %													
Government	.6	1.2	.3	.4	1.8	1.2	0	4.1	2.2	5.3	15.7	9.3	5.1
Military	.1	0	.5	.9	0	0	0	0	0	0	3.1	72.1	1.1
Total	.7	1.2	.8	1.3	1.8	1.2	0	4.1	2.2	5.3	18.8	81.4	6.2

*Columns may not total 100.0 because of rounding.

Biographical information on individuals occupying positions of authority in top institutions in each sector of society reveals that there are multiple recruitment paths to top institutional positions. Table 7–5 shows the principal lifetime occupational activity of individuals at the top of each sector of society. (This categorizing of people according to their lifework depends largely on their own designation of principal occupation in *Who's Who.*)

As we might expect, the corporate sector supplies most of the occupants of top positions in the corporate sector (82.3 percent). The corporate sector also supplies a majority of the top leadership in civic and cultural organizations (74.2 percent), a majority of the trustees of private and renowned educational institutions (66.5 percent), and about half of the trustees of the major foundations (47.7 percent). However, the corporate world provides less than 10 percent of governmental elites.

Top leaders in government are recruited primarily from the legal profession (61.5 percent); some have based their careers in government itself (15.7 percent) or in education (10.1 percent). This finding is important. Government and law apparently provide independent channels of recruitment to high public office. Thus, high position in the corporate world is not a prerequisite to high public office.

The mass media provide another separate path to elite membership. A majority of presidents and directors of television networks, wire services, and the influential press have been associated throughout their lives with the mass media. Of course, the nation's top lawyers have spent most of their lives in the legal profession.

Educators supply only a small fraction of the top leadership of the nation. Of the top governmental leaders, only 10.1 percent were educators, and educators comprise about 8 percent of the trustees of civic and cultural associations and about 23 percent of the trustees of foundations. Indeed, educators do not even supply a majority of the membership of university boards of trustees. Only 12 percent of our educational elites were drawn from the ranks of educators. Corporations only occasionally call upon educators to join corporate boards; less than 10 percent of corporate directors are educators.

LIFE AT THE TOP

"All societies offer rewards to men assuming leadership positions," writes sociologist Suzanne Keller.

> Some rewards are tangible material benefits such as money, land, cattle, or slaves, while others are intangible such as social honor and influence. . . . Rewards play a two-fold role in the recruitment of elites: they motivate individuals to assume the responsibilities of elite positions; and they maintain the values of hierarchical social position.[19]

[19] Keller, *Beyond the Ruling Class*, pp. 183–84.

Institutional leaders receive compensation in many forms. Corporate executives usually receive a bonus based on company performance, in addition to their salary. Then there are stock options, low-interest loans, and deferred compensation paid out over future years to reduce the current tax bite. There are indirect forms of compensation, too—the so-called perquisites of office, or "perks," which may include personal aides and assistants, plush offices and equipment, paid club memberships, plush boxes at sporting events, expense accounts, and the use of company cars and planes.

Corporate CEO compensation packages provide strong evidence that corporations are run by the top managers for themselves, not for the stockholders. The median yearly compensation package for the top one hundred CEOs in 1992 was $4.5 *million!*[20] These multimillion-dollar packages usually include salaries of $1 million to $1.5 million, plus bonuses of $1 million to $2 million, plus stock and stock options which allow executives to purchase company stock at a lower-than-market price. These compensation packages vary from year to year in value, so identifying the nation's highest paid CEOs requires a multi-year perspective. (It also requires considerable research, because CEOs often deliberately try to hide their high compensation in financial reports of their corporations.) *Forbes* magazine reported the five-year total compensation packages for the nation's five highest paid CEOs: Time Warner, Steven J. Ross—$138 million; Toys R Us, Charles Lazarus—$89 million; H.J. Heinz, Anthony J.F. O'Reilly—$88 million; Walt Disney, Michael D. Eisner—$73 million; Reebok, Paul B. Foreman—$58 million.[21]

Perhaps multimillion-dollar packages might be justified if compensation were tied to performance. But performance has little to do with financial rewards among CEOs. There is very little relationship between a corporation's profit performance, or even its stock price, and the CEO's salary and bonus. (Stock and stock options provide only a modest incentive to CEOs; if their corporation's stock market price rises, the value of these items rises.) Few CEOs ever suffer pay cuts when the corporation loses money. And "golden parachutes" (compensation packages designed to protect top managers if they are ousted) are becoming common.

The salaries of governmental leaders are considerably lower than those of corporate executives, although the perks are roughly equivalent. The President of the United States receives a salary of $200,000 plus $50,000 for personal expenses relating to duties, plus $100,000 for travel and $20,000 for entertainment, a total of $370,000. Expenses of the White House staff—which includes salaries, office expenses, and travel for special assistants, aides, and secretaries—run $10 million or more per year. The Vice-President received $176,200 in salary plus expenses in 1992. Each Cabinet member received

[20] *Forbes*, May 25, 1992, p. 182.
[21] Ibid., p. 176.

$143,800 in salary. The Chief Justice of the Supreme Court received $166,200 in 1992; the other Justices each received $159,000. Members of Congress—both senators and representatives—were paid $129,500 in 1992, with cost of living increases scheduled for future years. And they are each supplied another $200,000 or more to hire staff assistants and to run their offices. Committee chairs may spend over $2 million per year running their committees.

However, it is important to note that most top leaders in corporations and government work long and hard. The norm is sixty to seventy hours per week, traveling six to ten days per month, and spending many weekends devoted to business.[22] Most top elites put their jobs before their families or themselves. On their way to the top, most have relocated six or more times. Most top leaders express the belief that their families' lives have suffered because of their careers. Because they have worked so hard all their lives, retirement is often difficult.

SOCIAL CLUBS: ELITES AT PLAY

Institutional leaders are "joiners." The overwhelming majority of those who hold top positions in America belong to one or more social clubs. More important, over one third of the people at the top belong to just a few very prestigious private clubs. Corporate directors, network moguls, Cabinet members, foundation presidents, and superlawyers rub shoulders at places such as the Links and the Knickerbocker in New York, and the Metropolitan, Cosmos, and Burning Tree in Washington. They relax together on a summer outing under California redwoods at the Bohemian Grove. These private clubs provide an opportunity for informal interaction among elites in different segments of society. The importance of these clubs in developing elite consensus and cohesion is the subject of a great deal of speculation. E. Digby Baltzell writes: "At the upper class level in America . . . the club lies at the very core of the social organization of the access to power and authority."[23] Ferdinand Lundberg says: "The private clubs are the most 'in' thing about the . . . elite. These clubs constitute the societal control centers of the elite."[24]

Perhaps the most persuasive case for the importance of such private social clubs is set forth by sociologist G. William Domhoff:

> The Bohemian Grove [a luxury retreat on 2,700 acres of giant redwoods maintained by the Bohemian Club of San Francisco], as well as other watering holes and social clubs, are relevant to the problem of class cohesiveness in two ways. First, the very fact that rich men from all over the country gather in such close

[22] Based on a *Wall Street Journal*–Gallup Poll survey of chief executives of 1,300 large U.S. companies. *Wall Street Journal*, August 19, 1980, p. 31.

[23] E. Digby Baltzell, *The Protestant Establishment* (New York: Random House, 1964), p. 354.

[24] Ferdinand Lundberg, *The Rich and the Super-Rich* (New York: Bantam Books, 1968), p. 339.

TABLE 7–6　Club Memberships of Top Leaders

	Corporate					Public Interest					Government		
	Indus-try	Bank-ing	Utilities	Insur-ance	Invest-ment	Media	Law	Founda-tions	Educa-tion	Civic	Govern-ment	Military	All
Club Membership %													
None	34.9	30.3	34.6	37.9	16.8	36.1	30.5	30.6	35.8	33.8	76.3	85.9	36.2
One to four	33.3	37.1	39.8	40.2	51.3	39.3	48.4	43.3	29.0	32.8	20.7	11.8	35.4
Five or more	31.8	32.6	25.6	21.9	31.9	24.6	21.1	26.1	35.2	33.4	3.0	2.3	28.4
Exclusive Clubs* %													
None	64	57.4	65.4	70.9	57.5	65.8	65.3	65.8	56.3	63.0	95.7	95.1	64.7
One or more	36	42.6	34.6	29.1	42.5	34.2	34.7	34.2	43.7	37.0	5.3	4.9	35.3

*Links (N.Y.), Century (N.Y.), Knickerbocker (N.Y.), Piping Rock (N.Y.), River (N.Y.), Metropolitan (D.C.), Pacific Union-Bohemian (S.F.), Brook (N.Y.), Burlington (S.F.), California (L.A.), Casino (Chi.), Chagrin Valley (Clev.), Chicago (Chi.), Denver (Den.), Detroit (Det.), Eagle Lake (Hous.), Everglades (Fla.), Hartford (Conn.), Hope (R.I.), Idlewild (Dallas), Maryland (Md.), Milwaukee (Mil.), Minneapolis (Minn.), New Haven Town (Conn.), Philadelphia (Phil.), Rittenhouse (Phil.), Racquet (St. L.), Rainier (Seattle), Richmond (Va.), Cuyamuca (San Diego), Charleston (S.C.), Rolling Rock (Pitts.), Saturn (Buf.), St. Louis (St. L.), Somerset (Bos.), Union (Clev.), Woodhill (Minn.). Listing courtesy of G. William Domhoff.

circumstances as the Bohemian Grove is evidence of the existence of a socially cohesive upper class. It demonstrates that many of these men do know each other, that they have face-to-face communications, and that they are a social network. In this sense we are looking at [clubs] as a *result* of social processes that lead to class cohesion. But such institutions also can be viewed as facilitators of social ties. Once formed, these groups became another avenue by which the cohesiveness of the upper class is maintained.[25]

It is our judgment, however, that club membership is a result of top position-holding in the institutional structure of society rather than an important independent source of power. An individual is selected for club membership *after* acquiring an important position in society; position and power do not come as a result of club memberships. Personal interaction, consensus-building, and friendship networks all develop in the club milieu, but the clubs merely help facilitate processes that occur anyway. Nonetheless, the club memberships of persons at the top are worthy of attention.

Corporate leaders are more likely to be members of private social clubs than are governmental leaders. Table 7–6 shows that over two thirds of our corporate elites held private club memberships; nearly a third of them held five or more memberships. In contrast, only 23.7 percent of top governmental leaders held such memberships, and even fewer military chiefs were club members. Doubtless this differential reflects the greater importance of social interaction in the corporate world (and perhaps the fact that businesspersons can shift the exorbitant costs of such memberships to their corporations while government officials cannot). The fact that a majority of top governmental and military elites are *not* club members undercuts the importance attributed to club membership by many "power elite" writers. If a majority of top governmental elites do *not* sip cocktails at the Metropolitan Club, it is difficult to argue that the real decision-making in Washington takes place in that club's lounge.

Nonetheless, the fact that nearly half of the top elites in the corporate, legal, educational, foundation, and mass media sectors of society belong to one of *forty* selected clubs is impressive testimony to the prestige of these clubs.

SUMMARY

The elitist literature on power stresses the disproportionate numbers of top leaders drawn from the upper and upper-middle strata of society. But even classical elite theorists acknowledge the necessity of some opportunities for upward mobility in society, if only to strengthen support for the political system among the masses. The pluralist literature on power describes a more open leadership system where individuals from all social backgrounds can

[25] G. William Domhoff, *The Bohemian Grove and Other Retreats* (New York: Harper & Row, 1974), p. 88.

rise to the top if they have the necessary skills, information, and talents. However, pluralists acknowledge that opportunities to acquire such qualities are unequally distributed among classes in society. Pluralists also argue that social class is a poor predictor of decision-making behavior. We have not resolved this debate, but perhaps we have added some more factual information about the social composition of top institutional leaders.

On the whole, those at the top are well-educated, older, affluent, urban, WASP, and male. There are only a few African Americans in corporate board-rooms, although they represent 12 percent of the U.S. population. African Americans have been much more successful in government than in the corporate world. Only recently have women gained entrance into the board-rooms of large corporations, but less than 10 percent of corporate directors are women, and no woman heads a top 100 corporation. Even in government, despite three Cabinet posts and two Supreme Court seats, women still occupy only about 10 percent of the key positions. Women are more likely to be found as trustees of universities, foundations, and cultural organizations, but even in these sectors women leaders are far outnumbered by men. Top women leaders are upper and upper-middle class in origin, like their male counterparts. However, women leaders tend to have more education and they are younger. Women leaders are more likely to have been recruited from education, the mass media, or law than from the (mostly male) ranks of corporate management.

There is a slight tendency for corporate elites to be more urban and "upper class" than governmental elites. There are more Ivy Leaguers in corporate boardrooms than in government, and there appear to be more private prep school types in corporate management than in government. Governmental leaders tend to have more advanced degrees, not only in law but also in academic and professional fields.

There are multiple recruitment paths to the top of the nation's institutional structure. The corporate world, however, supplies a majority of the top leaders in the corporate sector itself, as well as in civic and cultural organizations, foundations, and universities. However, top governmental leaders are recruited primarily from the law, and to a lesser extent from government itself and education. The mass media, the law, and education all provide separate recruitment channels. In short, the corporate world, while an important recruitment channel, is not the exclusive road to the top.

8 Conflict and Consensus among Institutional Leaders

CONFLICT OR CONSENSUS AMONG ELITES?

How much agreement exists among people at the top about the fundamental values and future directions of American society? Do America's top leaders agree on the *ends* of policies and programs and disagree merely on the *means* of achieving those ends? Or are there significant differences among American elites over the goals and purposes of our society?

Social scientists frequently give conflicting answers to these questions—not because of differences in the results of their research, but because of differences in the interpretation of these results. Although it is sometimes difficult to survey elite attitudes and opinions (individuals at the top do not have much time to spend with pollsters), nonetheless, social scientists have produced a number of good studies of the values of corporate executives, governmental officials, political party leaders, university intellectuals, and even newspersons.

Pluralists contend that these studies reveal significant conflicts between Democrats and Republicans, liberals and conservatives, corporate directors and labor leaders, intellectuals and bankers, and other leadership groups, over a wide range of policy issues. They cite studies showing significant differences between various segments of the nation's elite over tax policy, welfare programs, government regulation of business and labor, energy and environmental questions, alternative approaches to national health care, and the appropriate measures to deal with inflation and recession.

By contrast, elitists contend that despite these differences over *specific* policy questions, all segments of American leadership share a broad consensus about the *fundamental values* of private property, limited government, separation of church and state, individual liberty, equality of opportunity, advancement based on merit, and due process of law. Moreover, since the Roosevelt era, American elites have generally supported liberal social welfare programs, including social security, fair labor standards, unemployment compensation, a federally aided welfare system, government regulation of public utilities, and countercyclical fiscal and monetary policies. Today, elite consensus also includes a commitment to equality of opportunity for women and minorities and a desire to end direct discrimination. Finally, elite consensus includes a desire to exercise influence in world affairs, to expand international trade, and to promote democracy abroad.

We contend that there is, indeed, a broad consensus among America's leaders on fundamental values and future directions of the nation. Disagreement among various segments of the nation's elite occurs *within a framework of consensus* on underlying values. The range of disagreement is relatively narrow, and disagreement is generally confined to *means* rather than ends. It is doubtful that any elite, however hierarchical, is ever free of competing ambitions or contending ideas. Indeed, some conflict may be essential to the health of an elite system. Sociologist Suzanne Keller writes:

> The point need not be labored that doubt and conflicts are necessary: societies advance both as a result of achievements and as a result of disagreements and struggles over the ways to attain them. This is where power struggles play a major indispensable role. Loyalty to common goals does not preclude conflict over how they are to be realized.[1]

So we expect to find conventional "liberal" and "conservative" arguments occurring within a broad and unifying consensus.

THE LIBERAL ESTABLISHMENT

The traditional philosophy of America's elite has been liberal and public-regarding. By this we mean that institutional leaders have shown a willingness to take the welfare of others into account as an aspect of their own sense of well-being. They have been willing to use governmental power to correct perceived wrongs done to others. This is a familiar philosophy—elite responsibility for the welfare of the poor and downtrodden, particularly minority populations. The liberal establishment believes that it can change people's lives through the exercise of governmental power: end discrimination, abolish poverty, eliminate slums, ensure employment, uplift the poor, educate the masses, and instill dominant culture values in all citizens. The prevailing liberal impulse is to *do good*, to perform public services, and to assist the poorest in society.

Leadership for liberal reform has always come from America's upper social classes. This leadership is more likely to come from established "old families" rather than "new rich," self-made people. Before the Civil War, abolitionist leaders were "descended from old and socially dominant Northeastern families" and were clearly distinguished from the emerging "robber barons"—the new leaders of the Industrial Revolution. Later, when

[1] Suzanne Keller, *Beyond the Ruling Class: Strategic Elites in Modern Society* (New York: Random House, 1968), p. 146.

the children and grandchildren of the robber barons inherited positions of power, they turned away from the Darwinist philosophy of their parents and toward the social welfarism of the New Deal. Liberalism was championed not by the working class, but by men such as Franklin D. Roosevelt (Groton and Harvard), Adlai Stevenson (Choate School and Princeton), Averill Harriman (Groton and Yale), and John F. Kennedy (Choate School and Harvard).

The "elite consensus" defies simplistic Marxian interpretations of American politics; wealth, education, sophistication, and upper-class cultural values do *not* foster attitudes of exploitation, but rather of public service and do-goodism. Liberal elites are frequently paternalistic toward segments of the masses they define as "underprivileged," "culturally deprived," "disadvantaged," and so on, but they are seldom hostile toward them.

Today's upper-class liberalism was shaped in the era of Franklin Delano Roosevelt. Roosevelt came to power as a descendant of two of America's oldest families, the Roosevelts and the Delanos, original Dutch patrician families of New York whose landed wealth predates the English capture of New Amsterdam. The Roosevelts and other patrician families whose wealth was gained well before the Industrial Revolution never fully accepted the Social Darwinism, "public be damned," rugged individualism of the industrial capitalists. They were not schooled in the scrambling competition of the upwardly mobile nouveau riche, but instead in the altruism and idealism of comfortable and secure wealth and assured social status. In describing FDR, historian Richard Hofstadter summarizes upper-class liberalism:

> At the beginning of his career he took to the patrician reform thought of the progressive era and accepted a social outlook that can best be summed up in the phrase "noblesse oblige." He had a penchant for public service, personal philanthropy, and harmless manifestos against dishonesty in government; he displayed a broad easy-going tolerance, a genuine liking for all sorts of people; he loved to exercise his charm in political and social situations.[2]

This liberal consensus, of course, is not strictly or necessarily altruistic. *The values of welfare and reform are functional for the preservation of the American political and economic system.* The radical criticism of the liberal establishment is that its paternalism toward the poor and minorities is in reality self-serving; it is designed to end poverty and discrimination while preserving the free enterprise system and the existing class structure.

THE NEOCONSERVATIVES

While American politics continues in the liberal tradition, that tradition is broad enough to encompass critics of "excessive" government interference in society. The war in Vietnam, the Great Society, urban rioting, campus unrest,

---

[2] Richard Hofstadter, *The American Political Tradition* (New York: Knopf, 1948), pp. 323–24.

Watergate, and inflation all combined in the 1960s and 1970s to raise doubts about the size and scope of governmental power. Elite interest in liberal reforms was tempered by the failures and costs of well-meaning yet ineffective (and sometimes harmful) public programs. Elites learned that society's problems cannot be solved simply by passing a law, creating a new bureaucracy, and spending a few billion dollars. War, poverty, ill-health, discrimination, joblessness, inflation, crime, ignorance, pollution, and unhappiness have afflicted society for a long time. Elites no longer assume that these problems can be erased from society by finding and implementing the "right" public policies.

In the 1980s neoconservatism tempered elite enthusiasm for large-scale government programs designed to cure society's ills. Neoconservative elites continued to hold liberal, reformist values, but they no longer had the confidence and ambition (bordering on arrogance) of the liberals of the 1960s. They developed more respect for the free-market system, and became more respectful of traditional values and institutions, including religion, family, and the community. They believed in equality of opportunity where everyone is free to strive for whatever they wish, but they drew back from absolute equality, where the government ensures that everyone gets equal shares of everything. Finally, neoconservatives came to believe that the United States must maintain a strong national defense if democracy is to survive in a world that is often hostile to American values.[3]

The neoconservatives disapproved of the unequal treatment suffered by racial minorities but generally opposed affirmative-action and busing programs that involved racial quotas. Neoconservatives were skeptical that laws, bureaucracies, regulations, and public spending could improve the nation's health or guarantee employment or protect the environment. They believed that government was being overloaded with tasks, many of which should be left to the individual, the family, the church, or the free-market system. Government had attempted to do too much for its citizens, and by failing to meet its promises, government had lost respect and legitimacy.[4]

In its beginning, the neoconservative position was a reaction of a few intellectuals to the turbulence of the 1960s. The early movement included sociologists Nathan Glazer, Irving Kristol, and Daniel Bell; political scientists James Q. Wilson, Aaron Wildavsky, and Daniel Patrick Moynihan (now a U.S. senator from New York); and political sociologist Seymour Martin Lipset. They captured control of an established liberal journal, *Commentary*, and created a new journal of their own, *The Public Interest*. A neoconservative base emerged in the American Enterprise Institute, a Washington policy-planning organization that grew to challenge the liberalism of the more prestigious Brookings Institution (see Chapter 9).

[3] Irving Kristol, "What Is a Neoconservative?" *Newsweek*, January 19, 1976, p. 87.
[4] Peter Steinfels, *The Neoconservatives* (New York: Simon & Schuster, 1979).

The message of these neoconservative intellectuals might not have been heard in elite circles if the nation had not faced rampaging inflation and declining productivity. But by 1980, the United States had experienced a decade-long inflation—the worst in its history. Personal savings were disappearing rapidly. The incentive to invest was crippled by high taxes. Factories and machines became outmoded, and U.S. products could no longer compete with products from Europe and Japan in the world (and even the U.S.) market. Americans as a whole spent too much and saved too little. Federal tax and budget policies promoted immediate consumption instead of investment in the future. A large segment of the federal government's budget (up to three quarters of it) was declared "uncontrollable"—notably the social insurance, welfare, and pension programs. Heavy taxes discouraged work, investment, and productivity.

The trend toward neoconservatism in elite thinking did not alter the underlying commitment to liberal, reformist values. But it represented a more realistic view of what can be achieved by government, and a more traditional view about the importance of personal initiative, enterprise, work, and family. These views were not limited to the Reagan administration. They enjoyed wide acceptance among the nation's top leaders in every sector of society.

The Reagan administration came to Washington with a well-developed policy agenda. Government, Reagan argued, was the problem, not the solution. Government taxing, spending, and monetary policies promoted immediate consumption, instead of investment and economic growth. Government taxing and spending had to be lowered and inflation brought under control. And indeed double-digit inflation was cured with a stiff dose of high interest rates, and later both inflation and interest rates declined dramatically. In the Economic Recovery Tax Cut Act of 1981, personal income taxes were reduced on the average by 25 percent. More important, in this act and later in the Tax Reform Act of 1986, top marginal tax rates were reduced from 70 percent to 28 percent and many loopholes were closed. Unemployment fell and the numbers *and percentages* of Americans with jobs reached unprecedented high levels. The United States enjoyed the longest continuous expansion of the gross national product in its history.

But the combination of lower taxes, increased defense spending, and continued high levels of social welfare spending produced unprecedented federal deficits. Indeed, the national debt *more than doubled* during the Reagan administration. Huge government deficits kept real interest rates high; the United States became the world's largest debtor nation; and future generations were burdened with heavy interest payments. Elites began to worry that America's prosperity was based on shaky debt foundations, that the nation had mortgaged its future, that a future economic crisis might rival the worst in history.

THE NEOLIBERALS

Today many liberals retain their faith in the power of government to "do good" and to solve society's problems, yet they reject many traditional liberal programs as unworkable. Neoliberalism "is an attempt to combine the traditional Democratic compassion for the downtrodden and outcast elements of society with different vehicles than the categorical aid programs or quota systems or new federal bureaucracies."[5] More than anything else, neoliberalism is a search for *new ideas* for government programs to restore the nation's economic health, uplift the poor, end discrimination, distribute income more equally, and provide education and medical care to all.

Chief among the neoliberal concerns is the nation's economy. Unlike old liberals, who placed social issues first on their agenda, the neoliberals are aware that little progress on social problems can be expected unless the economy is healthy. Instead of the "no growth" attitudes of liberals in the 1970s with their hostility toward industry, science, and technology, the neoliberals argue that government must take an active role in promoting and directing the nation's industrial growth.

Instead of the traditional liberal confrontations between government and business, the neoliberals propose direct government-business cooperation to bolster productivity, encourage investment, promote innovation, and boost international sales. Government might direct grants and loans to stimulate new economic development and industrial revitalization; it might seek to "invest" in new technologies, for example, fiber-optic information "superhighways." Since the neoliberal proposals encourage shifts in the labor force, they usually add government "human capital" programs to retrain and relocate workers.

Among the more prominent neoliberal thinkers are economist Lester Thurow, author of *The Zero Sum Society*; economist Robert Reich, fellow Oxford University Rhodes scholar with Bill Clinton and now secretary of labor; Ira Magaziner, another Oxford University Rhodes scholar friend of Bill Clinton, who tried (unsuccessfully) to get Rhode Island to adopt his neoliberal agenda, and who heads Hillary Clinton's health-care task force; and Charles Peters, editor of the *Washington Monthly*, the leading neoliberal journal. These neoliberals are generally critical of the traditional "interest group" liberals who would sacrifice America's growth, productivity, and competitive edge in world markets in order to satisfy the demands of union leaders, protectionist-seeking industries, and other special interests. The struggle between the neoliberals and traditional liberals is being fought mainly *within* the Democratic party.

---

[5] Randall Rothenberg, *The Neoliberals* (New York: Simon & Schuster, 1984).

POLITICAL ELITES: DEMOCRATS AND REPUBLICANS

Within the national consensus on behalf of private property, free enterprise, rewards according to merit, individual liberty, and due process of law, there are identifiable differences of opinion over specific policies and programs. Conventional politics in the United States centers on *party leaders*: Democratic and Republican party leaders differ over "liberal" and "conservative" dimensions. Interestingly, Democratic and Republican rank-and-file *voters* show less disagreement over the issues than party leaders. For example, Democratic and Republican party *leaders* can be clearly differentiated as liberals and conservatives. The mass public is more conservative than liberal in self-identification; Democratic voters are evenly split between these labels, while Republican voters tend to describe themselves as conservative. But Republican voters are not as conservative as Republican leaders, and Democratic voters are not as liberal as Democratic leaders. (See Table 8–1.)

The same pattern—Democratic and Republican party elites differing with each other, with the mass public somewhere in the middle—occurs on many domestic and foreign policy issues. Democratic leaders want to expand the size and services of government; Republican leaders want smaller government and fewer services; the mass public is evenly divided. Democratic leaders say the government is doing too little for blacks; Republican leaders disagree and so does the mass public, although not as strongly as Republican

TABLE 8–1 Democratic and Republican Party Elites Differ with Each Other and the Mass Public over "Liberal" and "Conservative" Labels and Specific Issues

	Democratic Leaders*	Mass Public			Republican Leaders*
		Democrats	Total	Republican	
Describe self as:					
"conservative"	5%	22%	30%	43%	60%
"liberal"	39	25	20	12	1
Prefer:					
small government, fewer sewers	16	33	43	59	87
bigger government, more sewers	58	56	44	30	3
Agree that government is paying too little attention to needs of blacks	68	45	34	19	14
Favor keeping military and defense spending at least at current levels	32	59	66	73	84

SOURCE: Results reported in the *New York Times*, August 14, 1988.

*Republican and Democratic delegates to presidential nominating convention in 1988.

leaders. Democratic leaders are prepared to cut defense spending; Republican leaders favor keeping it at least at current levels, and so does the mass public. In short, political elites have substantial policy disagreements on specific domestic and foreign policy issues.

FACTIONALISM AMONG ELITES

How much conflict exists among America's elites? Are American elites generally cohesive, with only traditional Democratic and Republican affiliations and conventionally liberal and conservative attachments dividing them? Or are there serious conflicts among elites—serious splits that threaten the national consensus and the stability of the system itself?

The pluralist view is that competition is a driving force in the American political system. The very purpose of the political system, according to pluralist theory, is to manage this competition, to channel it through the institutional structure, to modify its intensity, to arrange compromises, and to balance conflicting interests. In short, pluralism recognizes and encourages competition as a system of checks and balances within American society.

In general, pluralists contend that competition will be limited by several forces that act to maintain an "equilibrium" in the political system. First of all, there is supposed to be a large, nearly universal *latent group* in American society that supports the constitutional system and the prevailing rules of the game. This group is not always visible, but it can be activated to administer overwhelming rebuke to any faction that resorts to unfair means, violence, or terrorism. Secondly, *overlapping group membership* is also supposed to maintain the system in equilibrium. Many individuals belong to a number of groups and, therefore, group leaders must moderate their goals and philosophies to avoid offending members who have other group affiliations. Finally, pluralists offer the notion of *checks and balances* that arise from competition itself. No single segment of society—no single group of powerful leaders—could ever command a majority. Thus, the power of corporations is checked by government, government by parties and civic groups, the mass media by government and advertisers, and so on. These "countervailing" centers of power function to check the influence of any single segment of the nation's elite.

Elitists, of course, see a much greater cohesion and unity among various segments of the nation's leadership. Yet elitism does not imply a single, monolithic body of power-holders. Elitism does not pretend that power in society does not shift over time, or that new elites cannot emerge to compete with old elites. Indeed, it is unlikely that there ever was a society in which various individuals and factions did not compete for power and preeminence. A "circulation of elites" is clearly necessary to ensure a renewal of elite leadership through the contribution of slightly different interests and experiences that new members bring to their roles.

Elite theory contends, however, that serious splits among elites—disagreements over the fundamental values and future directions of American society—are rare. Indeed, perhaps the only really serious split in the nation's elite led to the Civil War—the split between Southern planters, landowners, exporters, and slave owners and Northern manufacturers, merchants, and immigrant employees; over whether the nation's future, particularly its Western land, was to be devoted to a plantation, exporting, slave economy or to a free, small farmer, market economy for domestic manufactured goods. This conflict led to the nation's bloodiest war. However serious we believe our present internal conflicts to be, they do not match the passions that engulfed this nation over a century ago.

COWBOYS AND YANKEES

Elite factionalism occurs along a number of fault lines. One of the more important factional divisions occurs between the newly rich, entrepreneurial Southern and Western *cowboys* and the established, managerial Eastern *yankees*. We believe this factionalism transcends partisan squabbling among Democrats and Republicans, or traditional riffs between Congress and the President, or petty strife among organized interest groups. The conflicts between *cowboys* and *yankees* derives from differences in their sources of wealth and the newness of the elite status of the *cowboys*.

New opportunities to acquire wealth and power develop as a result of technological changes and adjustments in the economy. In recent decades, major new areas of opportunity have developed in independent oil drilling operations, the aerospace industry, computer technology and business machines, real estate development, particularly in the "Sunbelt" from southern California and Arizona through Texas to Florida, and discount drugs and merchandising, fast foods, and low-cost insurance.

The new wealth of the *cowboys* is frequently unstable. Wealth that is institutionalized in giant corporations—corporations that form the basis of an industrialized economy, such as autos, steel, oil, and chemicals—is likely to remain intact over generations with only minor fluctuations in value. But many of today's *new* rich have acquired their wealth in relatively new and unstable industries. Independent oil operations and the aerospace industry are highly cyclical businesses. The computer industry has shown remarkable change over time. And fortunes in real estate, drugstores, discount merchandising, and low-cost insurance can fluctuate dramatically.

By contrast, the power of established *yankees* is institutionalized and stable. The *yankees* include the descendants of the great entrepreneurial families of the Industrial Revolution (the familiar Rockefellers, Fords, Mellons, du Ponts, Kennedys, Harrimans, and so forth). Other *yankees* have been recruited through established corporate institutions, Wall Street and Washington law firms, Eastern banking and investment firms, well-known foundations, and Ivy League universities.

The *cowboys* do not fully share in the liberal social welfarism of the dominant Eastern Establishment. The *cowboys* are "self-made" individuals who have acquired wealth and power in an intense competitive struggle that continues to shape their outlook on life. Their upward mobility, their individualism, and their competitive spirit shape their view of society and the way they perceive their new elite responsibilities. In contrast, the *yankees* have either inherited great wealth or have attached themselves to established institutions of great wealth, power, and prestige. The *yankees* are socialized, sometimes from earliest childhood, in the responsibilities of wealth and power. They are secure in their upper-class membership, highly principled in their relationships with others, and public-regarding in their exercise of elite responsibilities.

The *cowboys* are new to their position; they lack old-school ties, and they are not particularly concerned with the refinements of ethical conduct. The *yankees* frequently regard the *cowboys* with disdain—as uncouth and opportunistic gamblers and speculators, shady wheeler-dealers and influence-peddlers, and uncultured and selfish bores.

The *cowboys* are newly risen from the masses—many had very humble beginnings. But it is their experience in *rising* from the masses that shapes their philosophy, rather than their mass origins. As we would expect, they are less public-regarding and social welfare–oriented than the *yankees*, and they tend to think of solutions to social problems in individualistic terms—they place primary responsibility for solving life's problems on the individual. *Cowboys* believe that they "made it" themselves through initiative and hard work and advise anyone who wants to get more out of life to follow the same path. The *cowboys* do not feel guilty about poverty or discrimination; clearly neither they nor their ancestors had any responsibility for these conditions. Their wealth and position was not given to them—they earned it themselves and they have no apologies for what they have accomplished in life. They are supportive of the political and economic system that provided them the opportunity to rise to the top; they are very patriotic—sometimes vocally anti-Communist—and moderate to conservative on most national policy issues.

THE BILLIONAIRE COWBOYS

The personal wealth of the *cowboys* places them at the top of lists of America's wealthiest individuals (Table 2–14). But their wealth is not yet institutionalized in the fashion of the great Establishment families—the Rockefellers, the Mellons, the du Ponts. The billionaire *cowboys* do *not* control the nation's largest corporations, banks, utilities, insurance companies, foundations, and policy-planning organizations. Nonetheless, they represent a potential challenge to the Establishment as they consolidate and institutionalize their wealth over time.

A few prominent examples of the operations of the Sunbelt *cowboys* illustrate their freewheeling independence and the instability of their wealth.

The Bechtels. Representative of the swashbuckling style of the true Sunbelt *cowboys* is the father and son construction team that heads the Bechtel Corporation. Steven D. Bechtel and his son Steven D. Bechtel, Jr. control a little-known, family-held corporate colossus, which is the *world's* largest construction company. The senior Bechtel never obtained a college degree, but he acquired engineering know-how as a builder of the Hoover Dam. Bechtel conceived of and built the San Francisco Bay Area Rapid Transit, and he and his son built the Washington, D.C., METRO subway system.

Steven D. Bechtel, Jr. received an engineering degree from Purdue University in 1946 after service in the U.S. Marine Corps during World War II. He worked in many positions in the Bechtel Corporation before replacing his father as chairman.

The Bechtel Corporation has built an entire industrial city—Jubayl in Saudi Arabia; a copper industry including mines, railroads, and smelters in Indonesia; and the world's largest hydroelectric system in Ontario, Canada. Bechtel was fired as the contractor for the Trans-Alaska pipeline when cost overruns first occurred; but the final price of $8 billion turned out to be eight times higher than the original estimate, and it seems in retrospect that Bechtel would have done a more cost-effective job if it had been allowed to complete the work. The Bechtel Corporation remains family-owned and, therefore, refuses to divulge to the SEC or other prying bureaucracies its real worth.

The Bechtels have recruited established leaders to direct their far-flung enterprises. Before he became secretary of state, George Shultz was serving as president of the Bechtel Corporation. Before he became secretary of defense, Casper Weinberger was serving as vice-president of Bechtel. Both men had gone to Bechtel after serving in President Nixon's Cabinet, and both men have excellent Eastern Establishment connections. So even though the Bechtels themselves remain independent, their personal wealth and the colossal size of their privately owned corporation allow them to hire the top leadership in the nation.

The Hunts. The late billionaire H.L. Hunt was once asked by reporters whether he was worried about his son's extravagance (Lamar Hunt had lost over $1 million in one year as the owner of the new American League football team, the Kansas City Chiefs). "Certainly it worries me," replied the legendary oil magnate. "At that rate he'll be broke in 250 years."

The senior Hunt began drilling for oil in Smackover, Arkansas, in 1920. His very first well (which he won in a poker game) produced a gusher. By 1937, the independent Hunt Oil Company of Dallas, Texas, was worth millions, and at his death in 1974, H.L. Hunt was believed to be one of the richest men in America. His sons, Nelson Bunker, William Herbert, and Lamar, have continued to amass vast personal wealth. "Bunky" Hunt, who regularly refuses interviews and declines publicity, admitted to a congressional committee that he was probably worth over a billion dollars, but he added, "A billion dollars isn't what it used to be." He refused to say exactly how much he was worth: "Senator, it's been my experience that anyone who knows how much they're worth, ain't worth very much."

Operating out of the First National Bank of Dallas, the Hunts manage a vast array of businesses, including the Hunt Energy Corporation and Placid Oil; 3.5 million acres of real estate, including prime downtown Dallas properties; 100,000 head of cattle; and 700 thoroughbred horses. But in 1979, Bunky Hunt and his brother William Herbert decided on an even more ambitious scheme—to corner the world market in silver.

The Hunts began to buy silver at $6 an ounce. Their purchases were so vast that they decided to buy a leading Wall Street investment firm, Bache Halsey Stuart Shields, to facilitate their operations. When silver jumped to $11 an ounce, they contacted their oil-rich Arab friends and recommended more heavy buying. By early 1980, the Hunts had forced the price of silver to $50 an ounce, and their holdings were worth an estimated $7.5 billion. However, much of their holdings were in the form of "futures contracts"— guarantees to pay a set price for silver at a certain date in the future. Rising interest rates in the United States attracted many investors away from silver (and gold) and into high-interest-paying bank certificates and money market funds. Increasingly the Hunts were called upon to pay cash for the unpaid portions of their futures contracts. Finally, on March 27, 1980, "Silver Thursday," the Hunts and their Bache brokers were unable to meet their debts. Panic ensued on Wall Street, as well as in the Federal Reserve System, the U.S. Treasury, and the Commodities Future Trading Commission. The price of silver tumbled. Bache was barely saved from bankruptcy, and many investors lost millions. A $1.1 billion loan was made to the Hunts to keep them from dumping their silver on the market and further depressing the price. Their scheme to corner the silver market failed.

The wealth of the Hunts and many other *cowboys* is unstable; it is not tied to large institutions. At one time Bunky Hunt was the world's wealthiest man, worth an estimated $16 billion. Today, much of the Hunt empire and its assets are tied up in bankruptcy court. Other Texas oilmen have also fallen: Clint Murchison, Jr., was forced to sell the Dallas Cowboys and later to file bankruptcy; John Connally, former Texas governor, secretary of the treasury, and oil and real estate entrepreneur, was also forced into bankruptcy. The problems of these new-wealth *cowboys* have been attributed to declining worldwide oil prices and deflation in land and real estate values.

The Bass Brothers. The original Bass fortune was created in typical *cowboy* fashion. Sid Richardson was a Texas oil wildcatter who had worked the fields for many years before finding his gusher. He borrowed, traded, and financed oil leases, and bought out the New York Central railroad, winning and losing fortunes over his lifetime. He backed winners in politics, including former Texas Governor John B. Connally and President Lyndon B. Johnson. He never married, but he took in his only nephew, Perry Bass, as a partner. When Sid Richardson died in 1959, he left his Texas oil wells to Perry Bass's four sons.

Over time the four Bass brothers amassed a vast empire in oil and gas (Texaco, Northwest Energy, Consolidated Oil and Gas, Charter Co.); high tech (GTECH, Prime Computers); real estate (downtown Ft. Worth; Americana Hotels; Pier 39, San Francisco; Punta Gorda, Florida); clothing (Munsingwear, Nike); fast foods (Church's Fried Chicken); manufacturing (LTC, Fairchild, Champion Parts, Allis Chalmers); banking (InterFirst); and entertainment (Walt Disney). And their personally owned oil wells kept flowing.

The rapid expansion of the Bass fortune is generally attributed to the skills of the oldest Bass brother—Sid Richardson Bass, named after the family's founder. All of the brothers—Sid, Edward, Robert, and Lee—were schooled at Andover and Yale. Sid Richardson Bass is also a Stanford M.B.A., a trustee of the Yale Corporation, a trustee of New York's Museum of Modern Art, and head of Bass Brothers Enterprises, the umbrella group for the many Bass companies and corporations.

The Basses may not have invented "greenmail," but they have been one of its leading practitioners. "Greenmail" is the profit made by a corporate raider who begins buying up a company's stock, threatens a takeover and ouster of the current management, and then sells his stock back to the worried management at a large profit. The Basses were involved in major threats to the management of Texaco and Walt Disney Productions. The Basses have adopted Ft. Worth as their family project, turning the "cowtown" with its stockyards and familiar scents into a complex of gleaming new towers with fashionable shops and restaurants. The Basses are deeply involved in Texas politics through their Good Government Fund and the Bass Brothers Political Action Committee. They support both Democrats (former U.S. Senator Lloyd Bentsen, former Speaker of the House Jim Wright) and Republicans (U.S. Senator Phil Gramm).

To date, the Bass family has displayed considerable unity, even though each brother is associated with different projects. In Ft. Worth they are described simply as "the boys".

H. Ross Perot: Challenging the Establishment? No one better fits the *cowboy* image than the diminutive billionaire tycoon H. Ross Perot. He has spent most of his lifetime, as well as substantial outlays from his massive fortune, in various challenges to the nation's corporate and political establishment. In the 1992 presidential election, Perot financed his own campaign against "politics as usual" and garnered the largest independent vote since Teddy Roosevelt in 1912. He basks in his celebrity status, paying for his own television time when not appearing on talk shows, and underwriting the finances of his national organization, United We Stand America.

Ross Perot is the son of a Texarkana horse trader and cotton broker who taught his offspring the value of hard work at an early age. Young Ross was not a standout scholar or athlete in high school but worked at breaking horses and selling newspapers. He escaped Texarkana Junior College through drive and self-discipline and won an appointment to the U.S. Naval Academy. Upon graduation, he served four years of active duty in the Navy, although he admits that he was disenchanted with military life. His petition for early release from active duty was rejected; he claims to have had a dispute with his commanding officer over the use of the crew's social fund to redecorate the captain's cabin. He sold computers for IBM in Dallas and quickly became a high-volume salesman. But he soon became disenchanted with IBM's emphasis on selling hardware, believing instead that customers wanted software especially designed for their own business. Acting on his own insight, he quit IBM and formed his own software company, Electronic Data System Inc., on his thirty-second birthday in 1962. But his big break came three years later when Congress passed the Medicare and Medicaid programs as part of President Lyndon Johnson's "Great Society." EDS soon became the leading subcontractor providing computer software to process Medicare and Medicaid claims in Texas, California, and other states. In 1968 EDS went public with Wall Street sale of its stock, and Perot became a billionaire.

EDS fluctuated violently on the stock market, first rising from $17 a share to $162 and then crashing back to $29. At one point in his career, Perot had the dubious distinction of being the only man ever to *lose* $1 billion.[6] Annoyed at these stock market fluctuations, he purchased du Pont Walston Inc., one of the largest brokerage firms on the New York Stock Exchange. But Perot failed as an investment broker; du Pont Walston collapsed, and Perot temporarily disappeared from the list of wealthiest Americans. But EDS gradually recovered, and Perot's interests in oil, gas, and real estate prospered. In 1984 he sold EDS to General Motors for $2.5 billion and a seat on the GM board.

Perot hoped to use his GM post to reform corporate America, to bring to the nation's largest industrial corporation the same initiative, energy, and competitiveness that drove the *cowboy* entrepreneur. But GM's established management was not ready for Perot; his public attacks on GM's "archaic" management style were not appreciated in the boardroom. GM Chairman Roger Smith won approval from the board to buy out Perot. Perot left GM, reportedly bitter and vengeful. He went back into the computer business, creating Perot Systems to compete with EDS, now a GM subsidiary.

Perot's swashbuckling style was not limited to business. In 1979 Perot solved his own Iranian hostage crisis by flying to Iran, breaking some of his employees out of jail, and smuggling them to the Turkish border. The exploit

---

[6] "The Man Who Lost a Billion," *Fortune*, September 12, 1973.

inspired a book and TV miniseries, *On the Wings of Angels*. Perot also undertook to reform the Texas school system; he forced Texans to reevaluate traditional priorities by successfully sponsoring a law to require high school football players to pass courses. Perot acquired a taste for secret, covert operations and penchant for conspiracy theories. He became an active force in the Vietnam POW-MIA movement, believing that a widespread conspiracy existed to suppress information about living Americans who were left behind in the jungle.

It was really no surprise that Ross Perot decided to challenge the two-party system. "Challenging the system" is something that Ross Perot had done all of his life. And he had won more battles than he had lost. As a "man of action" he was frustrated with gridlock politics in Washington, especially the reluctance of Democrats and Republicans, liberals and conservatives, and Presidents and Congresses to confront the government's huge annual deficits.

No independent candidate has ever made it to the White House, although independent presidential candidates have affected the outcome of the race between major party candidates. For example, Teddy Roosevelt's 1912 "Bull Moose" effort split off enough votes from Republican William Howard Taft to allow Democrat Woodrow Wilson to win. But the American two-party system historically has discounted independent candidates. So when Ross Perot announced on *Larry King Live* that he would run if his supporters got his name on the ballot in all fifty states, most politicians and pundits gave him little chance of success.

Perot initially seemed to defy all of the conventional wisdom about independent presidential candidates. Party loyalties among voters had been weakening over the years, and in 1992 there were as many self-described Independents as there were self-described Democrats or Republicans. Perot motivated tens of thousands of supporters in a grass-roots effort that succeeded in placing his name on the ballot in all fifty states. And Perot himself promised to resolve the financial obstacle by spending "whatever it takes" from his own huge fortune to mount a "world-class campaign." He would eventually spend about $80 million, an amount well above the $55 million distributed by the Federal Elections Commission to each of the major party candidates, but close to what they spent after party funds, independent expenditures, and "soft money" were counted.

Perot's popular support mushroomed to 35 percent in the polls by late spring, higher than any independent candidate in the history of modern polling. He recruited professional campaign managers Hamilton Jordan (who had managed Jimmy Carter's successful 1976 campaign) and Ed Rollins (who had handled Ronald Reagan in 1984). His twangy Texas quotes captivated audiences, yet he carefully avoided taking clear policy positions. Rather than address specific issues, Perot promised to "fix things," appealing to voters as a successful "can do" businessman challenging the political "establishment."

But "Perot mania" began to fade as the media commenced to tear down the candidate they had helped to create. First the media reported on Perot as a "welfare billionaire" who had made his fortune from government contracts to computerize Medicaid and Medicare programs; then Perot was described as a political insider who has used his wealth and influence to develop the Alliance Airport near Ft. Worth; later he was attacked for his Rambo-like involvement in covert actions and hostage rescue efforts. Finally, he was rapped for hiring private investigators to search for dirt on his political and business opponents, including President Bush's sons. Perot himself blamed Republican "dirty tricksters" for the negative publicity, and no doubt many of the media leads were supplied by his political opponents. Perot would not listen to professional advice; he fired Ed Rollins. By mid-summer, Perot's media image had taken a beating and he was below 25 percent in the polls and mired in third place.

On July 16, at the start of the Democratic Convention, an angry Perot chose to exit the presidential race that he had never formally entered. But he never withdrew his name from the ballot in any state; on the contrary, he continued to fund his petition drives. Most of his supporters were deeply disappointed with the temperamental tycoon. Many were angry: "He's let people down. He's betrayed them. He's forced the alienated to be more alienated."[7] Perot seemed stunned by the anger of his former supporters; he did not like to be branded a "quitter." Throughout the summer, he teased the media with hints that he might jump back into the race. In September, he staged a "poll" of his "volunteers" and then cited the results as a call to reenter the campaign.

In "Perot II—the Sequel," Perot launched the first real electronic campaign—shunning the daily flying circus of cross-country airport speeches, rallies, photo ops, and press conferences in favor of TV talk-show appearances, spot commercials, and paid half-hour "infomercials." The talk-show formats, especially call-in shows, were usually friendly. And to the surprise of the professionals, Perot's infomercials captured huge audiences. With pointer in hand, Perot flipped through charts depicting the nation's economic problems, promising to "fix things" in effective, plain Texas talk. Perot despised the national news media; he fashioned an end-run around news reporters, buying media time himself to present his message directly to the American people. Even before the first presidential debate, Perot's poll figures began to rise again.

Perot's blunt talk clearly "won" the first of the three televised presidential debates. "If its time for action, I have the experience that counts. If its time for gridlock and talk and finger-pointing, I'm the wrong man." In all three debates, Clinton and Bush treated Perot with kid gloves, not wanting to alienate his middle-class supporters. The debates rehabilitated Perot's candidacy; he won back almost two of every three supporters he had had before dropping out.

---

[7] Head of Perot's New York petition drive as quoted in *Congressional Quarterly Weekly* report, July 18, 1992, p. 2079.

Historically, independent candidates have lost the votes of people who expressed a preference for them in the polls, but in the voting booth decided not to "waste" their votes on a long shot. In the last days of the campaign, Perot skillfully countered this tendency with paid TV commercials claiming that the real "wasted vote" would be a vote for "politics as usual." He also aired five half-hour "infomercials" touting his character as husband, father, businessman, benefactor, and man of action.

Perot ended up with the highest vote, 19 percent, ever won by a third candidate in modern times. Moreover, the Perot campaign played a major part in increasing voter turnout for the first time in over thirty years. Perot's candidacy prevented Bill Clinton from claiming majority support, holding the winner to 43 percent of the total votes cast. But Perot's voters were spread across the nation. He failed to win in a single state and thus came up with *no* electoral votes.

Perot's penchant for challenging the establishment remains undiminished. His organization, United We Stand America, continues to add members, and Perot himself continues to make his political presence felt on talk shows and paid "infomercials." Perot's carping at the Clinton administration complicates problems for the Democrats, but the prospect of his running for President again in 1996 terrorizes Republicans, who fear that he will split the anti-Clinton vote. Leaders of both parties hope that his unpredictable temperament will cause him to self-destruct.

THE NEW TYCOONS

Established corporate management has long professed a concern for the public interest and a devotion to the "corporate conscience." Indeed, the Business Roundtable[8] issued a formal *Statement on Corporate Responsibility*, which asserted that "the long-term viability of the business sector is linked to its responsibility to the society of which it is a part."[9] It quotes its own former chairman and the former chairman of General Electric, Reginald Jones:

> A corporation's responsibilities include how the whole business is conducted every day. It must be a thoughtful institution which rises above the bottom line to consider the impact of all of its actions on all, from stockholders to the society at large. *Its business activity must make social sense just as its social activities must make business sense.*[10]

But these sentiments are encountered more often among established corporate managers than among self-made entrepreneurs. They are senti-

---

[8] The Business Roundtable is discussed in "The Civic Associations" in Chapter 5, and in "The Business Roundtable" in Chapter 9.

[9] Business Roundtable, *Statement on Corporate Responsibility*, New York, October 1981.

[10] Ibid, p. 14. Italics in original.

ments more likely to be expressed by *yankees* in New York corporate board-rooms than by *cowboys* lunching at the Dallas Petroleum Club. New tycoons, whether they make their home in Manhattan or Houston, are more likely to believe that they best serve society by serving their own economic interests. They share with a few "classical" economists—most notably Nobel Prize–winner Milton Friedman—the belief that entrepreneurs best serve the nation by pursuing profit, increasing productivity, and striving for optimum efficiency.

Donald Trump. Perhaps no one better exemplifies the energy, vision, and daring of America's new generation of self-made tycoons than Donald Trump. The most celebrated real estate baron of our time, Donald Trump literally changed the face of our world—from Manhattan's dazzling Trump Tower and Grand Hyatt to the glitzy casinos of Atlantic City. And Trump's rise to wealth and power at a very young age testify to the extraordinary opportunities in America.

Donald Trump started with a mere $50 million—a stake derived from his father's modest yet successful New York building and real estate business. He turned this stake into $1 billion before reaching age thirty. "I gave Donald free rein," said his father. "He has great vision and everything he touches seems to turn to gold. Donald is the smartest person I know."[11]

Young Donald attended private schools in New York City and graduated from New York Military Academy as an honor cadet. As a boy he reportedly hung around his father's construction sites. He started college at Fordham University in New York, but at his father's urging, transferred to the Wharton School at the University of Pennsylvania. Bored with classes, he renovated property in his spare time, worked in his father's office during summers, and absorbed the real estate business. At twenty-two, with his Wharton School degree in hand, he was ready to rebuild New York City. He convinced his father to remortgage apartment buildings to generate cash for expansion; Donald Trump wanted to leave the "outer boroughs"—Queens, the Bronx, Brooklyn—to invade Manhattan.

Trump had already developed a reputation as the boy wonder of New York real estate when the opportunity arose to become a true real estate mogul. In 1974 New York City was on the verge of bankruptcy, and one of the nation's oldest corporate institutions—the Penn Central railroad—was already bankrupt. Other Manhattan real estate owners were liquidating their holdings or lying low waiting for more promising times. Then Donald Trump appeared, in his early trademark burgundy-colored suits and matching shoes, his initials "DLT" on his shirts, cuff links, and chauffeur-driven Cadillac limousines, offering to buy Penn Central's Manhattan properties. These he purchased for Depression-era prices, and he proceeded to develop, in a deal with the Hyatt Corporation, his first major hotel, the Grand Hyatt. Trump was twenty-eight years old when he negotiated these deals and then pushed a

---

[11] Jerome Tuccille, *Trump* (New York: Jove, 1985), p. 57.

major tax abatement for his new buildings through City Hall. Construction of the magnificent Trump Tower in Manhattan quickly followed, and then Trump turned his sights on Atlantic City. The voters of New Jersey passed a referendum permitting casino gambling in the dilapidated old resort city. Trump moved in quickly, obtained the necessary casino license from the state, and built the dazzling casino-hotel Harrah's. He purchased Resorts International, retained its Taj Mahal property in Atlantic City, and sold its remaining casinos to game-show mogul Merv Griffen. In one of his first failures, he created the USFL to challenge the NFL for the allegiance of the nation's professional football fans; his team, the New Jersey Generals, prospered but the league floundered.

Typical of many new wealth entrepreneurs, Trump does not hide his assets. Indeed he believes that using his own name on a property increases its value. Currently Trump owns the following: in Manhattan, the Trump Tower, the Trump Plaza, and the Trump Parc Hotel; in Atlantic City, casinos Trump Plaza and Trump's Castle and the new Taj Mahal; in Palm Beach Florida, Trump Towers and the Mar-a-Lago private mansion, golf course, and beach; as well as the Trump Princess, reportedly the world's greatest private yacht, a ghostwritten book *Trump: The Art of the Deal*, and even a bicycle race—the "Tour de Trump."

Trump has demonstrated that the entrepreneurial spirit can prevail over the bureaucratic mindset in government. Trump is politically shrewd and media smart. He regularly succeeds in overcoming the obstacles to development thrown up by armies of bureaucrats in New York City, New York State, and New Jersey. His empire is largely private, operating under a maze of corporate enterprises, most of which bear his own name.

THE NEW CLASS: AN EMERGING ELITE?

The creation and dissemination of ideas and information has become a central function in advanced industrial societies. Indeed, the importance of this function in modern society has led to the argument that professions in the mass media and entertainment industries, the foundations and think tanks, government bureaucracies and public interest groups, compose the vanguard of an ascendant "New Class" that will eventually displace the old economic leaders as society's ruling elite.[12]

The power of the New Class in a "post-industrial" society is based upon its mastery of knowledge and information, creative ideas, and technical expertise. However, it is generally recognized that the New Class is not yet a cohesive group, nor does it directly control the institutions and resources that are needed to support its work. The New Class is dependent upon governmental and corporate support—research, contracts, grants. Government

---

[12] Daniel Bell, *The Coming of Post-Industrial Society* (New York: Basic Books, 1973); B. Bruce-Briggs, ed., *The New Class* (New Brunswick: Transaction Books, 1979); Irving Kristol, *Two Cheers for Capitalism* (New York: Basic Books, 1978).

bureaucracies expand in part because of the demands of these increasingly powerful policy entrepreneurs, program administrators, and public-interest lobbyists. Political scientist Aaron Wildavsky writes about the New Class:

> Its defining existential condition is that high income and professional standing alone do not enable its members to maintain the status and privilege to which they aspire. Their money cannot buy them what they want, so their task, as they define it, is to convince others to pay collectively for what they cannot obtain individually. Thus government lies at the center of their aspirations and operations.[13]

The New Class is *not* an institutional elite; it does *not* exercise formal authority over any significant segment of the nation's material resources; and it is *not* included in our definition of the nation's elite. But we do not dismiss the arguments of the New Class theorists: that ideas, information, and expertise may become "a new form of property" in a "post-industrial" society; that power, wealth, and celebrity may eventually transfer to the holders of this intangible form of property; and that this new elite may hold "significantly different values" from existing elites.

According to sociologist Daniel Bell, the New Class is critical of American business, government, the military, and organized religion; the New Class has contributed to a decline in public confidence in these institutions, as well as a loss of popular faith in traditional values.

However, there is only very limited empirical evidence that the New Class espouses any different values than traditional economic elites. Political scientists Stanley Rothman and S. Robert Lichter surveyed various segments of the New Class—reporters, journalists, and television news producers, in the most influential outlets;[14] top Hollywood movie writers, directors, and producers;[15] and public-interest-group lobbyists and lawyers.[16] If anything, these New Class members came from even *more* privileged social-class backgrounds than traditional economic elites, and they benefited even more from educations at private prep schools and prestigious universities. And the New Class is overwhelmingly white and male.

The New Class generally agrees with traditional elites about the value of the private enterprise system (see Table 8–2). And the New Class certainly supports the notion of unequal incomes based on merit. Socialist ideas about equality in the distribution of wealth are poorly received among these highly competitive and achievement-oriented people. But it is true that the New Class supports a larger role for government in society than traditional elites.

[13] Aaron Wildavsky, "Using Public Funds to Serve Private Interests," in *The New Class*, ed. Bruce-Briggs, p. 79.

[14] Stanley Rothman and S. Robert Lichter, "Media and Business Elites," *Public Opinion*, (October–November 1981), pp. 42–46.

[15] Stanley Rothman and S. Robert Lichter, "What Are Movie-Makers Made Of?" *Public Opinion* (December–January 1984), pp. 14–18.

[16] Stanley Rothman and S. Robert Lichter, "What Interests the Public Interests," *Public Opinion* (April–May 1983), pp. 44–48.

TABLE 8–2 New Class and Traditional Elite Attitudes

Percent Agreeing	Traditional Elite Business Execs	New Class		
		Media[1]	Hollywood[2]	Public Interest[3]
Private enterpise				
Big corporations should be publicly owned.	6%	13%	15%	37%
Private enterprise is fair to workers.	89	70	67	NA
Less regulation of business would be good.	86	63	49	18
Meritocracy				
People with more ability should earn more.	90	86	94	71
Role of government				
Government should guarantee jobs.	29	48	38	80
Government should reduce gap between rich and poor.	23	68	59	94
Social-cultural values				
Homosexuality is wrong.	60	25	28	12
Homosexuals should not teach in public schools.	51	15	13	8
Adultery is wrong.	76	47	42	55
Women have a right to decide on abortion.	80	90	96	95

[1] Composed of 240 journalists and broadcasters at "the most influential media outlets." See *Public Opinion* (October–November 1981), pp. 42–46.

[2] Composed of 149 writers, producers, and directors of the 50 top-grossing films from 1965 through 1982. See *Public Opinion* (December–January 1984), pp. 14–18.

[3] Composed of 157 leaders or top staffers of 74 public interest groups ("PIGs") and public interest law firms. See *Public Opinion* (April–May 1983), pp. 44–48.

Perhaps the most obvious distinction between the New Class and traditional elites is found in moral and cultural values. As anyone who has observed the positive portrayal of homosexuality, abortion, and adultery in television, movies, and books would suspect, the New Class is significantly more cosmopolitan than traditional elites.

The New Class theory might be summarized as follows:[17]

1. In a complex and highly technical society, knowledge and expertise are functionally important, and those who have it can challenge traditional institutional elites for control of policy-making.

---

[17] This summary parallels Clarence N. Stone, "The New Class or the Old Convergence," *Power and Elites*, 1 (September 1984), 1–22.

2. The New Class can develop constituencies for its services and can capture key governmental programs and agencies.

3. The New Class is attitudinally different from traditional economic elites, and working through government and the mass media it can develop its own agenda for social reform and a new ethos for a post-industrial society.

Our reasons for rejecting this New Class notion, in favor of our own institutional elite theory, can be organized along similar lines:

1. The complexity of society actually makes technocratic solutions very uncertain and unreliable.[18] Decision-makers prefer pragmatic, fragmented, sequential decision-making; they are disillusioned with expert advice and frequently skeptical of highly abstract or theoretical solutions to social problems. The technocrats are not on top, but merely on tap, for call by institutional leaders when and if they decide to use them.

2. The New Class has little "common consciousness." Its members are divided between "professional estates" (scientific, technological, scholarly, administrative, legal, cultural) and between various institutional locations (business, media, government, universities, lobbying organizations, law firms, and so on). Moreover, their presumed access to government power is certainly no greater than that of economic elites. Government may have need of expertise, but it also has need of economic resources and the cooperation of those who control those resources.

3. The New Class is deeply committed to the values of individualism and personal merit and supportive of a society in which the most talented, hard-working, creative, and enterprising individuals receive disproportionate rewards. These are the same values that have always inspired America's traditional elites. The New Class has the same social advantages and educational credentials as traditional elites. Its support of the "new morality" in television, films, and books does not threaten the institutional positions or economic interests of traditional elites.

SUMMARY

Elitist and pluralist scholars disagree over the extent and significance of conflict among the nation's leaders. Pluralists observe disagreements over specific programs and policies; they contend that this competition is a significant aspect of democracy. Competition among elites makes policies and programs more responsive to mass demands, because competing elites will try to mobi-

---

[18] See David Braybrock and Charles E. Lindblom, *A Strategy for Decision* (New York: Free Press, 1970).

lize mass support for their views. Masses will have a voice in public policy by choosing among competing elites with different policy positions. Moreover, competitive elites will check and balance each other and help prevent abuses of power. In contrast, elitist scholars observe a fairly broad consensus among the nation's leaders on fundamental values and national goals. Elitists contend that the range of disagreement among elites is relatively narrow and generally confined to means rather than ends.

It is our own judgment, based on our examination of available surveys of leadership opinion as well as public statements of top corporate and governmental executives, that consensus rather than competition characterizes elite opinion. Despite disagreements over specific policies and programs, most top leaders agree on the basic values and future directions of American society.

The established liberal values of the nation's leadership include a willingness to take the welfare of others into account as a part of one's own sense of moral well-being, and a willingness to use governmental power to correct the perceived wrongs done to others—particularly the poor, blacks, and other minorities. Popular notions of corporate and financial leaders as exploitative, reactionary robber barons are based on nineteenth-century stereotypes.

Contemporary neoconservative and neoliberal political statements are merely variations on the underlying liberal consensus of the nation's top leadership. Neoconservatives express less confidence that government bureaucracies and spending programs can achieve liberal values. Neoliberals also express doubts about traditional taxing, spending, and regulatory programs; they call for "new ideas" to achieve the liberal values shared by all top leaders. Disagreement among various sectors of national leadership—businesspersons, Democratic and Republican politicians, bureaucrats, mass media executives, and labor leaders—is confined to a relatively narrow set of issues—the size of government budgets, specific details of tax reform, and the adequacy of current defense spending. There is widespread agreement on the essential components of welfare-state capitalism.

Nonetheless, there is evidence of elite factionalism. In recent years, a major fault line among the nation's leaders is the division between the newly rich Southern and Western *cowboys* and the established Eastern *yankees*. The *cowboys* have acquired their wealth since World War II in independent oil operations, the aerospace and computer industries, Sunbelt real estate from California through Texas to Florida, and discount stores. These *cowboys* do not fully share the liberal values of the established *yankees*. They are self-made persons of wealth and power—individualistic, highly competitive, and politically conservative. The *yankees* have enjoyed wealth for generations or have slowly climbed the rungs of the nation's largest corporations, law firms, banks, and foundations. They have acquired a sense of civic responsibility, and they look upon the *cowboys* as unprincipled gamblers, shady wheeler-dealers, and uncultured influence-peddlers.

Established corporate management generally professes a devotion to "corporate responsibility." They wish to exercise power in public affairs, to be respected in Washington, to cultivate a favorable media image. In contrast, many of the new self-made tycoons believe that they best serve the nation by making their enterprises profitable.

Despite the personal wealth and celebrity which many self-made newly rich have achieved, they have made few inroads into established institutional power positions. New wealth is often unstable; fluctuations in the prices of oil or real estate can have a drastic effect on the fortunes of these new tycoons. Established institutional management enjoys a more stable power base. While occasionally threatened by wealthy independent corporate raiders, on the whole, the nation's established corporate leadership has generally succeeded in maintaining its dominant power position.

9

How Institutional Leaders Make Public Policy

POLICY AS ELITE PREFERENCE OR GROUP INTERACTION?

Are the major directions of public policy in America determined by a relatively small group of like-minded individuals interacting among themselves and reflecting their own values and preferences in policy-making? Or are the major directions of American policy a product of competition, bargaining, and compromise among a large number of diverse groups in society? Does public policy reflect the demands of "the people" as demonstrated in elections, opinion polls, and interest-group activity? Or are the views of "the people" easily influenced by communications flowing downward from elites?

The elitist model of the policy process would portray policy as the preferences and values of the dominant elite. According to elitist political theory, public policy does not reflect demands of "the people," but rather the interests, sentiments, and values of the very few who participate in the policy-making process. Changes or innovations in public policy come about when elites redefine their own interests or modify their own values. Of course, elite policy need not be oppressive or exploitative of the masses. Elites may be very public-regarding, and the welfare of the masses may be an important consideration in elite decision-making. Yet the central feature of the model is that the *elites* make policy, not the masses. The elite model views the masses as largely passive, apathetic, and ill-informed about policy. Public opinion is easily manipulated by the elite-dominated mass media, so that communication between elites and masses flows *downward*. The "proximate policy-makers"— the President, Congress, the courts, and bureaucracy—knowingly or unknowingly respond primarily to the opinions of elites.

No serious scholar today claims that the masses make policy—that each individual can participate directly in all of the decisions that shape his or her life. The ideal of the New England town meeting where the citizenry convenes periodically as a legislature to make decisions for the whole community is irrelevant in today's large, complex industrial society. Pure democracy is, and always has been, a romantic fiction. Social scientists acknowledge that all societies, even democratic societies, are governed by elites.

By contrast, the pluralist model of the policy process portrays public policy as the product of competition, bargaining, and compromise among many diverse *groups* in society. Few individuals can participate directly in policy-making, but they can join groups that will press their demands upon government. Interest groups are viewed as the principal actors in the policy-making process—the essential bridges between individuals and government. Public policy at any time reflects an equilibrium of the relative influence of interest groups.

The individual can play an indirect role in policy-making by voting, joining interest groups, and working in political parties. Parties themselves are viewed as coalitions of groups: the Democratic party, a coalition of labor, ethnic groups, blacks, Catholics, central-city residents, black intellectuals, and southerners; the Republican party, a coalition of middle-class, white-collar workers, rural and small-town residents, suburbanites, and Protestants. According to this model, mass demands flow *upward* through the interest groups, parties, and elections to the proximate policy-makers.

AN OLIGARCHICAL MODEL OF NATIONAL POLICY-MAKING

Any model of the policy-making process is an oversimplification. The very purpose of a model is to order and simplify our thinking about the complexities of the real world. Yet too much simplification can lead to inaccuracies in our thinking about reality. Some models are too simplistic to be helpful; others are too complex. A model is required that *simplifies*, yet at the same time *identifies*, the really significant aspects of the policy process.

Let us try to set forth a model of the policy-making process derived from the literature on national elites—an "oligarchical model of the national policy-making process." Our model will be an abstraction from reality—not every major policy decision will conform to our model. But we think the processes described by the model will strike many knowledgeable readers as familiar, that the model indeed actually describes the way in which a great many national policies are decided, and that the model at least deserves consideration by students of the policy-making process.

Our "oligarchical model" of national public policy-making is presented in Figure 9–1. The model assumes that the initial resources for research, study, planning, and formulation of national policy are derived from corporate and personal wealth. This wealth is channeled into foundations, universities, and policy-planning groups in the form of endowments, grants, and contracts. Moreover, corporate presidents, directors, and top wealth-holders also sit on the governing boards of the foundations, universities, and policy-planning groups to oversee the spending of their funds. In short, corporate and personal wealth provides both the financial resources and the overall direction of policy research, planning, and development.

The foundations are essential linkages between wealth and the intellec-

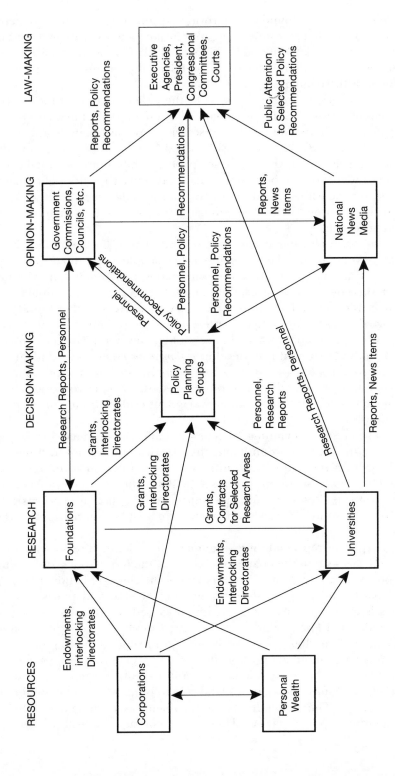

FIGURE 9-1 The Policy Process: The View from the Top

tual community. The foundations provide the initial "seed money" to identify social problems, to determine national priorities, and to investigate new policy directions. At a later period in the policy-making process, massive government research funds will be spent to fill in the details in areas already explored by these initial studies.

Universities necessarily respond to the policy interests of foundations, although of course they also try to convince foundations of new and promising policy directions. Nonetheless, research proposals originating from universities that do *not* fit the previously defined "emphasis" of foundation interests are usually lost in the shuffle of papers. While university intellectuals working independently occasionally have an impact on the policy-making process, on the whole, intellectuals respond to policy directions set by the foundations, corporations, and government agencies that underwrite the costs of research.

The *policy-planning groups* are the central coordinating points in the policy-making process. They bring together people at the top of the corporate and financial institutions, the universities, the foundations, the mass media, the powerful law firms, the top intellectuals, and influential figures in the government. They review the relevant university- and foundation-supported research on topics of interest, and more important, they try to reach a consensus about what action should be taken on national problems under study. Their goal is to develop *action recommendations*—explicit policies or programs designed to resolve or ameliorate national problems. At the same time, they endeavor to build consensus among corporate, financial, media, civic, intellectual, and government leaders around major policy directions.

Certain policy-planning groups—notably the Council on Foreign Relations, the Business Roundtable, the American Enterprise Institute, and the Brookings Institution—are influential in a wide range of key policy areas. Other policy-planning groups—the Population Council (world population control), Resources for the Future (environmental concerns), and the Urban Institute (urban problems), for example—specialize in certain policy issues.

Corporate representatives—company presidents, directors, or other high officials—sit on the boards of trustees of the foundations, universities, and policy-planning groups. The personnel interlocking between corporation boards, university trustees, foundation boards, and policy-planning boards is extensive. (We have already described interlocking among the Rockefeller and Ford foundations and the Council on Foreign Relations, the Business Roundtable, and the Brookings Institution in Chapter 5.)

Policy recommendations of the key policy-planning groups are then distributed to the mass media, federal executive agencies, and the Congress. The mass media play a vital role in preparing public opinion for policy change. The media define the "problem" as a problem and thus set the agenda for policy-making. They also encourage political personalities to assume new policy stances by allocating valuable network broadcast time to those who will speak out in favor of new policy directions.

The White House staff, congressional committee staffs, and top executive administrators usually maintain close contact with policy-planning groups. Frequently, before the results of government-sponsored research are available, federal executive agencies, with the assistance of policy-planning groups, will prepare legislation for Congress to implement policy decisions. Particular versions of bills will pass between executive agencies, the White House, policy-planning groups, and the professional staffs of the congressional committees that eventually will consider the bills. The groundwork is laid for making policy into law. Soon the work of the people at the top will be reflected in the actions of the "proximate policy-makers."

THE COUNCIL ON FOREIGN RELATIONS
AND THE TRILATERAL COMMISSION

The center of our oligarchic model of national policy-making in the fields of foreign affairs, national security, and international trade is occupied by the Council on Foreign Relations and its multinational arm, the Trilateral Commission. In Chapter 5 we described the top leadership of the CFR, including its many interlocking directorships with leading corporations, banks, and investment firms. Now let us describe the role of the CFR and the Trilateral Commission in the policy-making process.

The Council on Foreign Relations. Political scientist Lester Milbraith once observed that the influence of the CFR throughout government is so pervasive that it is difficult to distinguish the CFR from government programs: "The Council on Foreign Relations, while not financed by government, works so closely with it that it is difficult to distinguish Council actions stimulated by government from autonomous actions."[1] Of course, the CFR denies that it exercises any control over U.S. foreign policy. Indeed its by-laws declare that "The Council shall not take any position on questions of foreign policy and no person is authorized to speak or purport to speak for the Council on such matters."[2] But policy initiation and consensus building do not require the CFR to officially adopt policy positions.

CFR meetings are secret. The remarks of government officials who speak at CFR meetings are held in confidence. A CFR rule states:

> Full freedom of expression is encouraged at Council meetings. Participants are assured that they may speak openly, as it is the tradition of the Council that others will not later attribute their statements to them in public media or forums or

---

[1] Lester Milbraith, "Interest Groups in Foreign Policy," in *Domestic Sources of Foreign Policy*, ed. James Rosenau (New York: Free Press, 1967), p. 247.

[2] Council on Foreign Relations, *Annual Report*, 1992, p. 174.

knowingly transmit them to persons who will. All participants are expected to honor that commitment.[3]

The history of CFR policy accomplishments is dazzling. It developed the Kellogg Peace Pact in the 1920s, stiffened U.S. opposition to Japanese Pacific expansion in the 1930s, designed major portions of the United Nations' charter, and devised the "containment" policy to halt Soviet expansion in Europe after World War II. It also laid the groundwork for the NATO agreement and devised the Marshall Plan for European recovery. In the Kennedy and Johnson administrations, the Council took the lead in formulating U.S. policy in Southeast Asia—including both the initial decision to intervene militarily in Vietnam and the later decision to withdraw. Council members in the Kennedy-Johnson administration included Secretary of State Dean Rusk, National Security Adviser McGeorge Bundy, Assistant Secretary of State for Far Eastern Affairs William P. Bundy, CIA Director John McCone, and Undersecretary of State George Ball.

The Council consensus up to November 1967 was clearly in support of the U.S. military commitment to South Vietnam. Following the Tonkin Gulf Resolution and the introduction of U.S. ground combat troops in February 1965, President Lyndon Johnson created a private, informal group of CFR advisers, with the assistance of CFR chairman John J. McCloy, which later became known as the "Senior Advisory Group on Vietnam." The group was not an official governmental body, and it included more private elites than public officeholders. Twelve of the fourteen members of the Senior Advisory Group were CFR members; only Johnson's close personal friend Abe Fortas and General Omar Bradley were *not* CFR members. As the war continued unabated through 1967, the Council, at the urging of George Ball, recruited Professor Hans Morganthau of the University of Chicago to conduct a new private study, "A Reexamination of American Foreign Policy." Following the Tet offensive in February 1968, President Johnson called a special meeting of his Senior Advisory Group. The Group met for two days, March 25 and 26, during which time key members Douglas Dillon, Cyrus Vance, Arthur Dean, Dean Acheson, and McGeorge Bundy switched from "hawks" to "doves." They presented their new consensus to end the war to the President. Five days later, on March 31, 1968, President Johnson announced a de-escalation of the war and his personal decision to retire from public office.

At this point, the CFR, which was doubtlessly relieved that Johnson and his immediate advisers were left as the scapegoats of the Vietnam disaster, immediately launched a new group, the "Vietnam Settlement Group," headed by investment banker Robert V. Roosa and Wall Street lawyer Cyrus Vance. The group devised a peace proposal allowing for the return of prisoners and a stand-still ceasefire, with the Viet Cong and Saigon dividing the territory under their respective controls. Secretary of

---

[3] Council on Foreign Relations, *Annual Report*, 1982, p. 188.

State Kissinger avoided directly attributing U.S. policy to the CFR plan, but the plan itself eventually became the basis of the January 1973 Paris Peace Agreement.

Following Vietnam, the CFR, under David Rockefeller's tenure as chairman, began its "1980s Project." This was an ambitious program even for so powerful a group as the CFR. But money from the Ford, Lilly, Mellon, and Rockefeller foundations provided the necessary resources. The project officially began in 1975 and lasted until 1980, and it included an international campaign on behalf of "human rights"; an effort to restrict international arms sales; and a study of "North-South global relations"—relations between richer and poorer countries. Upon taking office in 1977, the Carter administration set all of these policies in motion. It restricted international arms sales; it encouraged private and World Bank loans to less developed countries; and, most important, it initiated a worldwide "human rights" campaign in which U.S. trade and aid were curtailed in countries that did not live up to human rights standards. Not only did the Carter administration adopt the CFR program in full, but it also brought CFR members into the government to administer these programs, including Cyrus Vance (secretary of state), Harold Brown (secretary of defense), Walter Mondale (Vice-President), Zbigniew Brzezinski (national security adviser), W. Michael Blumenthal (secretary of the treasury), Sol Linowitz (negotiator of the Panama Canal Treaty), Andrew Young (U.N. ambassador), and Paul Warnke (negotiator of the SALT II Agreement).

But the CFR itself, still under Rockefeller's direction, gradually became aware of the crumbling foreign and military policies of the United States during the Carter administration. In 1980, the CFR issued a stern report citing "sharp anguish over Americans held hostage by international outlaws" (Iran) and "the brutal invasion of a strategic nation" (Afghanistan).[4] It described U.S. defenses as "a troubling question." More important, the CFR announced the end of the "1980s Project," with its concern for "human rights," and initiated a new study program on U.S.–Soviet relations. Even before Carter left office, leading CFR members had decided that the "human rights" policy was crippling U.S. relations with its allies but was not affecting policies in Communist countries. Moreover, the CFR recognized "the relentless Soviet military buildup and extension of power by invasion, opportunism, and proxy," and recommended that the U.S–Soviet relationship "occupy center stage in the coming decade."[5] Thus, elite support for a harder line in foreign policy and a rebuilding of America's defenses had been developed through the CFR even before Ronald Reagan took office.

The CFR announced its new hard line toward the Soviet Union in a 1981 report, *The Soviet Challenge: A Policy Framework for the 1980s*. It recom-

---

[4] Council on Foreign Relations, *Annual Report*, 1979–80, p. 11.

[5] Ibid., p. 12.

mended a comprehensive, long-term military buildup by the United States, and it even argued that arms control should no longer be the "centerpiece" of U.S. policy toward the Soviets. It also recommended that the United States be prepared to use force in unstable areas of the world such as the Persian Gulf.

The Reagan administration, like those that preceded it, relied heavily on CFR advice. However, because of some conservative objections to the "internationalism" of the Council on Foreign Relations, CFR members on the Reagan team did not publicize their membership. Indeed, during the 1980 campaign, CFR and Trilateral Commission member George Bush was forced to resign from both organizations to deflect right-wing attacks that he was part of the CFR "conspiracy" to subvert U.S. interests to an "international government." Nonetheless, Reagan's Secretary of State George P. Shultz, Defense Secretary Casper Weinberger, Treasury Secretary Donald Regan, and CIA Director William Casey were CFR members.

When David Rockefeller stepped down as CFR chairman in 1985, his place was taken by Peter G. Peterson, chairman of the board of the Wall Street investment firm of Lehman Brothers Kuhn Loeb and a director of RCA, General Foods, 3M, Black and Decker, and Cities Services.

The CFR strongly supported the new thaw in U.S.–Soviet relations "spurred by the atmosphere of *glasnost*, the summit, and the Intermediate-range Nuclear Force treaty."[6] It welcomed a number of high Soviet officials to its meetings. NBC anchorman Tom Brokaw introduced Soviet Information Chief Gennadi Gerasimov, and arms negotiator Paul C. Warnke introduced chief Soviet negotiator Victor Karpov.

Today the Council takes pride in the success of the Cold War containment policy that was first outlined by CFR member George Kennen in his 1947 "X" article in *Foreign Affairs*. But it recognizes that the end of the Cold War necessitates another restructuring of fundamental policy goals. It seeks "to formulate a new organizing principle for American activities overseas in place of the East-West paradigm of the Cold War."[7] Above all, the Council seeks to keep the United States actively involved in international politics; that is, to avoid isolationism, trade barriers, and "xenophobia." Its members actively support U.S. aid to Russia and other former Soviet republics, the North Atlantic Free Trade Agreement and other efforts to stimulate global trade, an active U.S. role in peace efforts in the Middle East and in the republics of the former Yugoslavia, and the development of a strategy for dealing with the Islamic world.

In honor of the Council's seventy-fifth anniversary, a major new fund-raising campaign, headed by David Rockefeller and former Wall Street investment banker Douglas Dillon, was initiated to give the Council "the means to

---

[6] Council on Foreign Relations, *Annual Report*, 1988, p. 22.

[7] Council on Foreign Relations, *Annual Report*, 1992, p. 14.

reach abroad in a far more comprehensive way . . . as the United States begins to share more fully its international responsibilities."[8]

The Trilateral Commission. A discussion of the CFR would be incomplete without some reference to its multinational arm, the Trilateral Commission. The Trilateral Commission was established by CFR Board Chairman David Rockefeller in 1972, with the backing of the Council and the Rockefeller Foundation. The Trilateral Commission is a small group of top officials of multinational corporations and governmental leaders of industrialized nations, who meet periodically to coordinate economic policy between the United States, Western Europe, and Japan. According to David Rockefeller, a small, private group of international bankers, business leaders, and political figures—about 290 in all—can assist governments in a wide variety of decisions. "Governments don't have time to think about the broader longer-range issues," says Rockefeller, in typically elitist fashion. "It seemed to make sense to persuade a group of private, qualified citizens to get together to identify the key issues affecting the world and possible solutions."[9] Perhaps the most important contribution of the Trilateral Commission was the initiation of regular summit meetings between the heads of Western European nations, the United States, and Japan to discuss economic policy.

The Trilateral Commission's North American chairman is David Rockefeller; its North American members are a compendium of power and prestige: Robert E. Allen, chairman of AT&T; Harold Brown, former secretary of defense; Zbigniew Brzezinski, former national security adviser to the President; Henry Kissinger, former secretary of state; George P. Schultz, former secretary of state; Katherine Graham, chairman of the Washington Post Company; James E. Burke, chairman of Johnson & Johnson; Thomas S. Foley, speaker of the U.S. House of Representatives; James R. Houghton, chairman of Corning Glass; Paul Volcker, former chairman of the Federal Reserve Board; and Thomas G. Labrecque, chairman of Chase Manhattan, and others. Their European and Japanese counterparts are equally influential; for example, Takashi Ishihara, chairman of Nissan; Akio Morita, chairman of Sony; Yutaka Saito, chairman of Nippon Steel; Eiji Toyoda, chairman of Toyota; Giovanni Agnelli, chairman of FIAT. Bill Clinton served on the Trilateral Commission while governor of Arkansas, as have HUD Secretary Henry Cisneros and HHS Secretary Donna Shalala.

THE BUSINESS ROUNDTABLE

The Business Roundtable was established in 1972 "in the belief that business executives should take an increased role in the continuing debates about public policy." The organization is composed of the chief executives of the

[8] Ibid., p. 12.

[9] *Newsweek*, March 24, 1980, p. 38.

200 largest corporations in America and is financed through corporate membership fees. Former Du Pont chairman Irving Shapiro summarized the purposes of the Roundtable: "We wanted to demonstrate that there are sensible human beings running big companies, people who think beyond their own interests."[10]

The real impetus for the formation of the Business Roundtable, however, was the worsening inflation of the 1970s, a series of oil crises and resulting public criticism of the oil companies, and the growing consumer and environmental movements that threatened big business with costly regulations. The Roundtable came together from three existing business organizations: (1) the "March Group" of chief executive officers of large corporations, led by John Harper of Alcoa and Fred Borch of General Electric, which was fighting the creation of a federal consumer protection agency; (2) the Construction Users Anti-Inflation Roundtable, headed by Roger Blough of U.S. Steel, which was devoted to combating rising construction costs, especially the cost of labor; and (3) the Labor Law Study Committee, which was fighting changes in labor laws which permit common-site picketing.

Why did corporate America feel that it needed a central policy-planning organization? For many years, the U.S. Chamber of Commerce, the National Association of Manufacturers, the Business Council, and hundreds of industry associations such as the powerful American Petroleum Institute had represented business in traditional pluralist interest-group fashion. Why did business create this superorganization? The Business Roundtable itself says:

> The answer is that business leaders believed there was a need that was not being filled, and they invented the Roundtable to fill it. They wanted an organization in which the chief executive officers of leading enterprises would get together, study issues, try to come to a consensus, develop positions and advocate those positions. The executives who created the Roundtable believed that the U.S. economy would be healthier, there would be less unwarranted intrusion by government into business affairs, and the interests of the public would be better served if there were more cooperation and less antagonism. It was decided that one way business could be a more constructive force, and have more impact on government policymaking, was to bring the chief executives directly into the picture. The Roundtable therefore was formed with two major goals:
>
> —to enable chief executives from different corporations to work together to analyze specific issues affecting the economy and business, and
>
> —to present government and the public with knowledgeable, timely information, and with practical, positive suggestions for action.[11]

In brief, traditional interest-group representation was inadequate for

---

[10] *Time*, April 13, 1981, p. 76.

[11] Business Roundtable public statement, "What the Roundtable Is," dated January 1988—201 Park Avenue, New York, New York, 10166.

the nation's top corporate leadership. It wished to come together *itself* to decide upon public policy.

The power of the Business Roundtable stems in part from its "firm rule" that a corporate chief executive officer cannot send a substitute to meetings. Congress members are impressed when AT&T Chairman Robert Allen appears at a congressional hearing on business regulation; or when Citicorp Chairman John S. Reed speaks to a congressional committee about taxation; or when Robert C. Winters, chairman of Prudential, talks to Congress members about Social Security. Irving Shapiro of Du Pont served as Roundtable chairman during its early years. Now the chairman serves a two-year term; the most recent chairman is John D. Ong, chairman of B.F. Goodrich.

The Roundtable was at the forefront of "deregulation," tax cutting, and budget cutting in the Reagan years. One of Reagan's personal friends (Holmes Tuttle) reported: "The morning after the Inauguration, Justin Dart and I sat down with the President and gave him our impression of the budget. We kept saying the same thing: cut, cut, and then cut some more."[12] The Roundtable argued successfully that proposed environmental regulations should undergo economic impact analysis in order to learn what the cost of compliance really is, and whether this cost is worth whatever improvement the regulations bring.

The Roundtable perceives current federal deficits as a problem of excessive federal spending, requiring significant reductions in entitlement programs. Tax increases, particularly taxes on business, would harm the United States in international business competition. Robert Kilpatrick of the CIGNA Corporation chaired the Roundtable's Federal Budget Task Force, reasserting the Roundtable position that the major thrust of deficit reduction must be addressed at the spending side of the budget. The Roundtable favors "de-indexing" of all entitlement programs, including Social Security, so that Congress would not be forced to vote increases each year. And the Roundtable has taken the lead in opposing federally mandated worker health insurance. The Roundtable strongly supported the North American Free Trade Agreement.

Another pressing concern of the Roundtable's is "the abuse of capital markets" by hostile corporate raiders. The Roundtable represents managerial opposition to corporate takeovers, and the Roundtable does not hesitate to ask Congress for protection from the dreaded raiders. Roundtable member H.B. Atwater, chairman and chief executive officer of General Mills, testified before Congress in 1987 against "the few manipulators who put companies into play for short-term financial gain." He decried the adverse effects of leveraged buyouts on employees, communities, bond markets, and governments. (He tactfully avoided mentioning the adverse effects of hostile

---

[12] *Time*, April 13, 1981, p. 77.

takeovers on ousted top managers.) He named Carl Ichan and T. Boone Pickens as examples of "manipulators" who sought short-term profits at the expense of corporations and their employees.[13]

THE BROOKINGS INSTITUTION

The Brookings Institution remains the dominant policy-planning group for American domestic policy. This is true despite the growing influence of competing think tanks over the years. Brookings staffers dislike its reputation as a "liberal think tank," and they deny that Brookings tries to set national priorities. Yet the Brookings Institution has been very influential in planning the war on poverty, welfare and health-care reform, deficit reduction, and taxing and spending policies. The *New York Times* columnist and Harvard historian writing team, Leonard and Mark Silk, describe Brookings as the central locus of the Washington "policy network," where it does "its communicating: over lunch, whether informally in the Brookings cafeteria or at the regular Friday lunch around a great oval table at which the staff and their guests keen over the events of the week like the chorus of an ancient Greek tragedy; through consulting, paid or unpaid, for government or business at conferences, in the advanced studies program; and, over time, by means of the revolving door of government employment."[14]

The Brookings Institution began as a modest component of the progressive movement of the early twentieth century. A wealthy St. Louis merchant, Robert Brookings,[15] established an Institute of Government Research in 1916 to promote "good government," fight "bossism," assist in municipal reform, and press for economy and efficiency in government. It worked closely with the National Civic Federation and other reformist, progressive organizations of that era. Brookings himself was appointed to the War Production Board by President Woodrow Wilson.

The original trustees of Brookings included Frederic H. Delano (wealthy banker and railroad executive, a member of the first Federal Reserve Board, and an uncle of President Franklin Delano Roosevelt), James F. Curtis (banker and assistant secretary of the treasury under President Taft), Arthur T. Hadley (president of Yale University), Herbert Hoover (then a self-made millionaire engineer and later secretary of commerce and President of the United States), and Felix Frankfurter (Harvard law professor, later to become Supreme Court Justice).

The first major policy decision of the Brookings Institution was the

---

[13] Testimony of H.B. Atwater, chairman of the Business Roundtable Task Force on Corporate Responsibility, before the House Committee on Telecommunications and Finance, June 11, 1987.

[14] Leonard Silk and Mark Silk, *The American Establishment* (New York: Basic Books, 1980), p. 160.

[15] Brookings also served as chairman of the board of trustees of Washington University in St. Louis for twenty years, building a small college into a major university.

establishment of an annual federal budget. Before 1921, the Congress considered appropriation requests individually as they came from various departments and agencies. But the Brookings Institution proposed, and the Congress passed, the Budget and Accounting Act of 1921, which created for the first time an integrated federal budget prepared in the executive office of the President and presented to the Congress in a single budget message. This notable achievement was consistent with the early interests of the Brookings trustees in improving economy and efficiency in government.

The Brookings Institution assumed its present name in 1927, with another large gift from Robert Brookings, as well as donations from Carnegie, Rockefeller, and Eastman (Kodak). It also added Wall Street lawyer Dean Acheson to its trustees; he remained until his appointment as secretary of state in 1947. For many years, the full-time president and executive officer of Brookings was Robert D. Calkins, former dean of the School of Business at Columbia University.

Under the leadership of Robert Calkins, the Institution broke away from being "a sanctuary for conservatives" and recruited a staff of in-house liberal intellectuals. The funds for this effort came mainly from the Ford Foundation; later a Ford Foundation staff worker, Kermit Gordon, was named Brookings Institution president. (He served until his death in 1977.) First under Calkins and later under Gordon, Brookings fashioned itself as a policy-planning organization and rapidly gained prestige and prominence in elite circles. When Republicans captured the presidency in 1968, Brookings became a haven for unemployed liberal Democratic intellectuals and bureaucrats. "In the late sixties and early seventies, Brookings took on the appearance of a government-in-exile as refugees from the Johnson Administration found new offices in the Brookings edifice. . . ."[16] Charles L. Schultze, former chairman of the Council of Economic Advisers, began the publication of an annual "counter-budget" as a critique of the Nixon budgets. These are now published regularly under the title "Setting National Priorities." President Kermit Gordon, drawing on his experience as budget director under President Johnson, pressed forward with the notion of an alternative to the presidential budget. Brookings staffers Charles Schultze and Alice Rivlin developed a proposal for a new congressional budget process and a Congressional Budget Office. In 1974, Congress obligingly established new budgetary procedures and created new and powerful House and Senate Budget Committees, with a new joint Congressional Budget Office headed, of course, by Alice Rivlin. She returned to Brookings in 1983 after eight years of advising Congress on budget matters.

Brookings experienced a modest eclipse in power and influence during the 1980s. Brookings scholar Henry Aaron contends that social scientists gen-

---

[16] Silk and Silk, *The American Establishment,* p. 154.

erally were discredited by the failure of many of the Great Society programs to bring about their expected results.[17] This led to a breakdown in the liberal intellectual consensus on behalf of government intervention to solve social problems and contributed to the rising influence of neoconservative scholars. As the leading liberal think tank, Brookings suffered the popular disillusionment incurred by liberal reformers. Whatever the merits of Aaron's explanation, certainly we must add to it the disastrous economic performance of the 1970s—high inflation, low productivity, declining real incomes, and the general discredit this brought to Keynesian macroeconomics. As the Keynesians fell into disrepute, Brookings declined in influence. Finally, of course, Brookings's influence was weakened with the coming of the Reagan administration. If Brookings was the sole instrument of a truly consensual elite, it would have equal influence regardless of which administration was in office. But, in fact, Brookings's influence was minimal during the Reagan-Bush years.

The Clinton administration provided an opportunity for Brookings to reassert its dominant position in the policy-planning network. Alice Rivlin was appointed deputy director of the Office of Management and Budget (under director and former Congressman Leon Panetta) and helped craft the Clinton tax-increase and deficit-reduction legislation in 1993. Brookings staff were influential participants in developing Clinton's comprehensive healthcare package, and Brookings economists long supported the North American Free Trade Agreement.

Louis W. Cabot, former chairman of the board of trustees of the Brookings Institution, declared that "The top challenge for Brookings is to anticipate the major policy issues of the future. . . . Thanks to Brookings' modest endowment, we are able to set our own agenda and focus on what we believe to be the most important public policy issues."[18] Do the trustees determine research directions at Brookings? This is a very sensitive topic. Former Brookings Governmental Studies Director Gilbert Y. Steiner once asserted that "the trustees have precious little authority over anything and none at all over the findings and conclusions that are presented in Brookings books."[19] However, President MacLaury has acknowledged that the trustees are deeply engaged in the activities of Brookings, to the point of vetoing proposed research projects, and that interventions by the trustees have caused controversy within the institution. Brookings scholars, with their university backgrounds, expect academic freedom. But MacLaury was quoted in the *New York Times* as saying: "There is always the question about the role of the trustees, particularly with regard to academic freedom. But we are a think tank. We are not a university."[20] Chairman Louis W.

[17] Henry Aaron, *Politics and the Professors* (Washington: Brookings Institution, 1976).

[18] The Brookings Institution, *Annual Report*, 1988, p. 3.

[19] Gilbert Y. Steiner, "On Dye's Presidential Address," *Journal of Politics*, 41 (February 1979), 315–16.

[20] Quoted in the *New York Times*, December 14, 1983, p. 8.

Cabot states that "Our trustees enrich our research planning with pragmatic insights gained from experience in business and finance, government, the law, and academe. They provide the direction and commitment needed to keep Brookings and its work up to the standards we have set for ourselves."[21]

Brookings scholars are recruited for their potential contributions to policy-making, not for their teaching or even their scholarship per se. They are recruited to work on areas of interest to Brookings. They do not enjoy tenure. They need not obtain project grants or contracts in order to undertake a study, as scholars in most other think tanks must do. The power of the president, trustees, and benefactors does not extend to the management of policy research.

Yet according to the Brookings by-laws, the board of trustees "is responsible for general supervision of the Institution, approval of fields of investigation, and safeguarding the independence of the Institution's work." The president is given the responsibility for recommending policy research projects and selecting the staff; the board of trustees selects the president. These structural arrangements ensure that the trustees, and implicitly the financial contributors, maintain overall institutional control.

COMPETITION AMONG THE THINK TANKS

An oligarchic model does not preclude competition. Not only do individuals strive for power and preeminence, organizations do so as well. Competition among policy-planning organizations has grown over the years. The Council on Foreign Relations and the Trilateral Commission remain preeminent in foreign affairs and international trade issues. But in domestic policy, the historic influence of the Brookings Institution has been challenged in recent decades by the development of competing organizations, notably the American Enterprise Institute and the Heritage Foundation.

The American Enterprise Institute. For many years, Republicans dreamed of a "Brookings Institution for Republicans" which would help offset the liberal bias of Brookings itself. In the late 1970s, that role was assumed by the American Enterprise Institute (AEI). The American Enterprise Association, as it was first called, was founded in 1943 by Lewis H. Brown, chairman of the Johns-Manville Corporation, to promote free enterprise. William J. Baroody, Sr., a staffer at the U.S. Chamber of Commerce, became executive director in 1962 and adopted the name American Enterprise Institute. William J. Baroody, Jr., assumed the presidency of AEI after his father. In 1976, the AEI provided a temporary haven for many Ford administration refugees, including Treasury Secretary William E. Simon, Trans-

---

[21] The Brookings Institution, *Annual Report,* 1988, p. 4.

portation Secretary Carla Hills, CEA Chairman Herbert Stein, and AEI's "Distinguished Fellow," former President Gerald R. Ford. More important, however, the AEI began to attract distinguished neoconservative scholars, including sociologist Irving Kristol, commentator Michael Novak, economist Murray Weidenbaum (later chairman of the Council of Economic Advisers), and political scientists Seymour Martin Lipset, Ben Watlenberg, Austin Ranney, and Jeane Kirkpatrick (former U.N. ambassador). The AEI appealed to both Democrats and Republicans who were beginning to have doubts about big government. President William Baroody, Jr. distinguished the AEI from Brookings:

> In confronting societal problems those who tend to gravitate to the AEI orbit would be inclined to look first for a market solution . . . while the other orbit people have a tendency to look for a government solution.[22]

But Robert V. Roosa, former chairman of the Brookings Institution, and senior partner in the Wall Street investment firm of Brown Brothers, Harriman & Co., resented the implications that Brookings is "liberal," while the AEI is "conservative":

> AEI is selling against Brookings. They don't have to do that—they have a role to fill. . . . We do some things on the conservative side—and more now. . . . We say to corporations "We're on your side too."[23]

AEI's influence in the Clinton years rests upon the quality of its policy research. Arguably, AEI books and journals set the nation's standard for policy work. Its flagship bimonthly, *The American Enterprise*, publishes some of the best articles on public policy in a lively and engaging style and format. It also contains a "Public Opinion and Demographic Report" that regularly assesses the nation's condition and mood.

The Heritage Foundation. Conservative ideologues have never been welcome in the Washington establishment. Yet influential conservative businessmen gradually came to understand that without an institutional base in Washington they could never establish a strong and continuing influence in the policy network. Their estrangement from the centers of power was captured in a statement from the Heritage Foundation:

> In those days (1975) we jokingly used to say a phone booth was just about big enough to hold a meeting of conservative intellectuals in Washington . . . we were considered irrelevant by the "opinion-makers" in the media and the power-brokers in the Congress ignored us . . . A conservative "think tank," they

---

[22] Silk and Silk, *The American Establishment*, p. 179.
[23] Ibid.

said, was a contradiction in terms; conservatives had no ideas. History, of course, has proven them wrong.[24]

So they set about the task of "building a solid institutional base" and "establishing a reputation for reliable scholarship and creative problem-solving." The result of their efforts was the Heritage Foundation.

The Heritage Foundation was the brainchild of several congressional staffers and conservative publicists, including Edwin Feulner and Paul Weyrich. The funding came from Colorado businessman-brewer Joseph Coors, who was later joined by two drugstore magnates, Jack Eckerd of Florida and Lewis I. Lehrman of New York. Heritage boasts that it accepts no government grants or contracts and that it has a larger number of individual contributors than any other think tank. Prominent among its contributors are the Richard Mellon Scaife and the John M. Olin foundations.

Unquestionably, competition among think tanks is affected by the outcome of national elections. The Heritage Foundation would have been unlikely to win much influence in Washington had Ronald Reagan not been elected President. Heritage boasts that its 1980 book, *Mandate for Leadership*, set the policy agenda for the Reagan years. Heritage prides itself on being "on the top of the news" with quick *Backgrounders*—reports and memoranda ready at the drop of a press release. Scholarly books and monographs are not in style at Heritage. "Marketing is an integral part of Heritage's product," explains President Edwin Feulner. Despite the emphasis on current, topical, and brief analyses, the Heritage Foundation's flagship publication, *Policy Review*, has gained respect in academic circles.

Heritage is "unabashedly conservative." Resident scholars at Heritage are not particularly distinguished. President Feulner explains, "AEI has the big names—the Herb Steins, the Arthur Burnses. We have young Ph.D.s just out of graduate school on their first or second job."[25] There is very little direct evidence of Heritage influence in public policy. The Reagan administration came to Washington with the most conservative agenda in fifty years. The Heritage Foundation helped publicize that agenda, but there are no specific policy initiatives that can be traced to Heritage. At its tenth anniversary banquet in 1984, Reagan hailed the Foundation as changing "the intellectual history of the West" and testified to its "enormous influence on Capitol Hill and—believe me, I know—at the White House." George Bush was even more extravagant, telling Heritage, "You have been real world movers." But these plaudits were designed more to polish the conservative images of the President and Vice-President than to describe the real influence of Heritage. Heritage inflates its own image by

[24] Heritage Foundation, *Annual Report*, 1985, p. 1.

[25] Charles Holden, "Heritage Foundation: Court Philosophers," *Science*, 211 (1981), 1019–20.

taking credit for policies that would have been enacted anyway. Liberals unintentionally cooperate in this image-making by attributing sinister power to this conservative think tank.

THE POLICY-PLANNING TRUSTEES

A collective portrait of the trustees of CFR, the Business Roundtable, and the Brookings Institution in 1980 confirms the extensive interlocking between the policy-planning organizations and corporate, governmental, university, and civic institutions (see Table 9–1).

First of all, it is clear that the policy-planning organizations do in fact provide structured linkages with the corporate world. The trustees of these policy-planning organizations averaged over four corporate directorships each; only 6 percent of the policy-planning trustees were *not* members of corporate boards. *All* Roundtable directors are corporate directors; indeed, one must be a corporate chief executive officer as a condition of membership.

TABLE 9–1   The Policy-Planning Trustees: A Collective Portrait

	CFR N = 22	Brookings N = 18	Roundtable N = 44	Total N = 84
POSITIONS EVER HELD				
Corporate directorships				
Average number	3.2	5.0	4.3	4.1
(% with none)	(18.2%)	(11.1%)	(0%)	(6.0%)
Government offices				
Average number	3.0	1.2	0.4	1.2
(% with none)	(4.5%)	(50.0%)	(75.0%)	(51.2%)
University trusteeships				
Average number	1.0	1.0	1.3	1.2
(% with none)	(31.8%)	(38.9%)	(27.3%)	(32.1%)
Civic association offices				
Average number	5.2	5.7	5.3	5.1
(% with none)	(0%)	(0%)	(6.8%)	(2.4%)
Total institutional affiliations				
(average)	12.4	12.4	11.3	11.6
EDUCATION				
Percent college education	100.0%	100.0%	100.0%	100.0%
Percent prestigious university*	81.8%	77.7%	52.3%	69.0%
Percent law degree	22.7%	11.1%	11.4%	17.9%
Percent graduate degree				
(including law)	90.9%	66.7%	47.7%	58.3%

*Harvard, Yale, Chicago, Stanford, Columbia, M.I.T., Cornell, Northwestern, Princeton, Johns Hopkins, Pennsylvania, and Dartmouth.

SOURCE: Marquis, *Who's Who in America*, 1980–81. Data on eight directors were not available.

Second, the trustees of the policy-planning organizations have considerable government experience. They averaged 1.2 government posts during their careers; about half of all of the trustees reported some governmental experience. Almost all of the CFR directors held governmental posts at one time or another in their careers. Half of the Brookings trustees had served in government. This is an important comment on the four organizations: Clearly the CFR and Brookings trustees are more experienced in governmental affairs than the trustees of the Business Roundtable.

Third, the policy-planning trustees maintain an active interest in education. The average trustee held 1.2 university trusteeships; only 32 percent of our trustees had *not* held a university trusteeship.

Fourth, it is clear that the policy-planning trustees also form a bridge between their organizations and a wide range of civic and cultural organizations. The average trustee held five reported posts (not merely memberships) in civic and cultural associations. These included, for example, the Metropolitan Museum of Art; the Rockefeller, Ford, and Carnegie foundations; and other policy-planning groups such as the Urban Institute, American Assembly, and Resources for the Future. Only 3 percent did *not* report holding official posts in civic or cultural organizations. The coordinating function of the policy-planning trustees is made strikingly clear when we observe that the trustees averaged over eleven institutional positions each!

If we examine their educational backgrounds, we find that the policy-planning trustees are distinctively "Ivy League." Over two thirds of the directors of the CFR, the Business Roundtable, and the Brookings Institution graduated from just twelve prestigious universities. Nearly 20 percent of the policy-planning trustees are lawyers. More important, perhaps, is the prevalence of postgraduate degrees among the policy-planning trustees, including law degrees and an impressive number of M.B.A.s and Ph.D.s from prestigious universities. Over half of the trustees held advanced degrees, and this figure does *not* include the numerous honorary degrees that are regularly bestowed upon them. This finding supports speculations by other writers of the growing importance of expertise in policy-planning.

In brief, the policy planners have a great deal of experience in directing affairs in the corporate, governmental, university, and civic worlds. They are extraordinarily well educated, with the majority holding advanced degrees and most of these obtained from prestigious Ivy League universities. And, of course, the policy-planning trustees are overwhelmingly white, male, and middle-aged.

THE ROLE OF THE "PROXIMATE POLICY-MAKERS"

The activities of the "proximate policy-makers"—the President, Congress, federal agencies, congressional committees, White House staff, and interest groups—in the policy-making process have been described in countless books and articles. The term *proximate policy-maker* is derived from political scientist Charles E. Lindblom, who uses it merely to distinguish between citizens and elected officials: "Except in small political systems that can be run by something like a New England town meeting, not all citizens can be the immediate, or *proximate*, makers of policy. They yield the immediate (or proximate) task of decision to a small minority."[26] In typically pluralist fashion, Lindblom views the activities of the proximate policy-makers as the *whole* of the policy-making process. But our oligarchic model of public policy-making views the activities of the proximate policy-makers as only the *final phase* of a much more complex process. This is the open, public stage of policy-making, and it attracts the attention of the mass media and most political scientists. This public phase of policy-making is much easier to study than the private actions of corporations, foundations, universities, policy-planning groups, and mass media executives. Most pluralists concentrate their attention on this phase of public policy-making and conclude that it is simply a process of bargaining, competition, and compromise among governmental officials.

Undoubtedly, bargaining, competition, persuasion, and compromise over policy issues continue throughout this final law-making phase of policy-making. This is particularly true in the formulation of domestic policy; by contrast, the President is much freer to pursue elite recommendations in foreign and military policy areas without extensive accommodation of congressional and interest-group pressures. Of course, many elite recommendations fail to win the approval of Congress or even of the President in the first year or two they are proposed. Conflict between the President and Congress, or between Democrats and Republicans, or liberals and conservatives, and so forth, may delay or alter the final actions of the proximate policy-makers.

But the agenda for policy consideration has been set by other elites *before* the "proximate policy-makers" become actively involved in the policy-making process. The major directions of policy change have been determined, and the mass media have prepared the public for new policies and programs. The formal law-making process concerns itself with details of implementation: Who gets the "political" credit, what agencies get control of the program, and exactly how much money will be spent? These are not unimportant questions, but they are raised and decided within the context of policy goals and directions that have already been determined. These decisions of the "proximate policy-makers" tend to center about the *means* rather than the *ends* of public policy.

SUMMARY

Pluralist scholars focus their attention on the activities of "the proximate policy-makers"—the President, Congress, the courts, and bureaucracy. They observe competition, bargaining, and compromise among and within these

---

[26] Charles E. Lindblom, *The Policy-Making Process* (Englewood Cliffs, N.J.: Prentice Hall, 1968), p. 30.

public bodies over specific policies and programs. They observe the role of parties, interest groups, and constituents in shaping the decision-making behavior of these proximate policy-makers. But it is quite possible that the activities of the proximate policy-makers are merely the final phase of a much more complex structure of national policy formation.

Our oligarchical model of national policy-making attempts to trace elite interaction in determining the major directions of national policy. It portrays the role of the proximate policy-makers as one of implementing through law the policies that have been formulated by a network of elite-financed and elite-directed policy-planning groups, foundations, and universities. The proximate policy-makers act only after the agenda for policy-making has already been set, the major directions of policy changes have been decided, and all that remains is the determination of programmatic specifics.

The initial resources for research, study, planning, and formulation of policy come from donations of corporate and personal wealth. These resources are channeled into foundations, universities, and policy-planning groups. Moreover, top corporate elites also sit on the governing boards of these institutions to help determine how their money will be spent. The policy-planning groups—such as the Council on Foreign Relations, the Business Roundtable, and the Brookings Institution—play a central role in bringing together individuals at the top of the corporate and governmental worlds, the foundations, the law firms, and the mass media, in order to reach a consensus about policy direction.

10 Institutional Elites in America

INSTITUTIONAL POWER IN AMERICA

Power in America is organized into large institutions, private as well as public—corporations, banks, investment firms, governmental bureaucracies, media empires, law firms, universities, foundations, cultural and civic organizations. The nation's resources are concentrated in a relatively few large institutions, and control over these institutional resources is the major source of power in society. The people at the top of these institutions—those who are in a position to direct, manage, and guide institutional programs, policies, and activities—compose the nation's elite.

The *systematic* study of the nation's institutional elite is still in an exploratory stage. Although a great deal has been written about "the power elite," much of it has been speculative, impressionistic, and polemical. Serious difficulties confront the social scientist who wishes to move away from anecdote and ideology to serious scientific research on national elites— research that "names names," attempts operational definitions, develops testable hypotheses, and produces some reliable information about national leadership.

The first task confronting social science is to develop an operational definition of national elite. Such a definition must be consistent with the notion that great power resides in the institutional structure of society; it must also enable us to identify by name and position those individuals who possess great power in America. Our own definition of a *national institutional elite* produced 7,314 elite positions. Taken collectively, individuals in these positions controlled almost three quarters of the nation's industrial assets, more than one half of all the assets in communications and utilities, almost two thirds of all banking assets, more than three quarters of all insurance assets, and they directed the nation's largest investment firms. They commanded nearly half of all assets of private foundations and universities, and they controlled the television networks, the national press, and the major newspaper chains. They dominated the nation's top law firms and the most prestigious civic and cultural associations, and they occupied key federal government posts in the executive, legislative, and judicial branches and the top military commands.

Our selection of positions of institutional power involved many subjective judgments, but it provided a starting place for a systematic inquiry into the character of America's elite structure. It allowed us to begin investigation into a number of important questions: Who are the people at the top of the institutional structure of America? How did they get there? What are their backgrounds, attitudes, and values? How concentrated or dispersed is their power? Do they agree or disagree on the fundamental goals of society? How much cohesion or competition characterizes their interrelationships? How do they go about making important policy decisions or undertaking new policy directions?

HIERARCHY AND POLYARCHY AMONG INSTITUTIONAL ELITES

Before summarizing our data on institutional elites, it might be helpful to gain some theoretical perspectives on our findings by suggesting *why* we might expect to find evidence of either hierarchy or polyarchy in our results.

European social theorists—notably Weber and Durkheim—provide theoretical explanations of why social structures become specialized in advanced societies, and why coordination mechanisms are required. These theorists suggest that increasing functional *differentiation* of elites occurs with increasing socioeconomic development. In a primitive society, it is difficult to speak of separate economic, political, military, or administrative power roles; in primitive life, these power roles are merged together with other roles, including kinship, religion, and magical roles. But as separate economic, political, bureaucratic, and military institutions develop, and as specialized power roles are created within these institutions, separate elite groups emerge at the top of separate institutional structures. The increased division of labor, the scale and complexity of modern social organizations, and the specialization in knowledge, all combine to create functional differentiation among institutional elites. This suggests polyarchy among elites in an advanced society such as the United States.

Yet even though specialized elite groups are required to direct relatively autonomous institutional sectors, there must also be some social mechanisms to coordinate the exercise of power by various elites in society. This requirement of *coordination* limits the autonomy of various institutional elites. Thus, specialization acts to bring elites together, as well as to force them apart. Social theory does not necessarily specify *how* coordination of power is to be achieved in modern society. Nor does it specify *how much* unity is required to maintain a relatively stable social system or, conversely, how much competition can be permitted. Certainly there must be *some* coordination if society is to function as a whole. The amount of coordination can vary a great deal, however, and the mechanisms for coordination among elites differ from one society to another.

One means of coordination is to keep the relative size of elite groups small. This smallness itself facilitates communication. If there are relatively few people who actually direct institutional activity, then these people can have extraordinary influence on national policy. What's more, the small size of these groups means that institutional leaders are known and accessible to each other. Of course, policy-planning groups, governmental commissions, and advisory councils, or informal meetings and conferences, are instrumental in bringing "specialists" together. But how small *is* America's elite? C. Wright Mills, wisely perhaps, avoids any estimate of the size of "the power elite"; he says only that it is "a handful of men."[1] Floyd Hunter estimates the size of "top leadership" to be "between one hundred and two hundred men."[2] We have already indicated that our definition of the elite produces an estimated size of 7,314 positions occupied by 5,778 individuals—considerably more than implied in the power elite literature, but still few enough to permit a great deal of personal interaction.

Another coordinating mechanism is to be found in the methods by which elites are recruited. The fact that elites who are recruited to different institutional roles share the same social class and educational backgrounds should provide a basis for understanding and communication. Social homogeneity, kinship links, similarity of educational experience, common membership in clubs, common religious and ethnic affiliations, all help to promote unity of outlook. Yet at the same time we know that a certain amount of "circulation of elites" (upward mobility) is essential for the stability of a social system. This means that some heterogeneity in social background must be tolerated. But again social theory fails to quantify the amount of heterogeneity that can be expected.

Still another form of coordination is a general consensus among elites on the rules to resolve conflicts and to preserve the stability of the social system itself. Common values serve to unify the elites of various institutional systems. Moreover, agreement among elites to abide by the rule of law and to minimize violence has a strong utilitarian motive, namely to preserve stable working arrangements among elite groups. Finally, unifying values also legitimize the exercise of power by elites over masses, so the preservation of the value system performs the dual function of providing the basis of elite unity, while at the same time rationalizing and justifying for the masses the exercise of elite power. Unfortunately, social theory does not tell us *how much* consensus is required among elites to facilitate coordination and preserve a stable social system. Social theory tells us that elites must agree on more matters than they disagree, but it fails to specify how broad or narrow the range of issues can be.

[1] C. Wright Mills, *The Power Elite* (New York: Oxford University Press, 1956), p. 7.

[2] Floyd Hunter, *Top Leadership, U.S.A.* (Chapel Hill: University of North Carolina Press, 1959), p. 176.

Because social theory suggests *both* convergence and differentiation among institutional elites, it is possible to develop competing theoretical models of the social system—models which emphasize either hierarchy or polyarchy. For example, the notion of the "power elite" developed by C. Wright Mills implies *hierarchy* among economic, political, and military power-holders. The idea suggests unity and coordination among leaders of functionally differentiated social institutions. Mills speculates that a large-scale, centralized, complex, industrial society *necessitates* coordination:

> At the pinnacle of each of the three enlarged and centralized domains, there have arisen those higher circles which make up the economic, the political, and the military elites. At the top of the economy, among the corporate rich, there are the chief executives; at the top of the political order, the members of the political directorate; at the top of the military establishment, the elite of soldier-statesmen clustered in and around the Joint Chiefs of Staff in the upper echelon. . . . Each of these domains of power—the warlords, the corporation chieftains, the political directorate—tend to come together, to form the power elite of America.[3]

Thus, the hierarchical or elitist model rests upon the theoretical proposition that increasing complexity requires a high degree of coordination and consequently a great concentration of power.

In contrast, the polyarchical or pluralist model emphasizes differentiation in institutional structures and leadership positions—with different sets of leaders and different institutional sectors of society and with little or no overlap, except perhaps by elected officials responsible to the general public. According to this view, elites are largely specialists, and leadership roles are confined to a narrow range of institutional decisions. These specialists are recruited through separate institutional channels—they are not drawn exclusively from business or finance. Further, the functional specialization of institutional elites results in competition for power, a struggle in which competing elites represent and draw their strength from functionally separate systems of society. How do pluralists assume coordination is achieved among elites? The argument is that functionally differentiated power structures produce an equilibrium of competing elites. Resulting checks and balances of competition are considered desirable to prevent the concentration of power and assure the responsibility of elites.

In short, social theory postulates both hierarchy *and* polyarchy among elites in the social system. It is the task of systematic social science research to determine just *how much* convergence or differentiation exists among elites in the national system.

---

[3] Mills, *The Power Elite*, pp. 8–9.

WHO'S RUNNING AMERICA? SUMMARY OF FINDINGS

Our findings do not all fit neatly into either an hierarchical, elitist model of power, or a polyarchical, pluralist model of power. We find evidence of *both* hierarchy and polyarchy in the nation's institutional elite structure. Let us try to summarize our principle findings regarding the questions posed at the beginning of this volume.

Concentration of Institutional Resources.   The nation's resources are concentrated in a relatively small number of large institutions. Almost three quarters of the nation's industrial assets are concentrated in 100 industrial corporations; almost two thirds of U.S. banking assets are concentrated in the fifty largest banks; and over half of our assets in communications and utilities are concentrated in fifty corporations. More than three quarters of the nation's insurance assets are concentrated in just fifty companies; fifty foundations control 40 percent of all foundation assets; twenty-five universities control two thirds of all private endowment funds in higher education; and fifteen newspaper empires account for more than half of the nation's daily newspaper circulation. It is highly probable that thirty Wall Street and Washington law firms exercise comparable dominance in the legal field; that fifteen Wall Street investment firms dominate decision-making in securities; and that a dozen cultural and civic organizations dominate music, drama, the arts, and civic affairs. Federal government alone now accounts for 23 percent of the gross national product and two thirds of all government spending. More important, concentration of resources in the nation's largest institutions is increasing over time.

The Size of the Nation's Elite.   Approximately 6,000 individuals in 7,000 positions exercise formal authority over institutions that control roughly half of the nation's resources in industry, finance, utilities, insurance, mass media, foundations, education, law, and civic and cultural affairs. This definition of the elite is fairly large numerically, yet these individuals constitute an extremely small percentage of the nation's total population—less than three thousandths of 1 percent! However, this figure is considerably larger than that implied in the "power elite" literature.

Perhaps the question of hierarchy or polyarchy depends on whether one wants to emphasize numbers or percentages. To emphasize hierarchy, one can comment on the tiny *percentage* of the population that possesses such great authority. To emphasize polyarchy, one can comment on the fairly large *number* of individuals at the top of the nation's institutional structure; certainly there is room for competition within so large a group.

Interlocking versus Specialization.   Despite concentration of institutional resources, there is clear evidence of specialization among institutional leaders. Eighty-five percent of the institutional elites identified in our study were specialists, holding only one post of the 7,314 "top" posts. Of course, many of these individuals held other institutional positions in a wide variety of corporate, civic, and cultural organizations, but these were not "top" positions as we defined them. Only 15 percent of our institutional elites were interlockers—individuals holding more than one top post at the same time.

However, the multiple interlockers—individuals with six or more top posts—not surprisingly turned out to be giants in the industrial and financial world. Another finding is that there was a good deal of vertical overlap—top position-holders who have had previous experience in other top corporate, governmental, and legal positions—more so than there is horizontal (concurrent) interlocking. Only one quarter of governmental elites have held high corporate positions, and nearly 40 percent of the corporate elites have held governmental jobs. Yet even this vertical overlapping must be qualified, for most of the leadership experience of corporate elites was derived from *corporate* positions, and most of the leadership experience of governmental elites was derived from *government and law.*

There are, however, important concentrations of combined corporate, governmental, and social power in America. Large corporations such as AT&T have many interlocking director relationships with industrial corporations, banks, utilities, and insurance companies. In addition, there is concentration of power among the great wealthy, entrepreneurial families—the Rockefellers, Mellons, du Ponts, Fords. One of the most important of these concentrations over the years has been the Rockefeller family group, which has had an extensive network in industrial, financial, political, civic, educational, and cultural institutions.

Inheritors versus Climbers. There is a great deal of upward mobility in American society, as well as "circulation of elites." We estimate that less than 10 percent of top corporate elites inherited their position and power; the vast majority climbed the rungs of the corporate ladder. Most governmental elites—whether in the executive bureaucracy, Congress, or the courts—also rose from fairly obscure positions. Elected political leaders frequently come from parochial backgrounds and continue to maintain ties with local clubs and groups. Military leaders tend to have the largest percentage of rural, southern, and lower-social-origin members of any leadership group.

Separate Channels of Recruitment. There are multiple paths to the top. Our top elites were recruited through a variety of channels. Governmental leaders were recruited mainly from law and government. Corporate leaders emerged from the managerial ranks of industrial corporations, banks, insurance companies, and investment firms. Military leaders were recruited exclusively through the military ranks. Most top lawyers rose through the ranks of the large, well-known law firms, and mass media executives were recruited primarily from newspaper and television. Only in the foundations, universities, and cultural and civic associations was the formal leadership drawn from other sectors of society.

Social Class and Elite Recruitment.   Individuals at the top are overwhelmingly upper and upper-middle class in social origin. Even those who climbed the institutional ladder to high position generally started with the advantages of a middle-class upbringing. Nearly all top institutional elites are college-educated, and half hold advanced degrees. Elites are notably "Ivy League": 54 percent of top corporate leaders and 42 percent of top governmental leaders are alumni of just twelve well-known private universities. Moreover, a substantial proportion of corporate and government leaders attended one of just thirty-three private "name" prep schools.

Although women have made notable progress in recent decades in acquiring top institutional positions, they still hold fewer than 10 percent of corporate directorships, and none serve as chief executive officer of a top 100 corporation. Women have been somewhat more successful in gaining top government posts.

Very few African Americans occupy top positions in the institutional structure of the nation. While blacks have served in Cabinet posts in recent presidential administrations, only a very small number of blacks have been admitted to the boardrooms of corporate America. None serve as a chief executive officer of a top 100 corporation.

Corporate elites are somewhat more "upper class" in origin than are governmental elites. Governmental elites had slightly lower proportions of private prep school types and Ivy Leaguers than corporate elites, and governmental elites were less Eastern and urban in their origins than corporate elites. Governmental leaders in our study had more advanced professional degrees (generally law degrees) than did corporate elites.

Conflict and Consensus among Elites.   Elites in all sectors of American society share a consensus about the fundamental values of private enterprise, limited government, and due process of law. Moreover, since the Roosevelt era, elites have generally supported liberal, public-regarding, social welfare programs—including Social Security, fair labor standards, unemployment compensation, a federally aided welfare system, government regulation of public utilities, and countercyclical fiscal and monetary policies. Elite consensus also includes a desire to end racial discrimination—and to bring more minority Americans into the mainstream of the political and economic system.

In the 1980s neoconservative ideas dampened elite enthusiasm for large costly government programs aimed at curing the nation's social ills. In the 1990s neoliberal reforms give priority to stimulating economic growth over older liberal efforts to redistribute income.

Elite disagreement occurs *within* a consensus over fundamental values.

The range of disagreement is relatively narrow and tends to be confined to means rather than ends.

Factionalism among Elites. Traditional pluralist theory emphasizes competition between Democrats and Republicans, liberals and conservatives, labor and management, and other conventional struggles among interest groups. Elitist theory, on the other hand, emphasizes underlying cohesion among elite groups, but still admits of some factionalism. A recognized source of factionalism is the emergence of new sources of wealth and new "self-made" individuals who do not fully share the prevailing values of established elites. New wealth and old wealth have traditionally created fault lines within elites.

We have described elite factionalism in recent decades as a split between Sunbelt *cowboys* and established *yankees*. The *cowboys* accumulated their wealth and power in the years following World War II, in such enterprises as independent oil, the aerospace industry, computer and communications technology, discount drugs and merchandising, fast food chains, and real estate development in the Sunbelt (from southern California to Texas and Florida). The self-made *cowboys* are not as liberal or public-regarding or as social welfare–oriented as the *yankees*. The *yankees* inhabited older established institutions of power, most of which are headquartered in New York and Washington. The *yankees* were educated in the tradition of noblesse oblige—elite responsibility for the welfare of the masses. Despite the prominence of many new persons of wealth, established Eastern institutional wealth and power continue to dominate national life. New wealth is frequently unstable and highly sensitive to economic fluctuations.

An Oligarchic Model of National Policy-Making. Traditional pluralist theory focuses attention on the activities of the proximate policy-makers in the policy-making process, and the interaction of parties, interest groups, the President and Congress, and other public actors in the determination of national policy. In contrast, our oligarchic model of national policy-making views the role of the proximate policy-makers as one of deciding specific means of implementing major policy goals and directions which have *already been determined* by elite interaction.

Our oligarchic model assumes that the initial resources for research, study, planning, organization, and implementation of national policies are derived from corporate and personal wealth. This wealth is channeled into foundations, universities, and policy-planning institutions, where corporate representatives and top wealth-holders exercise ultimate power on the governing boards. Universities and intellectuals respond to the research emphases determined by the foundations.

Influential policy-planning groups—notably the Council on Foreign Relations, the Business Roundtable, and the Brookings Institution—may employ university research teams to analyze national problems. But their more important function is consensus-building among elites—bringing together individuals at the top of corporate and financial institutions, the universities, the foundations, and the top law firms, as well as the leading intellectuals, the mass media, and influential figures in government. Their goal is to develop policy recommendations having general elite support. These are then communicated to the proximate policy-makers directly and through the mass media. At this point government agencies begin their research into the policy alternatives suggested by the foundations and policy-planning groups. The role of the various public agencies is thus primarily to fill in the details of the policy directions determined earlier. Eventually, government agencies, in conjunction with the intellectuals, foundation executives, and policy-planning-group representatives, prepare specific legislative proposals, which then begin to circulate among the proximate policy-makers, notably White House and congressional committee staffs.

The federal law-making process involves bargaining, competition, persuasion, and compromise, as generally set forth in pluralist political theory. But this interaction occurs *after* the agenda for policy-making has been established and the major directions of policy changes have been determined. The decisions of proximate policy-makers are not unimportant, but they tend to center about the *means* rather than the *ends* of national policy.

POWER: INSIDER AND OUTSIDER VIEWS

Powerful people seldom publicly acknowledge their own power. They do not intend to mislead. Rather, they see their environment as pluralistic, competitive, and constantly changing. They do not see themselves as "elites"; they are acutely aware of their defeats, frustrations, and limitations. They view "ruling-class" theorists as hopelessly naïve, unschooled, and inexperienced.

From an insider's perspective, the policy "process" appears highly competitive, constantly changing, and occasionally chaotic, in the way that pluralists describe it.[4] Winning in the power "game" is the goal. Players in the game strive to influence policy in order to win prestige, celebrity, and a reputation for power. The competition is fierce. No one wins every battle; defeats, frustrations, and standoffs are experienced by even the most powerful players. Winners today are losers tomorrow. Insiders describe the Washington policy process from this individualistic viewpoint. There is no central direction to the process. Issues change almost daily; no one regularly controls the agenda.

To outsiders, however, the policy network appears highly structured. If there are hundreds who have acquired the status of Washington insiders, there are tens of thousands who have not. Students of the policy network who are themselves outside of that network tend to see a highly structured set of

[4] See Nelson Polsby, "Tanks but No Tanks," *Public Opinion* (April–May 1983), pp. 14–16.

relationships among corporations, foundations, think tanks, and government. They attribute little importance to the petty jostling for prestige, status, and influence among individuals—politicians, bureaucrats, businessmen, or intellectuals. They perceive this competition to be narrow in scope and bounded by institutional constraints. They perceive a consensus on behalf of economic growth, a stable business cycle, incentives for investment, economy and efficiency in government, a stable two-party system, and maintaining popular support for political institutions. Disagreement occurs over the means to achieve these ends, not over the ends themselves. Outsiders describe the policy network from an organizational and societal perspective, rather than from an individual perspective.

WHO'S RUNNING AMERICA?

Systematic research on national leadership is no easy task. We do not yet have sufficient evidence to confirm or deny the major tenets of elitist or pluralist models of national power. Our research on institutional elites produces evidence of both hierarchy and polyarchy in the nation's elite structure.

Our purpose has been to present what we believe to be interesting data on national institutional elites. We will leave it to our readers to relate this data to their own theory or theories of power in society. We do believe, however, that a systematic understanding of power and elites must begin with operational definitions, testable hypotheses, and reliable data if we ever expect to rise above the level of speculation, anecdote, or polemics in this field of study.

Index

LEADERSHIP INDEX